# Open Source Network Administration

# Prentice Hall PTR Series in
# Computer Networking and Distributed Systems

*Radia Perlman, Series Editor*

| | |
|---|---|
| **Kaufman, Perlman & Speciner** | *Network Security: Private Communication in a Public World, Second Edition* |
| **Dayem** | *Mobile Data and Wireless LAN Technologies* |
| **Dayem** | *PCS and Digital Cellular Technologies: Accessing Your Options* |
| **Dusseault** | *WebDAV: Next Generation Collaborative Web Authoring* |
| **Greenblatt** | *Internet Directories: How to Build and Manage Applications for LDAP, DNS, and Other Directories* |
| **Kadambi, Kalkunte & Crayford** | *Gigabit Ethernet: Migrating to High Bandwidth LANS* |
| **Kercheval** | *DHCP: A Guide to Dynamic TCP/IP Network Management* |
| **Kercheval** | *TCP/IP Over ATM: A No-Nonsense Internetworking Guide* |
| **Kretchmar** | *Open Source Network Administration* |
| **Liska** | *The Practice of Network Security: Deployment Strategies for Production Environments* |
| **Mancill** | *Linux Routers: A Primer for Network Administrators, Second Edition* |
| **Mann, Mitchell & Krell** | *Linux System Security: The Administrator's Guide to Open Source Security Tools, Second Edition* |
| **Maufer** | *A Field Guide to Wireless LANs for Administrators and Power Users* |
| **Skoudis** | *Counter Hack: A Step-by-Step Guide to Computer Attacks and Effective Defenses* |
| **Solomon** | *Mobile IP: The Internet Unplugged* |
| **Syme & Goldie** | *Optimizing Network Performance with Content Switching: Server, Firewall, and Cache Load Balancing* |
| **Tomsu & Schmutzer** | *Next Generation Optical Networks* |
| **Tomsu & Wieser** | *MPLS-Based VPNs: Designing Advanced Virtual Networks* |
| **Zeltserman** | *A Practical Guide to SNMPv3 and Network Management* |
| **Zeltserman & Puoplo** | *Building Network Management Tools with Tcl/Tk* |

# Open Source Network Administration

James M. Kretchmar

PRENTICE
HALL
PTR

**PRENTICE HALL**
Professional Technical Reference
Upper Saddle River, New Jersey 07458
www.phptr.com

*A CIP catalog record for this book can be obtained from the Library of Congress*

Editorial/Production Supervision: *Techne Group*
Executive Editor: *Mary Franz*
Editorial Assistant: *Noreen Regina*
Development Editor: *Jennifer Blackwell*
Marketing Manager: *Dan DePasquale*
Manufacturing Buyer: *Maura Zaldivar*
Cover Design Director: *Jerry Votta*
Full-Service Production Manager: *Anne R. Garcia*

© 2004 Pearson Education, Inc.
Publishing as Prentice Hall Professional Technical Reference
Upper Saddle River, NJ 07458

**Prentice Hall PTR offers excellent discounts on this book when ordered in quantity for bulk purchases or special sales. For more information, please contact: U.S. Corporate and Government Sales, 1-800-382-3419, corpsales@pearsontechgroup.com. For sales outside of the U.S., please contact: International Sales, 1-317-581-3793, international@pearsontechgroup.com.**

Company and product names mentioned herein are the trademarks or registered trademarks of their respective owners.

Printed in the United States of America

First Printing

ISBN 0-13-046210-1

Pearson Education Ltd.
Pearson Education Australia PTY, Limited
Pearson Education Singapore, Pte. Ltd.
Pearson Education North Asia Ltd.
Pearson Education Canada, Ltd.
Pearson Educación de Mexico, S.A. de C.V.
Pearson Education—Japan
Pearson Education Malaysia, Pte. Ltd.

# About Prentice Hall Professional Technical Reference

With origins reaching back to the industry's first computer science publishing program in the 1960s, and formally launched as its own imprint in 1986, Prentice Hall Professional Technical Reference (PH PTR) has developed into the leading provider of technical books in the world today. Our editors now publish over 200 books annually, authored by leaders in the fields of computing, engineering, and business.

Our roots are firmly planted in the soil that gave rise to the technical revolution. Our bookshelf contains many of the industry's computing and engineering classics: Kernighan and Ritchie's *C Programming Language*, Nemeth's *UNIX System Adminstration Handbook*, Horstmann's *Core Java*, and Johnson's *High-Speed Digital Design*.

PH PTR acknowledges its auspicious beginnings while it looks to the future for inspiration. We continue to evolve and break new ground in publishing by providing today's professionals with tomorrow's solutions.

*For my Father*

# CONTENTS

FOREWORD     xiii

ACKNOWLEDGMENTS     xvii

**1 INTRODUCTION**     **1**

  1.1   Network Administration     1

  1.2   Why Open Source?     2

      1.2.1   The Price Is Right     3

      1.2.2   Eggs in Your Basket     3

      1.2.3   You Might Find You Get What You Need     4

      1.2.4   The Question of Quality     5

      1.2.5   Is It Secure?     6

      1.2.6   Support     6

  1.3   Tools in This Book     7

  1.4   Environment     8

  1.5   Background     8

  1.6   Terminology and Conventions     9

**2 SNMP**     **11**

  2.1   Overview of SNMP     11

      2.1.1   SNMP     12

      2.1.2   Variables and the MIB     13

      2.1.3   Object Identifiers and Variable Hierarchy     15

      2.1.4   Variable Instances for Simple Variables     17

      2.1.5   Introduction to Tables     17

      2.1.6   Lexicographic Ordering and Get-Next-Request     19

      2.1.7   Traps     19

  2.2   What SNMP Can Help You Do     20

|  |  | 2.2.1 | The System Group | 20 |
|  |  | 2.2.2 | The Interfaces Group | 22 |
|  |  | 2.2.3 | ip.ipNetToMediaTable | 24 |
|  |  | 2.2.4 | The Bridge MIB | 25 |
|  | 2.3 | | Installing SNMP Tools | 26 |
|  |  | 2.3.1 | Building from Source | 27 |
|  |  | 2.3.2 | Build and Install | 28 |
|  | 2.4 | | Using SNMP Tools | 29 |
|  |  | 2.4.1 | Snmpget | 29 |
|  |  | 2.4.2 | Snmpset | 32 |
|  |  | 2.4.3 | Snmpwalk | 33 |
|  |  | 2.4.4 | Snmptrapd | 33 |
|  |  | 2.4.5 | Other Tools | 34 |
|  |  | 2.4.6 | Dealing with MIBs | 36 |
|  |  | 2.4.7 | Scripting with SNMP Tools | 36 |
|  | 2.5 | | Maintaining SNMP Tools | 37 |
|  | 2.6 | | References and Further Study | 37 |
| **3** | **MRTG** | | | **39** |
|  | 3.1 | | Overview of MRTG | 39 |
|  | 3.2 | | What MRTG Can Help You Do | 39 |
|  | 3.3 | | Installing MRTG | 41 |
|  |  | 3.3.1 | Building the PNG Library | 42 |
|  |  | 3.3.2 | Building the GD Library | 42 |
|  |  | 3.3.3 | Building MRTG | 43 |
|  | 3.4 | | Configuring MRTG | 43 |
|  |  | 3.4.1 | Generating the Configuration File | 44 |
|  |  | 3.4.2 | Other Configuration Options | 46 |
|  |  | 3.4.3 | Generating Initial Data | 47 |
|  |  | 3.4.4 | Generating Index Pages | 47 |
|  |  | 3.4.5 | Setting Up Regular Data Gathering | 49 |
|  | 3.5 | | Using MRTG | 50 |
|  |  | 3.5.1 | Faulty Data | 50 |
|  |  | 3.5.2 | Missing Data | 51 |
|  | 3.6 | | Maintaining MRTG | 51 |
|  | 3.7 | | References and Further Study | 52 |

**4   NEO**                                                                  **53**

   4.1   Overview of Neo                                                        53
   4.2   What Neo Can Help You Do                                               53
   4.3   Installing Neo                                                         57
   4.4   Using Neo                                                              59
         4.4.1   The Command Prompt                                             59
         4.4.2   The Location Syntax                                            59
         4.4.3   Variables                                                      64
         4.4.4   The Arpfind Command                                            66
         4.4.5   The Locate Command                                            66
         4.4.6   The Port Command                                               67
         4.4.7   The Device Summary Command                                     68
         4.4.8   The Device Info Command                                        71
         4.4.9   The Stats Command                                             72
         4.4.10  Online Help                                                   75
         4.4.11  Command Line Arguments                                        75
         4.4.12  Other Commands                                               76
         4.4.13  Using Neo in Degraded Network Conditions                      76
   4.5   Examples of Use                                                       77
   4.6   Maintaining Neo                                                        80
   4.7   References and Further Study                                           81

**5   NETFLOW**                                                             **83**

   5.1   Overview of NetFlow and Flow-Tools                                     83
   5.2   What NetFlow Can Help You Do                                          84
   5.3   How NetFlow Works                                                      84
         5.3.1   Flows                                                          84
         5.3.2   NetFlow and Switching Paths                                    86
         5.3.3   Exporting NetFlow Data                                         86
         5.3.4   NetFlow Versions                                              87
   5.4   Installing Flow-Tools                                                  88
   5.5   Configuring NetFlow on the Router                                     89
   5.6   Using Flow-Tools                                                       90
         5.6.1   Capturing Flows                                               90
         5.6.2   Viewing Flow Data                                             98
         5.6.3   Manipulating Flow Data                                       105
   5.7   References and Further Study                                         108

**6  OAK**                                                              **111**

  6.1   Overview of Oak                                                 111
  6.2   What Oak Can Help You Do                                        112
  6.3   Installing Oak                                                  114
  6.4   Using Oak                                                       114
        6.4.1   Configuring Syslog on Unix Workstations                115
        6.4.2   Configuring Syslog on Network Devices                  118
        6.4.3   An Introduction to Regular Expressions                 119
        6.4.4   Configuring Oak                                         122
  6.5   Maintaining Oak                                                 130
  6.6   References and Further Study                                    130

**7  SERVICE MONITORING**                                              **133**

  7.1   Overview of Service Monitoring                                  133
  7.2   What Service Monitoring Can Help You Do                         135
  7.3   Installing Sysmon                                               136
        7.3.1   Where to Place the Server                               136
        7.3.2   How to Install Sysmon                                   136
  7.4   Using Sysmon                                                    137
  7.5   Configuring Sysmon                                              141
        7.5.1   The Root Node                                           141
        7.5.2   Objects and Dependencies                                141
        7.5.3   Global Options                                          147
  7.6   Maintaining Sysmon                                              152
  7.7   Nagios                                                          152
  7.8   References and Further Study                                    154

**8  TCPDUMP**                                                         **155**

  8.1   Overview of Tcpdump                                             155
  8.2   What Tcpdump Can Help You Do                                    156
        8.2.1   Limitations of Tcpdump                                  158
  8.3   Installing Tcpdump                                              158
        8.3.1   You May Already Be a Winner                             158
        8.3.2   Which Version to Build                                  159
        8.3.3   The Pcap Library                                        159
        8.3.4   Tcpdump                                                 160
  8.4   Using Tcpdump                                                   160

| | | | |
|---|---|---|---:|
| | 8.4.1 | Running as Root | 161 |
| | 8.4.2 | Command Line Options | 161 |
| | 8.4.3 | Filters | 165 |
| | 8.4.4 | Command Line Examples | 166 |
| | 8.4.5 | Understanding the Output | 167 |
| | 8.4.6 | Viewing Packet Data | 168 |
| | 8.4.7 | Seeing It All | 169 |
| 8.5 | Examples of Debugging with Tcpdump | | 172 |
| | 8.5.1 | Packet Flooding | 173 |
| | 8.5.2 | A More Complicated Example | 174 |
| 8.6 | Maintaining Tcpdump | | 175 |
| 8.7 | Other Packet Analyzers | | 175 |
| 8.8 | References and Further Study | | 175 |
| **9** | **BASIC TOOLS** | | **177** |
| 9.1 | Ping | | 177 |
| | 9.1.1 | How Ping Works | 178 |
| 9.2 | Telnet | | 183 |
| 9.3 | Netcat | | 185 |
| | 9.3.1 | Installing Netcat | 185 |
| | 9.3.2 | Using Netcat | 186 |
| 9.4 | Traceroute | | 189 |
| | 9.4.1 | How Traceroute Works | 190 |
| | 9.4.2 | Installing Traceroute | 191 |
| | 9.4.3 | Using Traceroute | 192 |
| 9.5 | MTR | | 194 |
| | 9.5.1 | Installing MTR | 194 |
| | 9.5.2 | Using MTR | 195 |
| 9.6 | Netstat | | 197 |
| **10** | **CUSTOM TOOLS** | | **199** |
| 10.1 | Basics of Scripting | | 200 |
| | 10.1.1 | Running a Script | 201 |
| | 10.1.2 | Naming Conventions | 202 |
| | 10.1.3 | Local and Environment Variables | 202 |
| 10.2 | The Bourne Shell | | 203 |
| | 10.2.1 | Basics of the Bourne Shell | 203 |

| 10.2.2 | Using Variables | 204 |
| 10.2.3 | Local and Environment Variables | 205 |
| 10.2.4 | Exit Status | 206 |
| 10.2.5 | Conditionals | 207 |
| 10.2.6 | Arguments | 209 |
| 10.2.7 | Loops | 210 |
| 10.2.8 | Using Command Output | 210 |
| 10.2.9 | Working with Input and Output | 211 |
| 10.2.10 | Functions | 212 |
| 10.2.11 | Other Miscellaneous Items | 213 |
| 10.3 | Perl | 214 |
| 10.3.1 | Basics of Perl | 215 |
| 10.3.2 | Using Variables | 215 |
| 10.3.3 | Local and Environment Variables | 216 |
| 10.3.4 | Conditionals | 216 |
| 10.3.5 | Text Manipulation | 217 |
| 10.3.6 | Lists | 218 |
| 10.3.7 | Hashes | 220 |
| 10.3.8 | Reading from a File | 220 |
| 10.3.9 | Writing to a File | 221 |
| 10.3.10 | Arguments | 222 |
| 10.3.11 | Loops | 222 |
| 10.3.12 | Using Command Output | 223 |
| 10.3.13 | Subroutines | 223 |
| 10.3.14 | Exiting | 223 |
| 10.3.15 | Perl for Network Monitoring Scripts | 224 |
| 10.4 | Programming Monitors | 224 |
| 10.4.1 | Loop Timing | 225 |
| 10.4.2 | State Machines | 226 |
| 10.4.3 | Keeping It Running | 227 |
| 10.4.4 | Sending Nicer Mail with Sendmail | 228 |
| 10.5 | Running Programs from Cron | 229 |
| 10.6 | References and Further Study | 230 |
| **INDEX** | | **231** |

# FOREWORD

When I graduated from MIT in 1990, I joined the MIT Network Operations Group. It was there that, among other things, I started working on the Linux kernel as recreational programming. During my time with the Network Operations Group, I learned what it was like to have operational responsibilities. This is a valuable perspective that all developers should be exposed to, if only briefly.

During my first year or two with the Network Group, we evaluated a commercial network management system. Out of charity, I will not reveal the name of the product nor its vendor, but suffice it to say, it was a very complicated beast, which required huge amounts of disk space and computing power. It would display a picture of the campus, which when you clicked on a building, would zoom in and allow you to select a floor and display a floor plan, at which point you could click on a room, and finally, select a piece of network equipment. When selected, a picture of the device would appear, complete with flashing LEDs, which were emulated via SNMP monitoring. If there was a problem with a router, it would cause an alarm to ring and, on the campus map view, the building containing the bad network device would flash. If the building map was displayed, the floor with the problem would flash, and so on, until the faulty router was identified.

Unfortunately for the vendor of this very complicated, proprietary, network-management system, an experienced network engineer could localize the problem faster using simple tools like ping, traceroute, and an ASCII terminal. This was advantageous to us because we could also use them when we dialed in from home at 3 a.m.

Even implementers of this product realized how outrageous the entire interface was; rumor had it that by setting a certain magic configuration variable, the interface would display a picture of the Milky Way, and you could zoom into our local group of galaxies, pick our home galaxy, the star system on the edge of that galaxy, and so on, before finally zooming into the campus map level. No doubt it was the implementers' private protest against the set of requirements handed to them by some fuzzy-cheeked product manager who, obviously, had never configured a router or repaired a malfunctioning network in the middle of the night.

Not surprisingly, we decided to skip purchasing this very expensive, very unnecessary network management system. Instead, we stuck to our own collection of tools; some of which were freely downloaded from the Internet, and some of which we developed ourselves.

My personal contribution to this set of tools was the "ninit" program, a very simple tool. It watched over the named program, and restarted it if the need arose. It also collected periodic statistics, and tested the named program every 15 seconds to make sure it was still functioning correctly and responding to queries. If not, ninit would kill off the named process and restart it.

The ninit program was made famous in the Unix Haters Handbook (IDG Books, 1994), where it was lampooned as a demonstration of how unreliable Unix software is — or perhaps all software from BSD; or perhaps just Named — because it needed a watcher process. The Unix Haters may have had a point, but the ninit program was short, and it was sweet, and it restarted the name service on our servers at 3 a.m. so I didn't have to be awakened by a pager after our mail queues had exploded due to a lack of name service.

Many other people have advanced other explanations for the superiority of Open Source software, such as Linus Torvalds' observation that "with enough eyeballs, all bugs are shallow." While this is true, I think it is the last point which is the most important for explaining why Open Source network management tools work as well as they do: When the person to be aroused from bed to fix an operational problem is the person writing the tools, the very tight accountability loop means that they might not be architecturally beautiful (although often they are), nor have fancy graphical interfaces (very often not necessary), but they will certainly solve the problem at hand.

This book is a wonderful survey of a wide range of Open Source network management tools. Some of these tools may be well known to you already; others may be entirely new to you. All of them are extremely useful to a network operations team. I hope you enjoy going through these tools, and I encourage you to try them out in your own work. If you haven't tried some of these tools yet, you will be in for a very pleasant surprise.

Theodore Ts'o
Linux Kernel Developer
August 25, 2003

# ACKNOWLEDGMENTS

Many people made this book possible. First and foremost I wish to thank Radia Perlman, whose foresight turned lemons into the lemonade that is this book. Mary Franz, at Prentice Hall, made the idea a reality with tireless support and enthusiasm. Thanks also to Anne Garcia, Noreen Regina and Dmitri Korzh for helping me bring it all together. Additionally, thanks to Scott Mann, Ellen Mitchell, Matthew Crosby, and Gretchen Phillips who reviewed the material and consistently had helpful feedback.

A number of colleagues deserve thanks for their useful input and suggestions, including Matt Braun and Jon Rochils, as well as the entire Network Operations staff at MIT, especially Jeff Schiller and Bob Mahoney. Thanks to Marc Horowitz for the use of his tcpdump parsing script and Ted Ts'o for writing the foreword.

Thanks to all the friends whose support kept me going, including Ron Hoffmann, Erin Panttaja, Sola Grantham, Stephen Gildea, Anne LaVin, Jon Rochils, Jag Patel, Marc Tanner, Gisele Proulx, Edmund Golaski, Stan Zanarotti, and Karen Atkinson. Thanks to Mark and Dawna Nocera for the much needed weekly distractions that kept me on my toes. Thanks also to friends at the home away from home, especially Buff Weigand and Cannie Shafer. A special thank you goes to Rebecca Rogers, Penny Kulp and Tara Holm for keeping everything in perspective and for patience in listening to each excruciating detail along the way.

Many thanks to my brother Tom and my mother Barbara for their encouragement and enthusiasm throughout the project and for putting up with my crazy hours.

Finally, those who truly deserve acknowledgment are the many Open Source software developers whose labor of love has produced not only the subject matter of this book, but also the software that quietly keeps much of the Internet up and running. Keep at it!

The author would be happy to receive feedback with suggestions for improvements or corrections to mistakes. Send email to jmk@mit.edu.

This book was written using LaTeX, based on templates created by J. Kenneth Shultis.

James M. Kretchmar

# Chapter 1

# INTRODUCTION

## 1.1 Network Administration

In the past two decades the number of networked computers in the world has grown at an astonishing rate. In the mid 1980s when the personal computer became the hot new item, most people had no concept of connecting these machines. Today, a mere 20 years later, it is hard to imagine an organization with more than a few computers that does not connect them in some fashion. More often than not, these networks are also connected to the global Internet, allowing connectivity to any other Internet-connected machine anywhere else in the world.

When networking technology was not so widely used, there was little need for network management. There simply wasn't much to manage. And when things did go wrong, it was usually the hardware at fault. Today the hardware is much more reliable, and the problems are often caused by bad software or malicious users. At the same time, the need for reliability has increased. More people now rely on the network in order to accomplish their jobs; some networks even support life safety equipment. These two influences, the greater need for reliability and the fact that problems are more diverse and unpredictable than ever before, have led to a greater need for network management.

But even though the need is great, increased managability comes at a cost. Networked devices such as switches come in both managed and unmanaged flavors, and the managed ones are much more expensive. You must decide how much management capability you are willing to pay for based on the number of machines you will be connecting and the context and environment in which you will be connecting them. If you are connecting just three computers in your home, you will have little need for an expensive piece of hardware that has every management bell and whistle available. If something does go wrong, you can always reach over and unplug a problematic host. If instead you are connecting dozens of machines in a situation where you cannot simply remove one from the network by walking across the room or where you need be able to monitor the traffic levels of the connected devices, you probably will need at least some management capability from your network hardware. And obviously, if you are connecting hundreds or thousands of machines, you will have a definitive need for manageable devices so that you can ensure the stability of the network should a problem arise.

On the Massachusetts Institute of Technology (MIT) network, which has over 30,000 hosts connected to it, each host is attached to a managed network port.[1] As far as the field has advanced in the past few years, it is still the case that a single misbehaving host can cause a very large problem. Thus the ability to locate and potentially disable a problematic host is crucial.

## 1.2    Why Open Source?

Every piece of software described in this book is **open source** software. What is meant by the term open source? In short, it refers to software whose source code is available to the public without restriction. It also means the software can be modified by anyone for any use and that the modified program can also be redistributed as open source. There is a much more detailed definition available at `http://www.opensource.org/`, though this is only one interpretation, of course.

Though open source software is free, it still carries a license that governs its use. Usually, this license is there to ensure that the software continues to remain open. Additionally, open source software can be sold even though it is simultaneously available free. For example, you can buy copies of the Red Hat Linux distribution even though you can also download it at no cost. Why would anyone pay for something that could also be obtained free? In the case of Red Hat software, it is

---

[1]This is a little bit of a lie. On all of the networks that are run by the Network Operations team, every host is on a managed port. There a few networks that are run by individual labs, and the labs may choose to do things differently.

because you are also paying for support service from Red Hat, which does not come free.

## 1.2.1   The Price Is Right

The most obvious reason for using open source software is the price. Whereas other network administration tools can cost tens of thousands of dollars, open source software is available free. This isn't to say that you shouldn't pay for quality. If a tool comes along that is exactly the right tool for you, does everything you need, and greatly improves your ability to manage the network for a price that you can afford, by all means buy it. But if there is a tool available that is just as good or better and costs nothing, which one makes more sense?

The fact that the program is free has two subtle side effects. One is that you get to take the ultimate test drive. Not sure if a tool is right for you? No problem. Try it for as long as you like, and if you're not fully satisfied, you haven't paid a dime. The only loss is the time you invested in learning about the tool and setting it up. But increasing the knowledge and abilities of your staff in this manner is often a better investment than the one made in another company anyway.

The other benefit to using a piece of free software is that there is less pressure to stick with the product if a better one comes along. If you spent $20,000 on a tool last year but find something better this year, you may be tempted or pressured to stick it out with the old tool as long as possible.

## 1.2.2   Eggs in Your Basket

Buying a piece of software for which you do not have access to the source code is, at heart, a gamble. Imagine that something goes wrong with the software: A serious security vulnerability is discovered, or an irreversible change to your environment trips a bug that causes the software to stop working. If the company that produces the software is no longer in business or is unwilling to help, you're out of luck.

Here's an even more likely scenario: Imagine the company that produces the software is a very large company for which you are a very small customer. You have a support contract with the company, but if a problem is affecting *all* of the customers, the company's resources may be tapped out. Then who gets taken care of first? It's the big customers who spend lots of money. If you're a small customer, you will have to wait your turn, even if the problem is a critical one.

With an open source product, you have a fighting chance to deal with these problems on your own. This isn't to say it will necessarily be trivial. Some software problems are easy to solve and some are not. You may need a skilled programmer to help you out. But even if you do not have one on staff, you will still have the possibility of paying a consultant to help. Consider this option in contrast to having no recourse whatsoever.

One analogy is that buying closed source software is like buying a car with the hood welded shut, whereas with open source software, you can open the hood and poke around inside. Even if you can't fix anything on the car yourself, you can at least check the oil once in a while, and if an emergency does arise, you can have someone fix the car for you.

It is also true that because the popular open source packages are very widely used, a fixed version of the software will typically be available much faster than it will be for a proprietary product. The eyes of thousands of programmers tend to find bugs faster than the eyes of a dozen. Keep this in mind when choosing between different pieces of open source software. The more widely used the program is, the faster it will be repaired.

## 1.2.3   You Might Find You Get What You Need

Open source projects are often written by people who want to use the software themselves. Instead of relying on a marketing department to figure out what they want, the customers are writing exactly what they need. Since others also have access to the source, they can modify the software to fit their needs as well. And because the things you want to accomplish are probably also the goals of *someone* else out there, it is usually not hard find software that does what you want.

Similarly, when a piece of open source software does not do what you want, it is often easy to modify it to meet your needs. Not only that, but you can modify it as quickly as is required. A case in point: We recently had a piece of open source software that had an unfortunate file size limitation in the code, but we needed to use the program right away to gather data about an ongoing operational problem. A programmer on staff was able to fix the problem overnight and it was ready to go the next morning. This was by no means an exceptional event; it has happened time and time again. But if this had been a commercial piece of software, it would have taken days at the very best, but more likely weeks or months to get a change like this implemented.

## 1.2.4   The Question of Quality

The most common fear about using open source software, especially in a critical context such as production network administration, is that it is somehow not as good as commercial software. If you're paying for it, it must be of higher quality, right? From experience, we say the answer is no. Many open source programs are just as good as or better than their commercial counterparts. Take Multi Router Traffic Grapher (MRTG), for example, which is described in Chapter 3. It is essentially the industry-standard tool for graphing bandwidth use on network links. When free software is used in an industry in which you can pay hundreds of thousands of dollars for a single piece of equipment, it must be doing something right.

Of course, just as there is both good and bad commercial software available, there is both good and bad open source software. Proponents of open source believe that the open source development model helps create better quality software. Common arguments include that the very large number of people working on these projects is beneficial as is the openness of the system, which prevents developers from hiding code that isn't really up to par. On the other hand, a greater number of developers does not necessarily lead to a higher quality product,[2] and some open source software, such as a device driver, is understood by so few people that the code goes mostly unread anyway.

It is worth pointing out that the people who write these programs are usually professional programmers. They either work in a context where their product does not need to be sold commercially, as is often the case for software that comes from universities, or work in the corporate world during the day and spend their off-hours working on these tools. The software quality only benefits from the fact that it is a labor of love.

---

[2]Read *The Mythical Man-Month* (Addison-Wesley, 1995) by Frederick P. Brooks, Jr.

## 1.2.5   Is It Secure?

One common criticism of open source software is that because anyone
can read the source, it is easier for an attacker to find a vulnerability
and exploit it.  The expectation is that commercial software is more
secure because the security holes are hidden.  The truth, as has been
proven repeatedly in the past few years, is that this is not the case.  The
Internet has seen very serious security problems in both open source
and closed source software, some of which were responsible for very
visible, Internet-wide problems.  You probably read about a few of
them in the papers.  The only thing that differentiates the two is that
the open source bugs tend to have fixes available much more quickly,
which usually limits the amount of damage done.

This is where having the very large number of programmer eyes
really pays off.  Yes, the attackers can look for vulnerabilities in the
software, but so can the good guys, and there are far more of them
around.  This means there's a better chance that a bug will be found
and fixed than found and exploited.  At the same time, the good guys
will not devote much time to looking for vulnerabilities in proprietary
programs, but the attackers will.

## 1.2.6   Support

The downside to open source software is that it usually comes with no
support service.  If your open source tool fails, there is no one you can
call to complain to and no one to take the blame.  If it is important to
you to have a scapegoat available when software fails, open source is
not a good choice for you.

Instead, the first line of support for open source software is you
and your staff.  The more you have invested in learning about the
software and its inner-workings, the better chance you have of solving
a problem.  After that, you can appeal to the software maintainers for a
fix or consult online discussion forums related to the software.  Should
those fail, you can always resort to paying a consultant to help you.

Of course, if you can find open source software that *does* come with
support service, you will have the best of both worlds.

## 1.3   Tools in This Book

The tools in this book cover many aspects of network administration,
from traffic analysis to log monitoring.  Some of the tools, such as
MRTG and NetFlow, are very widely used and nearly industry standards.  Other tools, such as Neo and Oak, cover areas of network administration in which there is not yet a single tool that most administrators use.

All of the tools described in this book are open source software,
which means you may download and use them for free and you may
modify them if you desire.  The purpose of the book is to collect a good
set of network administration tools in one place. Open source software
developers are not known for spending serious time (or money) in self-
advertising.  So it can be a challenge to figure out which software is
worthwhile and which is not.  In addition to pointing out the good
software, this book explains how the software works and how to install
and use it.

The chapters are:

- **SNMP.** The Simple Network Management Protocol is the standard for remote administration of network devices.  Chapter 2
  includes a well-known set of tools for accessing information via
  SNMP.

- **MRTG.** The Multi Router Traffic Grapher is a very widely used
  tool for graphing bandwidth and other network statistics.

- **Neo.** This tool was written at MIT for high-level administration
  of switches, routers, and other devices that speak SNMP.

- **NetFlow.** NetFlow is a Cisco mechanism for collecting information about the internals of network traffic.  Chapter 5 describes a
  well-known package called Flow-Tools that collects and processes
  NetFlow information.

- **Oak.** Oak is a tool written at MIT for collecting syslog messages from servers and network equipment, condensing the information as appropriate, and notifying operators of problem conditions when they arise.

- **Service Monitoring.** The Sysmon program, covered in detail in Chapter 7, tests network hardware and server software to ensure they are functioning, and if they are not, it notifies the appropriate administrators. The Nagios program, a more complex tool that serves the same purpose, is briefly discussed as well.

- **Tcpdump.** This is a standard program for directly analyzing network traffic at the packet level.

- **Basic Tools.** Chapter 9 covers the basic tools of network administration, including the ping, telnet, netcat, traceroute, MTR, and netstat programs.

- **Custom Tools.** In Chapter 10, a brief, working knowledge of the Bourne shell and Perl scripting languages is presented.

If you encounter a bug in any one of the programs described in this book or find that a particular feature would be be a real benefit, do your part and mail the maintainers of the software. Don't be shy; they want to hear your feedback. However, do not expect that your problems will be solved overnight.

## 1.4   Environment

All of the examples given in this book were performed on machines running some flavor of the Unix operating system, in particular Solaris and Linux. All of the programs should work on other flavors of Unix as well, but the more exotic the variant, the more likely you will run into problems. A number of the programs advertise that they work under Windows too, and now that modern versions of MacOS run Unix under the hood, it should be possible to build the tools for those platforms as well.

## 1.5   Background

This book assumes you have an understanding of the basics of networking and does not go into detail about the Open System Interconnection (OSI) layered network model and other topics frequently included in books on networking. However, when an aspect of the underlying technology is particularly relevant, it is described in enough detail so that only a general familiarity with the material is necessary.

Each of the tools here is built from source, with explicit demonstrations in the text. The tools should build without much trouble, but a build process does occasionally fail. If it does, you may need some experience with building software in order to fix the problem. Often, it is simply a matter of instructing the build system to look for software in an unexpected location on the machine or of building a separate, required package that is not already installed on the machine. Sometimes the problem will be an error in the build system itself, in which case the maintainer of the software should be given a detailed report of the problem.

## 1.6 Terminology and Conventions

The terms *workstation, host, device,* and *node* are all used interchangeably in networking and in this text as well. The use of one instead of another is not meant to imply anything about the hardware in question, though the choice of word may reflect an expectation of common use.

# Chapter 2

# SNMP

## 2.1 Overview of SNMP

SNMP stands for Simple Network Management Protocol, and it is exactly what it sounds like: a relatively simple protocol used to manage devices on a network. The managed device is commonly a workstation, a switch, or a router but can be anything capable of speaking IP. For example, many printers and uninterruptible power supplies (UPSs) can be managed with SNMP. What exactly does it mean to be able to "manage" a device? It means an operator, or an SNMP **management agent** acting on behalf of an operator, can query the device for information and may also be able to instruct the device to make a change in configuration. In managing a router, an operator might use SNMP to query the router for the number of packets transmitted on an interface or instruct the router to make a change to its routing table.

The strength of SNMP lies in its simplicity and its standardization. Because the protocol is simple, it can be implemented in even the most basic devices. The fact that it is an Internet standard makes it an attractive tool for a site that has many devices from many different vendors. Each device may operate differently under the hood, but all devices must present the same management interface via SNMP. Then an operator can manage every device on the network in nearly the same way. The result of SNMP's ubiquity is that it is now the underlying technology for other management tools, including Neo and MRTG, which are discussed in later chapters.

There are currently three versions of SNMP: SNMPv1, SNMPv2, and SNMPv3. SNMPv2 is not drastically different from SNMPv1, and

SNMPv3, which adds security to the protocol, is not as widely deployed as the first two. This chapter focuses primarily on SNMPv1.

## 2.1.1   SNMP

When we talk about using SNMP for network management, we're really talking about a small collection of standards. SNMP itself is the protocol used to transmit management packets over the network. Other standards define how pieces of management information are named and organized. SNMP is built on top of the User Datagram Protocol (UDP). Because UDP is an unreliable protocol by design, there is nothing to ensure that SNMP packets will not be lost in transmission. Accordingly, most management agent software implements a timeout and retransmission to ensure that SNMP messages are received.

Three pieces of information are included in each SNMP packet before the actual management information. First is the version number, which for SNMPv1 is the value zero. Next is the SNMP **community name**. The community is a text string that serves as a rudimentary kind of authentication. The device being managed is configured ahead of time to allow certain communities access to certain management capabilities. For example, you may give a community called `my-secret` access only to retrieve management information from a device while you may give the community `really-secret` access to both change and retrieve it. The operator or management agent supplies the appropriate community name in the SNMP request, and upon receipt of the request, the device decides whether the given community has the necessary privileges.

It is important to note that in SNMPv1 and SNMPv2, the community name is not encrypted in the packet in any way. It is sent over the network as a cleartext password. This means that if these packets are in some way intercepted, an eavesdropper will easily be able to pick out the community name. If the managed device has no access restrictions in place other than the community name, the eavesdropper will now be able to use the community to perform management requests against the device. SNMPv3, in contrast, does have a real authentication mechanism so that an eavesdropper will not be able to gain privileged access. Unfortunately, SNMPv3 is not available on many manageable devices. This means the only options may be to:

- Disable some or all SNMP access

- Design your network in such a way that management traffic does not travel on networks where a malicious user may eavesdrop

- Use a firewall or other filter to block SNMP traffic from untrusted sources

- Enforce no special access restrictions and hope for the best

Network operators should consider what the security implications would be of unauthorized read- and write-level access to network devices and make management access decisions accordingly. Incidentally, should you wish to make your SNMP management open to everyone, the accepted default value for the community name is `public`.[1]

The third piece of information sent in the SNMP header indicates the type of request being sent and is called the **Protocol Data Unit (PDU) type**. PDU is just a fancy word for a packet. There are five valid choices for the PDU type, listed in Figure 2.1. A `get-request` asks the device to return a piece of information while a `set-request` asks the device to change a setting. The `get-response` is the device's response to one of those requests. The other two PDU types, `get-next-request` and `trap`, are discussed later in this chapter.

| PDU Type | Name | Function |
|---|---|---|
| 0 | `get-request` | Retrieve a variable's value |
| 1 | `get-next-request` | Retrieve the next variable and its value |
| 2 | `get-response` | Response from the managed device |
| 3 | `set-request` | Set a variable's value |
| 4 | `trap` | Spontaneous information from the device |

**Figure 2.1.** PDU Types in SNMPv1.

## 2.1.2   Variables and the MIB

While the SNMP standard defines a framework for talking to a device about management, we need a common way to talk about the

---

[1]At MIT we set the read-only community to public so that anyone may query devices for information. The read-write community is, of course, not open to the public.

information we wish to retrieve or change. Each piece of information available via SNMP is called an SNMP **variable**. There is a variable that indicates the operational status of an interface, for example, called `ifOperStatus`. Another variable, called `sysUpTime`, represents the amount of time the given device has been up and running.

Every SNMP variable is specified in the Management Information Base, more commonly called the **MIB**. The MIB is a separate standard from SNMP. The job of the MIB is to:

- Assign every variable a textual name

- Define a data type for the variable

- Describe the function of the variable and how the data type is used to achieve that function

- Define the access possibilities for the variable (e.g., read-only versus read-write)

Practically speaking, the MIB is a text file that lists SNMP variables and all the necessary information associated with them. The file is written in Abstract Syntax Notation One (ASN.1), a standard format for describing data, so that it is readable both by humans and by programs that act as SNMP agents. The data types themselves are further standardized by the Structure of Management Information (SMI) standard, which defines data types such as "TimeTicks" or "IpAddress."

The first MIB, the Internet Standard MIB, was published by the Internet Engineering Task Force (IETF) in 1998 as RFC 1066.[2] RFC 1158 and, later, RFC 1213 describe a new Internet MIB called MIB-II, which effectively replaces the original MIB. Any device speaking SNMP today is required to implement MIB-II.

There are now so many SNMP variables in use that it is not feasible to have one file that describes them all. Additionally, it is desirable for individual enterprises, such as private companies, to have control over their own set of variables. These variables might control products they produce, for example. So instead of one large MIB file, there are many

---

[2]This document was also revised very slightly and published in 1990 as RFC 1156, but these modifications did not reflect any technical changes in the system.

separate component files, some published by the IETF but also many published by vendors.

Note that the term MIB is sometimes used to refer to the Internet standard MIB, which now effectively means MIB-II. But other times, it refers to some particular portion of the MIB that is published separately. So while a purist might say there is only one MIB, it is common to hear someone talk about the "Bridge MIB" or an "Asante MIB." It is usually clear from context what is meant.

In the following sections we look at the MIB in closer detail, but still only as an introduction to the topic. For an in-depth discussion of MIBs, read *Understanding SNMP MIBS* (Prentice Hall PTR, 1996) by David Perkins and Evan McGinnis.

### 2.1.3  Object Identifiers and Variable Hierarchy

SNMP variable names must be globally unique. To help achieve this goal, they are arranged in a hierarchical fashion. The `sysUpTime` variable mentioned earlier is really named in full `.iso.org.dod.internet.`
`mgmt.mib-2.system.sysUpTime`. The `sysUpTime` variable belongs to a set of variables under the `system` group that all relate to management information about the state of the device as a whole. The `ifOperStatus` variable, which indicates the operational status of an interface, is found under the `interfaces` tree, which contains variables relating to interface-specific information.

The root of the variable hierarchy has no name, but it has three children, depicted in Figure 2.2. One is for use by the International Organization for Standardization (ISO), one for the Comité Consultatif International Téléphonique et Télégraphique (CCITT) (now the International Telecommunications Union [ITU]), and the third is for joint ISO and CCITT use. The scope of this naming scheme is actually much larger than that used by SNMP. All SNMP variables in use on the Internet fall under the `.iso.org.dod.internet` branch of the tree.

In addition to having a textual name, each branch of the tree has an integer associated with it. This number is used in communicating variable names over the wire in SNMP. The textual names are for human readability only. So `.iso.org.dod.internet.mgmt.mib-2.`
`system.sysUpTime`, when encoded in an SNMP packet, is sent as `.1.`

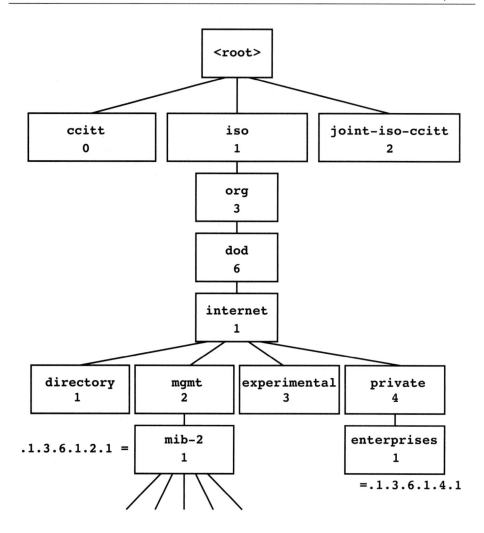

**Figure 2.2.** Object Identifier Hierarchy.

3.6.1.2.1.1.3. This string of integers is called the variable's **object identifier**, often abbreviated to **object ID** or **OID**.

The `mib-2` branch of the variable hierarchy is where the Internet standard MIB begins. The `private.enterprises` portion of the tree is where MIBs assigned to private organizations begins.

## 2.1.4   Variable Instances for Simple Variables

When making an SNMP request for a simple variable, such as `sysUp-Time`, you must append a final `.0` to the variable name, for reasons that will become clear when SNMP tables are discussed in Section 2.1.5. For example, `sysUpTime` must actually be requested as `sysUpTime.0` or at the protocol level, `.1.3.6.1.2.1.1.3.0`. The SNMP tools will require you to supply the final `.0` when you make requests.

## 2.1.5   Introduction to Tables

Some kinds of management information, such as the name of the system contact, can be easily stored in a single variable. Other kinds of information are better described in a table of values. For example, if a device has 24 ports, it would be convenient to represent traffic data as a table with 24 rows, one for each port.

The MIB has a facility for defining a table. Instead of going into great detail on how tables are designed, it's easier to look at a real example:

```
interfaces.ifTable.ifEntry.ifOperStatus.1 = up(1)
interfaces.ifTable.ifEntry.ifOperStatus.2 = up(1)
interfaces.ifTable.ifEntry.ifOperStatus.3 = up(1)
interfaces.ifTable.ifEntry.ifOperStatus.4 = down(2)
interfaces.ifTable.ifEntry.ifOperStatus.5 = down(2)
interfaces.ifTable.ifEntry.ifOperStatus.6 = up(1)
interfaces.ifTable.ifEntry.ifOperStatus.7 = up(1)
interfaces.ifTable.ifEntry.ifOperStatus.8 = up(1)
interfaces.ifTable.ifEntry.ifOperStatus.9 = up(1)
interfaces.ifTable.ifEntry.ifOperStatus.10 = down(2)
interfaces.ifTable.ifEntry.ifOperStatus.11 = up(1)
interfaces.ifTable.ifEntry.ifOperStatus.12 = up(1)
interfaces.ifTable.ifEntry.ifOperStatus.13 = up(1)
interfaces.ifTable.ifEntry.ifOperStatus.14 = up(1)
interfaces.ifTable.ifEntry.ifOperStatus.15 = up(1)
interfaces.ifTable.ifEntry.ifOperStatus.16 = up(1)
interfaces.ifTable.ifEntry.ifOperStatus.17 = down(2)
interfaces.ifTable.ifEntry.ifOperStatus.18 = down(2)
```

This is a portion of the `interfaces` group, which is a direct child of `mib-2` (see Figure 2.3). The `interfaces` group is made up of one simple variable (`ifNumber`, the number of interfaces on the system) and one

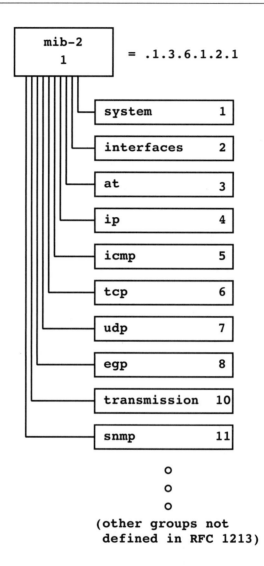

**Figure 2.3.** Children of mib-2 Defined in RFC 1213.

table called `ifTable`. The preceding output is only a small portion of
the `ifTable`, in particular the portion showing the operational status
of an interface. Instead of a `.0` on the end of each variable name, a
number is appended that acts as an index into a row of the table. For
the interface table, this index typically corresponds to the interface port
number. In the example, we can determine that port one is operational

while port ten is not. On Ethernet switches, this often means that port one has link while port ten does not.

The interface table has many columns other than the `ifOperStatus` column that contain additional data about the interface. The `ifSpeed` column, for example, indicates the bandwidth of the interface, and the `ifInOctets` column contains the number of bytes of data received by the interface.

### 2.1.6   Lexicographic Ordering and Get-Next-Request

Because each SNMP variable name is an ordered sequence of integers, it is possible to list variables in a lexicographic order. That is, every variable comes numerically before or after another variable, and so a complete ordered listing of all the variables a device uses can be made. This ordering gives purpose to the **get-next-request** PDU type. Using the **get-request** PDU type, we supply a variable name and the managed device returns the variable's value, along with the name of the variable we requested. When we make a request with the **get-next-request** PDU type, we supply a variable name and the managed device returns the value of the *next* SNMP variable it knows about, along with the name of that variable.

This is a convenient way to walk through a table. We continue asking for the next variable in the table until we either find a variable that is no longer of interest or run out of variables. If we start at the root, **get-next-request** will allow us to step through the entire tree of variables that a device supports. An example is given in Section 2.4.3, when the **snmpwalk** tool is discussed.

### 2.1.7   Traps

The **trap** PDU type is a special kind of SNMP message. Instead of generating an SNMP message in response to a query, a device can spontaneously send a trap to a listening SNMP agent. One useful example of a trap is the **linkDown** trap. When the link state on an interface changes from up to down, the managed device, if configured to use traps, sends an SNMP packet indicating the change. The listening SNMP agent can then use this information to inform an operator.

Because a trap is sent over UDP, just like any other SNMP packet, there is no guarantee that it will make it to its destination. But the problem is somewhat worse for traps than for other types of SNMP requests. SNMP agents that make a query with `get-request`, `get-next-request`, or `set-request` can wait for a response, and if one does not arrive, it can try the query again. A device sending a trap, however, has no mechanism to determine if the trap was received.

Also remember that under certain circumstances, a device may not be able to send a trap. If it unexpectedly loses power, for example, it will not have any opportunity to send a message.

## 2.2    What SNMP Can Help You Do

Protocol design aside, the practical power of SNMP lies in device information available to be retrieved and changed. Fortunately there is a great deal of device configuration available via SNMP. This section looks at some of the standard variables available on networked devices.

### 2.2.1    The System Group

The `system` group is a direct child of `mib-2` that contains variables related to general information about the device. RFC 1213 defines seven simple variables in this group, listed in Figure 2.4. The # column in this table designates the part of the object identifier appended to `mib-2` for the given variable. The RW column indicates whether the variable can be set with an SNMP `set-request`.

The function of most variables is clear. The `sysObjectID` variable returns an SNMP object ID that is unique to that particular kind of device. This object ID is designated by the vendor and therefore always

| Variable | # | RW | Function |
|---|---|---|---|
| sysDescr | 1 | | Text description of the device, including OS |
| sysObjectID | 2 | | An SNMP object identifier for this device |
| sysUpTime | 3 | | Device up time, in hundredths of a second |
| sysContact | 4 | Yes | Contact information for the device admin |
| sysName | 5 | Yes | Admin assigned name, typically the hostname |
| sysLocation | 6 | Yes | Physical location information for the device |
| sysServices | 7 | | Integer value representing available services |

**Figure 2.4.** Variables in the `System` Group.

starts with .1.3.6.1.4.1, which is the prefix for private enterprises. The `sysServices` variable designates which layers of network service are provided by the device. Its use requires some explanation. From RFC 1213:[3]

> The value is a sum.  This sum initially takes the
> value zero. Then, for each layer, L, in the range
> 1 through 7 that this node performs transactions
> for, 2 raised to (L - 1) is added to the sum.  For
> example, a node which performs primarily routing
> functions would have a value of 4 (2^(3-1)).  In
> contrast, a node which is a host offering
> application services would have a value of 72
> (2^(4-1) + 2^(7-1)).  Note that in the context of
> the Internet suite of protocols, values should be
> calculated accordingly:
>
>     layer  functionality
>        1   physical (e.g., repeaters)
>        2   datalink/subnetwork (e.g., bridges)
>        3   internet (e.g., IP gateways)
>        4   end-to-end  (e.g., IP hosts)
>        7   applications (e.g., mail relays)
>
> For systems including OSI protocols, layers 5 and
> 6 may also be counted.

Example values of the system group from a real device look like this:

```
system.sysDescr.0 = "Asante IntraSwitch 5324MT"
system.sysObjectID.0 = OID: enterprises.298.2.2.15
system.sysUpTime.0 = Timeticks: (186442210) 21 days, 13:53:42.10
system.sysContact.0 = "admins@example.com"
system.sysName.0 = "switch.example.com"
system.sysLocation.0 = "5-125T"
system.sysServices.0 = 10
```

The variables `sysContact`, `sysName`, and `sysLocation` are set by an operator using either SNMP or a separate management interface to the device. Notice that the `sysObjectID` variable points to an object ID under `enterprises.298`, which is assigned to Asante. The

---

[3]RFC 1213.   Management Information Base for Network Management of TCP/IP-based internets: MIB-II. K. McCloghrie, M.T. Rose. Mar-01-1991.

sysServices value is 10, indicating that layer 2 and layer 4 services are available. On this device, an Ethernet switch, the layer 2 service is packet switching and the layer 4 service is the IP functionality the device uses for management.

## 2.2.2   The Interfaces Group

The interfaces group is another direct child of mib-2. It contains variables related to information about individual interfaces on a piece of network hardware. A workstation or other simple network device with one network connection may have only one or two interfaces. A switch or router may have many.

The interfaces group has only one simple variable, ifNumber, which is the number of interfaces available on the system. An example from a router:

```
interfaces.ifNumber.0 = 91
```

and from a workstation:

```
interfaces.ifNumber.0 = 2
```

In this case, the workstation has two interfaces, one physical network interface, and one loopback interface.

The only other variable defined for the interfaces group is the table ifTable. The columns of this table are listed in Figure 2.5. Most of these are self-explanatory. One thing worth noting is that it is not always easy to relate the interface index number to the port number on a device. Sometimes the index number will be the same as the port number, such that when ifIndex is three, it will refer to port three on the device. Sometimes this is not the case, particularly on devices that have multiple boards and number each port as a board/port pair. There is no standard mechanism for making the conversion. Cisco devices, for example, use a simple formula to convert the board/port to an ifIndex number and vice versa. Extreme products use a similar formula but with different values so that port one on board one is ifIndex 1001, port two on board one is 1002, and port one on board two is 2001. Some devices provide the ability to use a separate SNMP lookup in the private enterprises portion of the MIB to perform the conversion.

| Variable | # | RW | Function |
|---|---|---|---|
| ifIndex | 1 | | Interface index number |
| ifDescr | 2 | | Text string describing the interface |
| ifType | 3 | | Integer representing the interface protocol |
| ifMtu | 4 | | The MTU of the interface |
| ifSpeed | 5 | | Nominal bandwidth of the interface |
| ifPhysAddress | 6 | | Layer 2 physical address of the interface |
| ifAdminStatus | 7 | Yes | Desired administrative state of the interface |
| ifOperStatus | 8 | | Current operational state of the interface |
| ifLastChange | 9 | | sysUpTime when OperStatus last changed |
| ifInOctets | 10 | | Total number of octets received by interface |
| ifInUcastPkts | 11 | | Number of unicast packets received |
| ifInNUcastPkts | 12 | | Number of non-unicast packets received |
| ifInDiscards | 13 | | Number of inbound packets discarded |
| ifInErrors | 14 | | Number of inbound packets with errors |
| ifInUnknownProtos | 15 | | Number of inbound packets of unknown protocol |
| ifOutOctets | 16 | | Total number of octets send by the interface |
| ifOutUcastPkts | 17 | | Number of unicast packets sent |
| ifOutNUcastPkts | 18 | | Number of non-unicast packets sent |
| ifOutDiscards | 19 | | Number of outbound packets discarded |
| ifOutErrors | 20 | | Number of outbound packets with errors |
| ifOutQLen | 21 | | Number of packets in the outgoing queue |
| ifSpecific | 22 | | A media dependent object identifier |

**Figure 2.5.** Variables in IfTable.

The interfaces group does not report current interface bandwidth usage. Originally the RFC called for ifSpeed to do just that, but in practice, it is always used to report the maximum speed possible on the link. On switches capable of supporting multiple link speeds, the value is usually set to the speed of the current link, in bits per second, or zero if no link is present.

In order to gather statistics on current interface bandwidth use, it is necessary to retrieve a byte count, such as ifInOctets, wait a designated period of time, retrieve a second byte count, and then subtract the difference and divide by the elapsed time. For example, we retrieve:

```
interfaces.ifTable.ifEntry.ifInOctets.6 = 4109645530
```

and then exactly 10 seconds later retrieve:

```
interfaces.ifTable.ifEntry.ifInOctets.6 = 4109669635
```

The average bandwidth use at this time is $\frac{4109669635 - 4109645530}{10} = 2410$ Bytes/s.

The `ifType` variable uses an integer to represent the protocol spoken by the interface. The value for Ethernet is 6, while PPP's is 23. The full table of supported values is listed in RFC 1213.

## 2.2.3   ip.ipNetToMediaTable

The `ip.ipNetToMediaTable` is used to translate IP addresses to hardware addresses. In the context of Ethernet, this means looking up the Ethernet address associated with a particular IP address in the device's Address Resolution Protocol (ARP) cache. An older method of doing this involved using the `at` group, which while usually still supported, is not as generic as the newer system. The `ip.ipNetToMediaTable` is shown in Figure 2.6. To show how this table would be used, sample data from a router follows. In order to save space, the variable names have been shortened; each variable name would begin with the prefix `ip.ipNetToMediaTable.ipNetToMediaEntry`.

```
ipNetToMediaPhysAddress.4.10.152.0.44 = 0:0:1d:dc:85:2d
ipNetToMediaPhysAddress.4.10.152.0.45 = 0:e0:63:2b:c9:c0
ipNetToMediaPhysAddress.4.10.152.0.46 = 0:e0:63:2b:ca:f8
ipNetToMediaPhysAddress.4.10.152.0.53 = 8:0:20:9e:f1:80
ipNetToMediaPhysAddress.4.10.152.0.54 = 8:0:69:2:e6:ec
ipNetToMediaPhysAddress.4.10.152.0.60 = 8:0:20:93:da:3f
ipNetToMediaPhysAddress.4.10.152.0.61 = 0:5:2:f6:c7:b
ipNetToMediaPhysAddress.4.10.152.0.62 = 0:1:e6:4f:9a:6a
```

In reading the first line of output, we learn that the IP address `10.152.0.44` has a cached Ethernet address of `0:0:1d:dc:85:2d`.

| Variable | # | RW | Function |
|---|---|---|---|
| `ipNetToMediaIfIndex` | 1 | Yes | Interface number for the address |
| `ipNetToMediaPhysAddress` | 2 | Yes | Physical address |
| `ipNetToMediaNetAddress` | 3 | Yes | IP address |
| `ifNetToMediaType` | 4 | Yes | Integer representing media type |

**Figure 2.6.** The `ip.ipNetToMediaTable`.

There are a couple of important things to note. First is that before the IP address, there is an interface index number. In this example, every address shown is on interface four. When making a query to determine the hardware address of a particular IP address, we'll need to know the interface it's on so that we can supply that part of the variable name. In practice, there are two ways to do this. One is to determine first which is the correct interface via some other SNMP query. On a router we might look up which interface we would route the packet to and assume that is the correct interface to use in looking up the hardware address. An easier, though brute-force, solution is to simply perform the lookup for every interface number on the device.

Also note that lookups can be performed only in the IP address to hardware address direction. If you wish to map a hardware address to an IP address, you must either retrieve the entire table until you find the hardware address you are looking for or hope that the vendor supplies a private MIB that allows reverse lookups, which most do not.

## 2.2.4   The Bridge MIB

The variable group starting with `dot1dBridge` is better known as the bridge MIB and is defined by RFC 1493. It is a direct child of `mib-2`, though it is not defined in RFC 1213. As expected, the bridge MIB contains information relevant to switching and bridging.[4] One table from the bridge MIB that is worthy of special mention is the forwarding database table, depicted in Figure 2.7. This table is indexed by physical address. For a particular address, `dot1dTpFdbPort` will return the port number to which the bridge will forward packets for that address. If that port and address mapping is learned dynamically by the bridge, `dot1dTpFdbStatus` is set to 3. Other values for `dot1dTpFdbStatus`

| Variable | # | RW | Function |
|---|---|---|---|
| `dot1dTpFdbAddress` | 1 | | Physical address |
| `dot1dTpFdbPort` | 2 | | Associated port |
| `dot1dTpFdbStatus` | 3 | | How the mapping was made |

**Figure 2.7.** The `dot1dTpFdbTable`.

---

[4]For all practical purposes, switching and bridging can be considered the same.

indicate the port mapping was made differently. For example, a value of 4 indicates the address belongs to the bridge itself and is therefore statically configured.

Sample output of `dot1dTpFdbTable` follows. The variable names have again been shortened; each variable name would begin with `dot1dBridge.dot1dTp.dot1dTpFdbTable`.

```
dot1dTpFdbEntry.dot1dTpFdbPort.8.0.9.50.98.244 = 25
dot1dTpFdbEntry.dot1dTpFdbPort.8.0.9.231.93.192 = 25
dot1dTpFdbEntry.dot1dTpFdbPort.8.0.32.5.9.147 = 7
dot1dTpFdbEntry.dot1dTpFdbPort.8.0.32.125.167.158 = 25
dot1dTpFdbEntry.dot1dTpFdbPort.8.0.32.138.134.127 = 25
dot1dTpFdbEntry.dot1dTpFdbPort.8.0.32.143.66.1 = 25
dot1dTpFdbEntry.dot1dTpFdbPort.8.0.32.147.187.7 = 13
dot1dTpFdbEntry.dot1dTpFdbPort.8.0.32.154.38.212 = 25
dot1dTpFdbEntry.dot1dTpFdbPort.8.0.32.160.9.193 = 1
dot1dTpFdbEntry.dot1dTpFdbPort.8.0.32.164.117.198 = 25
dot1dTpFdbEntry.dot1dTpFdbPort.8.0.32.178.66.134 = 25
dot1dTpFdbEntry.dot1dTpFdbPort.8.0.32.231.127.52 = 12
dot1dTpFdbEntry.dot1dTpFdbPort.8.0.43.28.153.246 = 25
dot1dTpFdbEntry.dot1dTpFdbPort.8.0.105.11.122.33 = 25
```

Be aware that the hardware addresses are shown here in decimal notation. The first line indicates that the hardware address `08:00:09:32:62:f4` (the hexadecimal version of `8.0.9.50.98.244`) is found behind port 25.

This table is immensely useful because it allows an operator to ask a switch which port a particular host is on. This is a vital tool for diagnosing and solving network problems. Neo, a network administration tool introduced in Chapter 4, provides a simple interface to perform these lookups.

## 2.3   Installing SNMP Tools

In order to make use of the management capabilities available from SNMP, you will need a set of tools that can make SNMP queries. At a minimum these tools will need to allow you to:

- Query a variable and view the response

- Set a variable and determine if it was successful

- Query entire tables with `get-next-request`

- Receive traps

It would also be beneficial if the tools could perform more advanced tasks, such as retrieving data from the `interfaces` group and presenting it in a clear format.

A widely used set of very good SNMP tools is the **net-snmp** package from the University of California at Davis. The project Web page is at `http://www.net-snmp.org/`. Until recently, these tools were called the **ucd-snmp** tools, and earlier versions still bear this name. Versions 4 and earlier are ucd-snmp; versions 5 and later are net-snmp.

The Web site for these tools has source distributions available, as well as binary distributions for some platforms. In particular, there are binary distributions available of version 5 for Linux and binary distributions of version 4 available for Linux, Solaris, HPUX, FreeBSD, Irix, and Windows. The most recent version is always available as a source distribution.

## 2.3.1   Building from Source

After the source distribution is downloaded, it must be uncompressed and extracted from the tar archive. This can be done as:

```
Solaris% gunzip -c net-snmp-5.0.8.tar.gz | tar xvf -
```

or on a system with gnu tar it can be done as:

```
Linux% gtar zxvf net-snmp-5.0.8.tar.gz
```

Of course, the actual filename will depend on the version you have chosen to download. In this case, a directory will be created called `net-snmp-5.0.8`. Change to that directory and type:

```
Solaris% ./configure
```

to configure net-snmp in preparation for building. After running for a while, it will ask you for input on several questions.

- **Default SNMP Version.** First, it will want to know the default version of SNMP to use, for which you can answer 1, 2, or 3. The version can always be overridden on the command line, so your answer will not prevent you from using any functionality later on. The default answer is version 3. In the examples in this chapter, we always set the version explicitly on the command line.

- **System Contact Information.** This will be the system contact returned for `system.sysContact.0` if you decide to run the SNMP daemon from the package. It is often set to the email address of the administrator.

- **System Location.** This will be the location returned for `system.sysLocation.0` if you decide to run the SNMP daemon from the package. It should be set to the physical location of the device.

- **Logfile Location.** This specifies the name of the file to which net-snmp will send logging information and error messages. The default answer is usually acceptable.

- **Snmpd Persistent Storage Location.** This is the name of the directory where net-snmp will keep statefull configuration files. The default answer is again acceptable.

## 2.3.2  Build and Install

After configuration is complete, you can type:

```
Solaris% make
```

to build the entire package. If you want to install it on your system, login to a root account and type:

```
Solaris# make install
```

By default, this will install into the following directories in `/usr/local/`:

- `bin/`: net-snmp applications

- `sbin/`: net-snmp daemons (`snmpd`, `snmptrapd`)

- `share/snmp/`: net-snmp configuration data

- `share/snmp/mibs/`: MIB files

- `lib/`: net-snmp programming libraries

- `include/`: net-snmp programming includes

- `man/`: net-snmp man pages

If you wish to place these files somewhere other than in `/usr/local`, you must run the configure script with the `--prefix` option, as in:

```
Solaris% ./configure --prefix=/usr/local/mydirectory
```

and then run the `make install`.

## 2.4  Using SNMP Tools

The following sections present examples of using the net-snmp tools. In each case, the program name is executed without a full pathname, assuming that `/usr/local/bin/` and `/usr/local/sbin/` are in your path. If they are not, you will need to type the full path to the program, as in:

```
Solaris% /usr/local/bin/snmpget -h
```

### 2.4.1  Snmpget

The `snmpget` program built by net-snmp can be used to retrieve the value of an SNMP variable. A simple example is:

```
Solaris% snmpget -v 1 -c public switch.example.com \
    system.sysUpTime.0
SNMPv2-MIB::sysUpTime.0 = Timeticks: (405064255) 46 days, \
    21:10:42.55
```

The backslash is inserted only to break up the command line for clarity. The first two arguments specify that we want to use SNMP version one. The `-c` argument tells `snmpget` to use the following string as the SNMP community; in this case, the community is `public`. This is followed by the name of the device we wish to query and, finally, the name of the SNMP variable to look up. Remember that a final zero must be appended to the variable name when a simple variable is referenced.

Though it is easier to remember the textual variable name, you may sometimes want to use the numeric object ID instead. `snmpget` will allow you to do this:

```
Solaris% snmpget -v 1 -c public switch.example.com \
    .1.3.6.1.2.1.1.3.0
SNMPv2-MIB::sysUpTime.0 = Timeticks: (405108049) 46 days, \
    21:18:00.49
```

Here snmpget automatically looks up the variable name in the appropriate MIB and displays it for you. If it can't find the variable name in
a MIB, it translates as much as possible and leaves the rest in numeric
form:

```
Solaris% snmpget -v 1 -c public switch.example.com \
    .1.3.6.1.2.1.17.1.2.0
SNMPv2-SMI::mib-2.17.1.2.0 = INTEGER: 33
```

When this happens, it means snmpget cannot find the MIB that contains this particular variable. You can, however, obtain the MIB and
direct net-snmp to use it. For more information on how to do this, see
Section 2.4.6 later in this chapter.

The snmpget command has a number of other command line options available, listed in Figure 2.8. These options are also available for
the snmpset and snmpwalk commands described in the next sections.
Additionally, the man pages for snmpget and snmpcmd, installed with
net-snmp, describe the options in more detail.

The -O option is particularly useful because it controls the output
format that these tools use. It is used in conjunction with the subop-
tions listed in Figure 2.9, which is from the net-snmp documentation.
For example, to instruct snmpget to print object IDs numerically:

```
Solaris% snmpget -O n -v 1 -c public switch.example.com \
    system.sysUpTime.0
.1.3.6.1.2.1.1.3.0 = Timeticks: (2367889214) 274 days, 1:28:12.14
```

Or, to instruct it to print a full variable name:

```
Solaris% snmpget -O f -v 1 -c public switch.example.com \
    system.sysUpTime.0
.iso.org.dod.internet.mgmt.mib-2.system.sysUpTime.0 = Timeticks...
```

And of course, running snmpget or any of the other tools with the -h
or --help flags will print a list of every option available.

| Argument | Function |
|---|---|
| -h, --help | Print the help message. |
| -H | Print configuration file options relevant to this program. |
| -V, --version | Print net-snmp software version number. |
| -v *version* | Specify SNMP version. Must be 1, 2c, or 3. |
| -c *community* | Specify the SNMP community. |
| -r *retries* | Specify the number of times to retry requests. |
| -t *timeout* | Specify the number of seconds to wait for a response. |
| -d | Dump SNMP packets in hexadecimal. |
| -D *module*[,...] | Debugging for the specified modules. Try ALL. |
| -m *mib*[:*mib*...] | Load named MIBs. Use ALL for everything. |
| -M *dir*[:*dir*...] | Include named directories when looking for MIBs. |
| -P *suboptions* | Set options for MIB parsing. |
| -O *suboptions* | Set output options. |
| -I *suboptions* | Set input options. |
| -C *suboptions* | Set application-specific options. |

**Figure 2.8.** Options Common to `snmpget`, `snmpset`, and `snmpwalk`.

| Arg | Function |
|---|---|
| a | Print all strings in ASCII format |
| b | Do not break OID indexes down |
| e | Print enums numerically |
| E | Escape quotes in string indices |
| f | Print full OIDs on output |
| n | Print OIDs numerically |
| q | Quick print for easier parsing |
| Q | Quick print with equal-signs |
| s | Print only last symbolic element of OID |
| S | Print MIB module-id plus last element |
| t | Print timeticks unparsed as numeric integers |
| T | Print human-readable text along with hex strings |
| u | Print OIDs using UCD-style prefix suppression |
| U | Don't print units |
| v | Print values only (not OID = value) |
| x | Print all strings in hex format |
| X | Extended index format |

**Figure 2.9.** Output Options for `snmpget`, `snmpset`, and `snmpwalk`.

## 2.4.2  Snmpset

The `snmpset` command can be used to set the value of a writable SNMP
variable. For example, if we wish to set the system contact on a device,
we can use `snmpset` as:

```
Solaris% snmpset -v 1 -c really-secret switch.example.com \
    system.sysContact.0 s admin@example.com
SNMPv2-MIB::sysContact.0 = STRING: admin@example.com
```

Here the `-v` and `-c` options are used just as with the `snmpget` command.
Note that the community used is different from that in the previous example and is decidedly not `public`. On this device, the `really-secret`
community has access to set SNMP variables, while `public` has access
only to read SNMP variables.

As with `snmpget`, the next two arguments designate the device and
variable we wish to query. For `snmpset`, though, we have two additional
arguments at the end indicating what value we wish to set. The first
argument specifies what kind of value the next argument will be. The
`s` means the value will be a text string. Figure 2.10 lists all the possible
values for this argument, which you can also view by running `snmpset`
`-h`. Finally the last argument is the value we wish to set. In this case,
we have set the system contact to be `admin@example.com`.

| Arg | Variable Type |
|-----|---------------|
| i | Integer |
| u | Unsigned integer |
| t | Timeticks |
| a | IP address |
| o | Object ID |
| s | String |
| x | Hexadecimal string |
| d | Decimal string |
| b | Bits |
| U | Unsigned 64 bit integer |
| I | Signed 64 bit integer |
| F | Float |
| D | Double |

**Figure 2.10.** Value Type Arguments for `snmpset`.

### 2.4.3 Snmpwalk

The `snmpwalk` command provides a useful way to retrieve a contiguous segment of variables from a device. It uses the `get-next-request` PDU type to continue requesting the next variable until the entire segment is retrieved. For example, the entire system group can be obtained with:

```
Solaris% snmpwalk -v 1 -c public switch.example.com system
SNMPv2-MIB::sysDescr.0 = STRING: Cabletron Systems, Inc. ...
SNMPv2-MIB::sysObjectID.0 = OID: SNMPv2-SMI::enterprises ...
SNMPv2-MIB::sysUpTime.0 = Timeticks: (690848548) 79 days, ...
SNMPv2-MIB::sysContact.0 = STRING: admin@example.com
SNMPv2-MIB::sysName.0 = STRING: switch.example.com
SNMPv2-MIB::sysLocation.0 = STRING: 5-125T
SNMPv2-MIB::sysServices.0 = INTEGER: 71
```

If we wanted to retrieve the entire ARP cache from a router, we could do it with:

```
Solaris% snmpwalk -v 1 -c public router.example.com \
    ip.ipNetToMediaTable.ipNetToMediaEntry.ipNetToMediaPhysAddress
```

Additionally, we can retrieve every MIB-II variable on the system with the `snmpwalk` command if we leave off the final argument completely:

```
Solaris% snmpwalk -v 1 -c public router.example.com
```

Also useful is retrieving every private enterprise variable on a device:

```
Solaris% snmpwalk -v 1 -c public router.example.com enterprises
```

This is sometimes a useful way to find out what SNMP support a device might have if you do not have the MIB available. Recently, some vendors have been occasionally hiding variables from SNMP walks in an effort to obscure certain variables that are otherwise accessible with a direct `snmpget`. There is no trick to finding these "hidden" variables; you must obtain them from a MIB or some other published source of information.

### 2.4.4 Snmptrapd

The `snmptrapd` program is a daemon that listens for SNMP traps and either logs the messages to syslog or stores them in a file. If run with no arguments, it will send the messages to syslog by default. Make sure to run the program as root so that it can listen on the privileged port it requires:

```
Solaris# snmptrapd
```

Your prompt will return immediately as the program turns itself into a daemon. If you wish to run the program so that it stores trap messages in a file instead of sending them to syslog, use the -o option:

```
Solaris# snmptrapd -o /var/tmp/trapd.log
```

In order for **snmptrapd** to receive any data, you must have a device configured to send traps to the listening machine. This is done differently on different devices. Typically, there will be a place in the configuration where you can specify the IP address of one or more trap recipients as well as the community name that should be used. Any community name is acceptable; the community name will simply show up in the logfile. You can choose a secret community name in order to provide a small additional amount of security.

When logging to a file, **snmptrapd** will store a message like the following upon receiving a trap:

```
2003-05-14 23:36:39 W92-165T-SW-13.MIT.EDU [10.10.0.31] \
    (via 10.10.0.31) TRAP, SNMP v1, community public
    SNMPv2-SMI::mib-2.17 Enterprise Specific Trap (1) \
        Uptime: 274 days, 7:25:01.00
```

If **snmptrapd** is logging to syslog instead, it will store a message like this:

```
10.10.0.31: Enterprise Specific Trap (1) Uptime: 274 days ...
```

This trap is an enterprise-specific trap that reports the system up time.

The message format that **snmptrapd** uses can be changed with additional arguments to the program. See the man page for full details on how to do this.

## 2.4.5  Other Tools

In addition to **snmpget**, **snmpset**, and **snmpwalk**, the net-snmp package comes with a number of other useful tools. Included are:

- **snmpgetnext**: Perform a single get-next-request query

- **snmpbulkget**: Perform a bulk-get request (not for SNMPv1)

- **snmpbulkwalk**: Perform a bulk-get walk (not for SNMPv1)

- `snmpd`: An SNMP listening daemon

- `snmpdelta`: Real-time monitor for integer values

- `snmpdf`: Retrieve disk information from remote workstations

- `snmptrap`, `snmpinform`: Send an SNMP trap

- `snmpnetstat`: Produce network information, as in netstat

- `snmpstatus`: Print general device status information

- `snmptable`: Produce a nicely formatted SNMP table

- `snmptest`: For SNMP debugging

- `snmptranslate`: Print detailed MIB information

For example, `snmpnetstat` can be used to print the routing table on a device:

```
Solaris% snmpnetstat -r -v 1 -c public router.example.com
Routing tables
Destination        Gateway             Flags    Interface
default            ROUTER-2.EXAMPLE.C UG        GigabitEthernet1/2
10.7.10/24         ROUTER-3.EXAMPLE.C UG        GigabitEthernet1/1
10.7.14/24         ROUTER-3.EXAMPLE.C UG        GigabitEthernet1/1
10.7.15/24         ROUTER-3.EXAMPLE.C UG        GigabitEthernet1/1
10.7.16/24         ROUTER-3.EXAMPLE.C UG        GigabitEthernet1/1
10.7.17/24         ROUTER-3.EXAMPLE.C UG        GigabitEthernet1/1
10.7.21/24         ROUTER-3.EXAMPLE.C UG        GigabitEthernet1/1
10.9/23            ROUTER-4.EXAMPLE.C UG        FastEthernet3/7
10.11/23           ROUTER-4.EXAMPLE.C UG        FastEthernet3/7
```

Or `snmpdelta` can be used to monitor the number of packets coming into an interface:

```
snmpdelta -c public -v 1 switch.example.com ifInUcastPkts.6
IF-MIB::ifInUcastPkts.6 /1 sec: 1
IF-MIB::ifInUcastPkts.6 /1 sec: 1
IF-MIB::ifInUcastPkts.6 /1 sec: 1
IF-MIB::ifInUcastPkts.6 /1 sec: 1
IF-MIB::ifInUcastPkts.6 /1 sec: 26
IF-MIB::ifInUcastPkts.6 /1 sec: 20
IF-MIB::ifInUcastPkts.6 /1 sec: 1
IF-MIB::ifInUcastPkts.6 /1 sec: 1
```

And `snmptable` can be used to print an entire table nicely:

```
Solaris%  snmptable -v 1 -c public switch.example.com ipNetTo...
SNMP table: IP-MIB::ipNetToMediaTable

ipNetToMediaIfIndex ipNetToMediaPhysAddress ipNetToMediaNet...
    27           0:5:dc:95:d0:a            10.7.21.106      ...
    27           0:5:dc:95:d0:a            10.7.21.108      ...
```

## 2.4.6   Dealing with MIBs

By default, the net-snmp tools store MIBs in `/usr/local/share/snmp/mibs`. The package comes with about 50 MIBs, but inevitably, you will find there are variables you want to use from other MIBs. First note that you do not need a MIB to access a variable as along as you access it by its numeric object ID. However, if you wish to use the textual name, it is necessary to have the appropriate MIB.

Where can you find a particular MIB? It depends on what you're looking for. All of the MIBs defined as IETF standards can be found at `http://www.ietf.org/`. Vendor MIBs are available from the vendor, sometimes by FTP or on the Web. One excellent source for MIBs is `http://www.simpleweb.org/`. It has all of the IETF MIBs well organized, as well as pointers to several vendor MIBs. Additionally, it has a nice tool for stepping through MIB variables and definitions.

Once you've downloaded a MIB, you can place it in the same directory as your other MIBs. You still must tell the net-snmp tools to look for it, though. If, for example, you download and install the bridge MIB in `/usr/local/share/snmp/mibs/` as `BRIDGE-MIB.txt`, you can tell `snmpget` to use it with:

```
Solaris% snmpget -m BRIDGE-MIB -v 1 -c public \
    switch.example.com dot1dBaseNumPorts.0
BRIDGE-MIB::dot1dBaseNumPorts.0 = INTEGER: 33
```

If we had left out the `-m BRIDGE-MIB` option, this query would not have worked.

## 2.4.7   Scripting with SNMP Tools

The net-snmp tools are ideal for use in network management scripts. For example, you may wish to write a script that monitors a set of

UPSs. You can use `snmpget` to query the appropriate variables and warn an operator if a UPS goes on battery power.

When using SNMP tools in your scripts, bear in mind that on some smaller devices (and even on some larger ones), it is possible to overburden the processor with SNMP requests. As a result, you must take care not to run repeated `snmpwalk`'s or `snmpget`'s without a break, or at least ensure that it won't cause an operational problem for your device if you do.

Also note that if your MIB files are not located on the same machine as your script (as would be the case if they were on a networked file system, for example), they may not be available just when you want your program to notice a problem. Either store the MIBs locally on the machine or make sure you use the tools with numeric object IDs only (for both input and output) so that the MIBs are not needed for variable lookups.

## 2.5   Maintaining SNMP Tools

The net-snmp package requires little maintenance. Occasionally, you may wish to add a MIB or update the software, but other than that, there is no routine maintenance necessary.

## 2.6   References and Further Study

There are a number of books available that discuss SNMP in greater depth, including *Essential SNMP* (O'Reilly and Associates, 2001) by Douglas R. Mauro and Kevin J. Schmidt. Both *TCP/IP Illustrated, Volume 1* (Addison-Wesley, 1994) by W. Richard Stevens and *Internetworking with TCP/IP* (Prentice Hall, 2000) by Douglas Comer have sections with details about the SNMP protocol and associated standards.

RFCs 1155, 1156, and 1157, available from `http://www.ietf.org/`, are the original standards for SNMP. RFC 1157 defines SNMP itself, and RFC 1156 is the standard for MIB-I, now replaced by RFC 1213 for MIB-II. RFC 1155 defines the SMI and should now be read in conjunction with RFC 1212, which describes a concise format for use in a MIB.

Additionally, `http://www.simpleweb.org/` has information on many MIBs, including a tool for browsing through MIB variables. It also has SNMP tutorials and references. Detailed information on using and writing MIBs can be found in the book *Understanding SNMP MIBS* (Prentice Hall PTR, 1996) by David Perkins and Evan McGinnis.

# Chapter 3

# MRTG

## 3.1  Overview of MRTG

MRTG is the Multi Router Traffic Grapher, a piece of free software released under the GNU General Public License.[1] It was written primarily by Tobias Oetiker and Dave Rand. MRTG produces Web pages that display graphs of bandwidth use on network links on daily, weekly, monthly, and yearly scales. This can be an invaluable tool for diagnosing network problems because it not only indicates the current status of the network but also lets you visually compare this with the history of network utilization.

MRTG relies on SNMP version one, and optionally SNMP version two, to obtain data from routers or other network hardware. Using the variables described in Chapter 1, MRTG sends SNMP requests every five minutes and stores the responses in a specialized data format. This format allows MRTG to present the daily, weekly, monthly, and yearly graphs without the data files forever growing larger. It does this by summarizing the older data as necessary. The graphs themselves are created in Portable Network Graphics (PNG) format and can be included in Web pages or used in other applications.

## 3.2  What MRTG Can Help You Do

In the middle of a crisis, or when you are debugging an immediate network problem, MRTG will allow you to view the traffic patterns of many networks at once and quickly determine if one or more is experi-

---

[1] The GNU General Public License can be found linked under "licenses" on `http://www.gnu.org/`.

encing an abnormal traffic load. The fact that the graphs display the history of the network is key. In practice, it can be difficult to tell from immediate bandwidth and packet-per-second counts alone whether a network is operating normally. If a 100Mb/s link is carrying 85Mb/s of traffic, is this heavy but normal use or is the network straining under an attack? By having the history of the network available, you can look for sudden changes that might account for an operational problem. A denial-of-service attack that attempts to exhaust the available bandwidth on a network nearly always presents as a sudden, sustained increase in traffic levels; the attackers do not have much to gain by slowly ramping up the attack over a period of time.

When you are not tending to an immediate problem, MRTG is useful for studying trends in traffic on your network. It will help you understand how traffic is distributed across your network, plan capacity needs for the future, and so on.

A sample MRTG graph of a day's worth of network traffic is depicted in Figure 3.1. Note that time progresses to the left, not to the right. This is the default configuration and it is indicated at the bottom of the graph both by the small arrow at the left and by the direction of the time scale. Some MRTG configurations choose to increase time to the right, so be sure examine the graph first. The data at the top of the graph represents the amount of traffic sent into an interface, while the data at the bottom represents the amount of traffic sent out from an interface. You can see that over the past day, this router interface

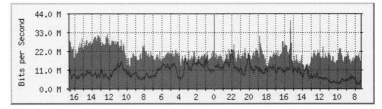

**Figure 3.1.** Sample Daily MRTG Graph.

typically received about 20Mb/s of traffic and sent about 10Mb/s. You will also notice that just after 3:00 p.m. yesterday, there was a short spike in traffic out of the interface.

While MRTG is most often used to collect data from router interfaces, it can also collect traffic data from switches or servers. In this way, you can monitor the bandwidth use of a particular machine. In fact, MRTG can be configured to collect any statistical data that a device makes available via SNMP.

## 3.3   Installing MRTG

MRTG is available at `http://www.mrtg.org/`. It relies on a few pieces of software not included in the distribution. In particular, it requires:

- Perl 5.005 or greater

- The GD library

- The PNG library

- The zlib library

You will not need external SNMP software because MRTG comes with its own SNMP implementation. Begin by unpacking the source in a convenient location:

```
Linux% gunzip -c mrtg-2.9.25.tar.gz | tar xvf -
Linux% cd mrtg-2.9.25
```

Install documentation is available from the `doc/` directory in the distribution, but on a modern Linux system, MRTG will build without any special instructions:

```
Linux% ./configure
Linux% make
```

Then as root you may log in and execute the following command:

```
Linux# make install
```

if you would like to install MRTG in the default location, `/usr/local/mrtg-2/`. If you are building MRTG for other platforms, you may find that a couple of necessary components are not already installed on your system. On Solaris, for example, you will first have to build the PNG and GD libraries before you can successfully build MRTG.

### 3.3.1   Building the PNG Library

The source for PNG is available at `http://www.libpng.org/pub/png/`
`libpng.html`. Download the latest version and unpack it:

```
Solaris% gunzip -c libpng-1.2.5.tar.gz | tar xvf -
Solaris% cd libpng-1.2.5
```

Then examine the `INSTALL` file. It contains a list of makefiles designed
for use with different systems. For example:

```
makefile.linux    => Linux/ELF makefile (gcc, creates \
   libpng12.so.0.1.2.5)
makefile.hpux     => HPUX (10.20 and 11.00) makefile
makefile.macosx   => MACOS X Makefile
```

Find the one that is the closest match to your system and make a note
of the name. In this example, we use `makefile.solaris`. Copy the
makefile file you wish to use to the current directory and try building
the package:

```
Solaris% cp scripts/makefile.solaris makefile
Solaris% make
```

If all goes well, there will be a file called `libpng.a` when you are finished.
If the build complains about not being able to find the zlib library, you
will need to retrieve it from `http://www.gzip.org/zlib/` and build it
before continuing. Once you have `libpng.a`, install it on your system
from a root account with:

```
Solaris# make install
```

### 3.3.2   Building the GD Library

The GD library is available at `http://www.boutell.com/gd/`. As
above, download the latest version and unpack it:

```
Solaris% gunzip -c gd-2.0.9.tar.gz | tar xvf -
Solaris% cd gd-2.0.9
```

Before running the configure script, you must indicate where GD should
find the PNG library by setting the `CFLAGS` and `LDFLAGS` environment
variables. Assuming you installed PNG in the default location, `/usr/`
`local/`, you will want:

```
Solaris$ CFLAGS=-I/usr/local/include export CFLAGS
Solaris$ LDFLAGS="-L/usr/local/lib -R/usr/local/lib" export \
   LDFLAGS
```

if you use the bash, Korn or Bourne[2] shell, but:

```
Solaris% setenv CFLAGS -I/usr/local/include
Solaris% setenv LDFLAGS "-L/usr/local/lib -R/usr/local/lib"
```

if you use the csh or tcsh shell.

Now install GD on your system with `make install` from a root account.

### 3.3.3   Building MRTG

Once the GD library is built with PNG, you can go on to build MRTG. Change back to the MRTG source directory and now run the configure script with `CFLAGS` and `LDFLAGS` still pointed at `/usr/local`:

```
Solaris$ CFLAGS=-I/usr/local/include export CFLAGS
Solaris$ LDFLAGS="-L/usr/local/lib -R/usr/local/lib" export \
   LDFLAGS
Solaris$ ./configure
Solaris$ make
```

And as root:

```
Solaris# make install
```

This will install all of the MRTG software in `/usr/local/mrtg-2`. You can specify an alternate location by running the configure script with the `--prefix` option:

```
Solaris$ ./configure --prefix=/var/tmp/my-mrtg
```

For the rest of this chapter, it is assumed that MRTG is installed in the default location.

## 3.4   Configuring MRTG

Once the MRTG software is installed, you will need to configure it to monitor your devices. This section describes the configuration process, which includes generating the config file, generating HTML index pages for the graphs, and setting up MRTG to gather data at regular intervals.

---

[2]The Bourne shell is `/bin/sh`.

### 3.4.1    Generating the Configuration File

MRTG has a versatile configuration language that makes it difficult to
write your own configuration from scratch. Fortunately, the distribution
comes with a handy program that will generate a configuration for you.

First you must decide where you would like MRTG to place its
generated data files and Web pages. Typically, you will want this to
be a directory on a Web server, and it may be publicly readable. You
must also decide where to place the MRTG configuration file, which
should *not* be publicly readable. It will contain SNMP community
names for your devices, which you may wish to keep secret. We will
place the MRTG pages and graphs in `/usr/local/apache/htdocs/`
`mrtg/` on our Web server and the configuration file in `/usr/local/`
`mrtg-2/cfg/mrtg.cfg`. The `/usr/local/mrtg-2/cfg/` directory does
not exist yet, so we create it, using the account MRTG will run from,
and we make sure others won't have access to the directory:

```
Solaris# mkdir /usr/local/mrtg-2/cfg
Solaris# chmod 700 /usr/local/mrtg-2/cfg
```

The `/usr/local/apache/htdocs/mrtg/` directory should also be created, but with permissions appropriate for your Web server to be able
to read it.

Now run the `cfgmaker` program to create the configuration file:

```
Solaris# /usr/local/mrtg-2/bin/cfgmaker \
    --global 'WorkDir: /usr/local/apache/htdocs/mrtg' \
    --global 'Options[_]: bits' \
    --global 'IconDir: icons' \
    --snmp-options=:::::2 \
    --subdirs=HOSTNAME \
    --ifref=ip \
    --ifdesc=alias \
    --output /usr/local/mrtg-2/cfg/mrtg.cfg \
      community@router1.example.com \
      community@router2.example.com \
      community@router3.example.com
```

It will spend a short while probing each device in order to build the
configuration.

Each option on the command line controls a feature in the configuration. The `--global` options control global configuration features.

`WorkDir` is the directory where MRTG will place data files, and the `bits` option instructs MRTG to report bandwidth in multiples of bits per second instead of bytes per second. The global option `IconDir` specifies the name of a directory in the `WorkDir` directory where MRTG icons will be stored. Copy the icons from the MRTG distribution to this directory now:

```
Solaris# mkdir /usr/local/apache/htdocs/mrtg/icons
Solaris# cp /usr/local/mrtg-2/share/mrtg2/icons/* \
   /usr/local/apache/htdocs/mrtg/icons/
```

and make sure the directory and files are readable to your Web server.

The `snmp-options` variable controls several aspects of SNMP behavior. The only modification we make to the default is to use SNMPv2, which will allow large counter values to work appropriately. If this option is not enabled, you may see incorrect data reported for high-speed network links. You can override the SNMP options set with the `snmp-options` variable for any particular router by appending the options to the name of the router later on the `cfgmaker` command line.

The `subdirs` option controls the organization of MRTG data. By default, MRTG will store all data files in the one specified `WorkDir`. But as each interface will have several different data files associated with it, and each router may hold several interfaces, this can quickly become unwieldy. Setting `subdirs=HOSTNAME` will cause each router to have its own subdirectory under `WorkDir` where all data files for interfaces on that router are stored.

When MRTG stores interface data, it picks a unique filename for each interface. The default name is based on the SNMP index number of the interface. However, there is a serious downside to accepting this as the default. On many routers, adding or removing a board will change SNMP index numbering of other interfaces; interface fifteen yesterday might become interface twenty today. When this happens, MRTG won't know which interface moved where, and the data will become hopelessly confused. One way to avoid this problem is by using the `ifref=ip` option. This tells MRTG to name interface data files by the IP address of the interface rather than the SNMP index number. Under this system, you can add or remove boards, and MRTG will still be able to access the appropriate data. You can even move a network to a new interface and have no problem. The section on maintaining

MRTG goes into greater detail on keeping MRTG consistent with your network configuration.

The `ifdesc=alias` option instructs MRTG to use the interface description when labeling graphs instead of using the default, the SNMP index number. This description will correspond to the string set using the `description` interface command on a Cisco router. If you don't typically set meaningful interface descriptions, you can choose another option for labeling your graphs; several alternate options are listed in Figure 3.2.

The last option to the `cfgmaker` command, `output`, simply specifies the name of the file to which the configuration should be written. Following that, we list each router to be monitored in the form *community@router* where *community* is the community name needed to perform SNMP requests.

| ifdesc | Label type |
|---|---|
| `nr` | Index number |
| `ip` | IP address |
| `eth` | Ethernet address |
| `descr` | Description (board name) |
| `name` | Abbreviated board name |
| `alias` | Config description |

**Figure 3.2.** Settings for the `ifdesc` Option.

## 3.4.2   Other Configuration Options

Examine `/usr/local/mrtg-2/cfg/mrtg.cfg` and you will see the results of the config generation. Many options are automatically set, and there are many other options not in use. The MRTG distribution comes with a full reference for configuration options, linked as MRTG Configuration Reference from the Web page in the `doc/` directory. If you decide to use some of these other options, set them by modifying the `cfgmaker` command line above and running the program again. This way when you move router interfaces around in the future, you can run the `cfgmaker` command to detect the changes without losing any modifications you might have made by hand.

### 3.4.3   Generating Initial Data

Once the configuration file has been created, you can run the `mrtg` program. From the command line, try:

```
Solaris% /usr/local/mrtg-2/bin/mrtg /usr/local/mrtg-2/cfg/mrtg.cfg
```

This will contact your routers and gather the first set of data. Do not be alarmed if you see a long list of errors; this is normal for the first two times you run the program. MRTG is warning you about older data files that it tries to move, but those data files do not yet exist. If you run the program twice more, it should no longer report errors.

After running the `mrtg` command, you will be able to find PNG files and HTML files in `/usr/local/apache/htdocs/mrtg`. A typical Apache Web server installation will allow you to view the pages at `http://server.example.com/mrtg`, where `server.example.com` is replaced with the name of the machine you are installing MRTG on.

If you view one of the HTML files in a Web browser, you will see the empty graphs for a particular interface. Digging out these HTML files is an awkward way to access the graphs because they have odd names like `router1.example.com_10.175.0.1.html`.[3] Fortunately, MRTG also comes with a program that generates an index Web page filled with graphs, one per interface.

### 3.4.4   Generating Index Pages

Index pages are created with the `indexmaker` program in the MRTG distribution. A simple example would be:

```
Solaris% /usr/local/mrtg-2/bin/indexmaker \
   --output /usr/local/apache/htdocs/mrtg/all.html \
   --columns=1 \
   /usr/local/mrtg-2/cfg/mrtg.cfg
```

This creates a single HTML file called all.html that contains the daily graph for all interfaces on all routers. Open this file in a Web browser and see how it looks. The graphs will not yet contain any data. Click

---

[3]This assumes you chose to reference interfaces by IP address. If you chose to reference interfaces differently, the name will take a different form but will still be too cumbersome for easy access.

on a graph and you will see the detailed daily, weekly, monthly, and yearly graphs for that interface.

If you have many interfaces, you may find it takes a long time for the index page to load. If this is the case, you may wish to break the graphs up into several different Web pages, perhaps one page per router. You can do this with the `--filter` option. The following example will create the page router1.html with only interfaces from router1:

```
Solaris% /usr/local/mrtg-2/bin/indexmaker \
    --output /usr/local/apache/htdocs/mrtg/router1.html \
    --filter name=~router1 \
    --columns=1 \
    --title="Bandwidth stats for router1.example.com" \
    /usr/local/mrtg-2/cfg/mrtg.cfg
```

Since you will want to generate the index pages for each router a few times while experimenting with MRTG and later when maintaining it, you can use a simple shell script to create an index page for each router. Create a file called `indexer.sh`:

```
#!/bin/sh
for i in router1 router2 router3; do
    echo "Indexing $i"
    /usr/local/mrtg-2/bin/indexmaker \
        --output /usr/local/apache/htdocs/mrtg/$i.html \
        --filter name=~$i \
        --columns=1 \
        --title="Bandwidth stats for $i" \
        /usr/local/mrtg-2/cfg/mrtg.cfg
done
```

and then type

```
Solaris% chmod u+x indexer.sh
```

to make the program executable. Run the program and it will create the index page for each of the routers listed on the third line. You can now open the `router2.html` page in a Web browser. You should see a page of graphs, one for each interface on router2. If you click on the graph of an interface, you will be taken to the page with its weekly, monthly, and yearly graphs.

If you use separate pages for each router, you'll also want to create a small Web page that links to the index page for each router. This you will have to do by hand. An example might be a `/usr/local/apache/` `htdocs/mrtg/index.html` that contains the HTML:

```
<!DOCTYPE HTML PUBLIC "-//W3C//DTD HTML 4.0 Transitional//EN">
<html>
<head>
  <title>MRTG Graphs</title>
  <meta http-equiv="Content-Type" content="text/html;
    charset=iso-8859-1">
  <meta http-equiv="Refresh" content="300">
  <meta http-equiv="Cache-Control" content="no-cache">
  <meta http-equiv="Pragma" content="no-cache">
  <meta name="robots" content="noarchive">
</head>
<body bgcolor="#FFFFFF" text="#000000">
  <h1>MRTG Graphs</h1>
  <blockquote>
    <a href="router1.html">router1</a> <br>
    <a href="router2.html">router2</a> <br>
    <a href="router3.html">router2</a> <br>
  </blockquote>
</body>
</html>
```

This page can now act as your starting point for using MRTG. Choose a router to examine from this page, which links to an index page with a graph for each interface on the router. Click on that graph and you'll see detailed information about the interface.

## 3.4.5  Setting Up Regular Data Gathering

The only task left is to make sure that MRTG contacts the routers and collects data every five minutes. There are two ways to do this. The first and preferred option is to add an entry to the crontab on your server. This is done differently on different systems. On Linux and Solaris, run the `crontab -e` command, which will start an editor from which you may edit the crontab. On other systems, you are expected to edit the crontab manually. Either way, you should be logged in as the user whose account you wish to run MRTG from. Add a line to the crontab:

```
0,5,10,15,20,25,30,35,40,45,50,55 * * * * \
   /usr/local/mrtg-2/bin/mrtg /usr/local/mrtg-2/cfg/mrtg.cfg \
      --logging /var/log/mrtg.log
```

Under Linux only, you can you use a nifty abbreviation:

```
*/5 * * * * \
   /usr/local/mrtg-2/bin/mrtg /usr/local/mrtg-2/cfg/mrtg.cfg \
      --logging /var/log/mrtg.log
```

Note that each crontab entry must be entirely on a single line. The backslashes in the example should not be included in your crontab; they are used here only to indicate that the line continues without breaking. Save the file and quit the editor, and now the MRTG program will run every five minutes to gather data from routers and update the graphs.

The other method for running MRTG at periodic intervals is to configure it to run as a daemon. This will keep the mrtg program running in the background once you have started it. This is a reasonable way to run MRTG but has the disadvantage that if the program were to accidentally exit, it would stop collecting data until restarted by hand. If you decide to run MRTG as a daemon, you will need to add the text "RunAsDaemon: Yes" to the config, preferably by adding --global 'RunAsDaemon: Yes' as an option to the cfgmaker command. Be sure to add the mrtg command to your system startup scripts so that the daemon will be started when the machine reboots.

## 3.5    Using MRTG

Using MRTG is, as they say, as easy as falling off a log. Click on the graphs you want and examine the data. There are a couple of subtle points to be aware of, though.

### 3.5.1    Faulty Data

When looking at the graphs, consider whether the data makes sense before blindly trusting it. We had an MRTG graph indicate that the traffic on an important network had dropped to zero. In reality, no such thing had occurred; the router software encountered a bug that caused it to stop reporting traffic data correctly via SNMP. This became clear after we examined traffic statistics for other devices on the network.

On a separate occasion, we found that over the period of a few weeks, the bandwidth use on one of our external links was steadily dropping. This was suspicious given the time of year and the fact that the demand for bandwidth seems to be consistently growing with time. It turned out that we had not configured MRTG to use SNMPv2 large counters, and we had hit a point on that link where there was so much traffic that it overloaded the capacity of the smaller counters.

If you are suspicious about the accuracy of MRTG data use tools such as the router command interface to obtain second and third opinions.

### 3.5.2 Missing Data

Traffic levels on a typical network are somewhat bursty, and as a result, the edge of the data in an MRTG graph is usually jagged. When MRTG cannot gather or store data from a router as scheduled, it fills in the same value it found for the previous interval. This tends to keep the data more in tune with reality than filling in a traffic rate of zero. If you notice a completely flat section of an MRTG graph, such as in Figure 3.3, consider that it is likely a period of time when MRTG could not retrieve or store data from the router. A perfectly constant traffic level is a rare exception. In this example, the file system where MRTG stores its data was unavailable between 8:30 p.m. and 1:00 a.m.

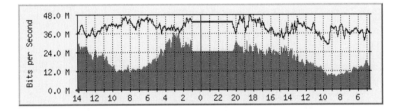

**Figure 3.3.** Graph with Missing Data.

## 3.6  Maintaining MRTG

MRTG requires more maintenance than most of the tools described in this book. Each time you move a network or router interface, you will have to make sure the change is reflected in the MRTG configuration. This is why it is to your advantage to save the `cfgmaker` command line and `indexer.sh` script described earlier. They will allow you to generate a new configuration and new index pages with a minimal amount of effort. You may even choose to run them nightly from the crontab so that changes will be reflected automatically.

Moving networks and interfaces can wreak havoc with MRTG's sense of which data files belong to which network. Your setting of `ifref` on the `cfgmaker` command line will give you control over how MRTG references interfaces. If you set `ifref` to `ip`, MRTG will track an interface by its IP address. This is a good choice since you'll be able to move a network to a new interface and MRTG will still track the data. Other options for the the `ifref` variable are the same as those listed in Figure 3.2, except that the `alias` setting is not available.

In the event that you do make a change that causes MRTG to lose its sense of which data belongs to which network, you can attempt to remedy the situation by finding the appropriate `.log` file under `/usr/local/apache/htdocs/mrtg/router*` and renaming it to be the data file that MRTG expects for the new network.

## 3.7   References and Further Study

The MRTG Web site at `http://www.mrtg.org/` and the MRTG software distribution both have detailed documentation on using MRTG, including information on `cfgmaker`, `indexmaker`, the configuration language and all other components of MRTG.

The PNG distribution and further information about PNG can be found at `http://www.libpng.org/`. The GD library is at `http://www.boutell.com/gd/`.

`http://www.perl.org/` is one of the many sites devoted to information related to Perl, the language in which most of MRTG is written.

# Chapter 4

# NEO

## 4.1 Overview of Neo

In Chapter 2, you saw how a networked device can be managed with SNMP. With `snmpget`, `snmpset`, and `snmpwalk`, you can retrieve operational information and make configuration changes. As useful as these programs are, they are not well suited for debugging day-to-day network problems. A tool is needed that handles all of the SNMP requests behind the scenes while presenting a simple interface to the user.

At MIT, we wrote just such a tool called Neo. Using Neo's simple commands, we can check bandwidth usage or determine on which switch port a particular host resides. For us, it has become the bread and butter of network administration. Neo is a text-based client that is well suited to an environment in which an operator may need to use a remote login session to manage the network.

Of course, Neo is helpful only if your devices can be managed with SNMP. If your devices have only a telnet interface or have no management interface at all, Neo will not be a useful tool for interacting with them.

## 4.2 What Neo Can Help You Do

Neo can perform a number tasks, and as a relatively new tool, it is constantly having more functionality added. The core functionality is currently:

- Determining on which switch port a host resides

- Translating an IP address to a hardware address

- Obtaining traffic statistics

- Obtaining board or port information

- Disabling or enabling a port

- Obtaining general device information

- Obtaining information about device power and environmental conditions

## Locating Hosts and the Forwarding Table

One of the benefits of network switches over repeaters is that switches send traffic destined for a particular host only to the port on which that host resides. A repeater, in contrast, sends all traffic to every port (see Figure 4.1). The switch must therefore know which host is on which port so that it can direct traffic appropriately. The switch figures this out using a process known as **station learning**. The idea is for the switch to build a **forwarding table** that maps each host to a port on the switch and to do so without any operator intervention. This allows a host to be plugged into a switch with no need to change the switch configuration manually.

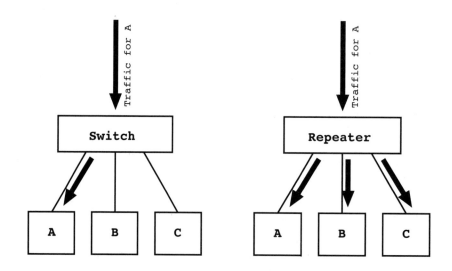

**Figure 4.1.** Switched Traffic Versus Repeated Traffic.

The process of learning which host is on which port begins with an empty forwarding table. In this state, the switch acts just like a repeater: Because it doesn't know which port traffic should be sent to, it sends the traffic to every port. Eventually, a host on the switch is expected to send some data of its own, either spontaneously or in response to data sent to it. When this happens, the switch notes the hardware address of the sending host and the port the traffic came from. This information is then stored in the forwarding table, and the switch now knows to send traffic destined for that address to that port. In this way, the source address of traffic is used to determine where traffic destined for that address should be sent in the future.

The switch makes information in the forwarding table available via SNMP as described in Chapter 2. Neo allows an operator to query this information easily. You can find the port on which a particular hardware address is located:

```
neo: locate 00:03:BA:09:1F:36 @switch13.example.com
Found on 6@switch13.example.com
```

or ask the switch for all hardware addresses present on a particular port:

```
neo: port search 2/5@switch2.example.com
00:04:76:CB:B1:CD
00:05:02:4B:C6:50
00:06:5B:1D:68:43
00:06:5B:1D:68:46
00:50:8B:AD:FE:8E
00:E0:63:2B:D7:C4
00:E0:63:2B:D7:DC
```

Neo syntax also allows many different devices to be searched in a single query in case the operator does not know on which switch a host will be:

```
neo: locate 00:03:BA:09:1F:36 @k:northannex
Found on 6@switch13.example.com
```

## Translating an IP Address to a Hardware Address

Neo can use the SNMP `ipNetToMediaTable` to ask a device for the hardware address associated with a particular IP address:

```
neo: arpfind host.example.com router.example.com
10.5.0.1 says 10.5.1.2 is 00:03:BA:09:1F:36
```

This is particularly useful when you need to locate a host and have only its IP address or host name. You can use Neo first to ask the nearest router for a host's hardware address and then use that hardware address in a `locate` command.

## Obtaining Traffic Statistics

It's often very helpful when you are debugging network problems to be able to view the amount of traffic being sent to or from particular ports. Neo is capable of presenting this data:

```
neo: stats switch.example.com
Probing devices ...
Getting first set of stats...
Getting second set of stats...
Port statistics:
```

| p | type | u | lnk | adm | ap kbs | ikbs | okbs | pps | ipps | opps | ierps | oerps |
|---|------|---|-----|-----|--------|------|------|-----|------|------|-------|-------|
| 1 | 100TX | | 100 | On | 20 | 0 | 20 | 26 | 0 | 26 | 0 | 0 |
| 2 | 100T | | 100 | On | 19 | 0 | 19 | 26 | 0 | 26 | 0 | 0 |
| 3 | 100TX | | 10 | On | 20 | 0 | 20 | 27 | 0 | 27 | 0 | 0 |
| 4 | 100TX | | - | On | 0 | 0 | 0 | 0 | 0 | 0 | 0 | 0 |
| 5 | 100TX | | - | On | 0 | 0 | 0 | 0 | 0 | 0 | 0 | 0 |
| 6 | 100TX | | 100 | On | 455 | 42 | 413 | 157 | 51 | 106 | 0 | 0 |
| 7 | 100TX | | 10 | On | 19 | 0 | 19 | 26 | 0 | 26 | 0 | 0 |
| 8 | 100TX | | 100 | On | 19 | 0 | 19 | 26 | 0 | 26 | 0 | 0 |
| 9 | 100TX | | 100 | On | 19 | 0 | 19 | 26 | 0 | 26 | 0 | 0 |
| 10 | 100TX | | - | On | 0 | 0 | 0 | 0 | 0 | 0 | 0 | 0 |
| 11 | 100TX | | 100 | On | 19 | 0 | 19 | 26 | 0 | 26 | 0 | 0 |
| 12 | 100TX | | 100 | On | 19 | 0 | 19 | 27 | 0 | 27 | 0 | 0 |
| 13 | 100?X | * | 100 | On | 382 | 368 | 14 | 84 | 71 | 13 | 0 | 0 |
| 14 | 100?X | * | - | On | 0 | 0 | 0 | 0 | 0 | 0 | 0 | 0 |
| 15 | loop | | 10 | On | 59 | 28 | 31 | 80 | 40 | 40 | 0 | 0 |

## Disabling or Enabling a Port

When a host or a network segment is causing an operational problem, the only solution may be to disable that part of the network in order to keep everything else up and running. Neo has commands for turning a port on or off:

```
neo: port disable 22@switch.example.com
22@switch.example.com disabled

neo: port enable 22@switch.example.com
22@switch.example.com enabled
```

### Power, Environmental, and General Device Information

Finally, Neo can ask devices about the status of power, environmental conditions, and other information.  On any device, Neo can print the system name, the address of the administrative contact, and other information from the SNMP `system` group.  On devices that support it, Neo can print the temperature of the device or the status of the power supplies.  On a managed UPS, Neo can retrieve detailed information about the battery lifetime and the operational status of the device.

### Other Functionality

Aside from these core functions, Neo has support for a few additional features such as accessing information from printers, performing domain name server (DNS) lookups, and executing shell commands.

## 4.3   Installing Neo

The source for Neo is available at `http://web.mit.edu/ktools/`. Download the latest version and uncompress the package:

```
Solaris% gunzip -c neo-1.2.12.tar.gz | tar xvf -
```

The unpacked source can then be found in a directory with the same name as the version you have downloaded.  Change to that directory:

```
Solaris% cd neo-1.2.12
```

And then configure and build the package:

```
Solaris% ./configure
Solaris% make
```

You may also then type:

```
Solaris% make install
```

which simply places the Neo binary in `/usr/local/bin/`.

Neo should build without trouble on most platforms and is regularly tested on Solaris and Linux in particular. Because Neo is a relatively new piece of software, the configuration and build process has not yet been tested at many sites. If you encounter a problem with either step, you are encouraged to send email to `bug-neo@mit.edu` with a detailed description of the failure.

If the configure script is not able to find the GNU readline library, Neo will successfully build without it, but command line editing will not be available. If your system does not have the readline library, you can download it at `http://www.gnu.org/` and install it on your system. Solaris, for example, does not come with the readline library, though Linux typically does.

If you have readline installed in a nonstandard location, you may need to set the **CFLAGS** and **LDFLAGS** environment variables before running the configure script. For example, if your shell is csh or tcsh, you would use:

```
Solaris% setenv CFLAGS -I/usr/local/include
Solaris% setenv LDFLAGS -L/usr/local/lib
Solaris% ./configure
```

But if your shell is bash or the Bourne shell, it would instead be:

```
Solaris% CFLAGS=-I/usr/local/include export CFLAGS
Solaris% LDFLAGS=-L/usr/local/lib export LDFLAGS
Solaris% ./configure
```

Neo builds its own small SNMP implementation and therefore does not require any external SNMP packages.

Once the binary is built, try running it to make sure it works. You should see output like this:

```
Solaris% ./neo

Welcome to neo version 1.2.12 (Atropine).
Consult 'help version' for information on features in this version.

neo:
```

If so, you have successfully built Neo and are ready to begin using it.

## 4.4   Using Neo

The following sections discuss Neo commands and syntax in detail.

### 4.4.1   The Command Prompt

Neo presents you with its own command prompt, which is the word "neo" followed by a colon. From this prompt, you can type commands for Neo to execute. If upon startup Neo did not print a warning about the readline library, you will have full command line editing available from the prompt. Figure 4.2 lists some of the common command line editing features; for a more detailed reference, consult `http://www.gnu.org/directory/readline.html`.

At any time while Neo is executing a command, you can type Control-C to interrupt the running command and return to the Neo prompt.

The Neo command prompt also allows a limited amount of command abbreviation. For example, the `device` command can be abbreviated `dev`, and the `port enable` command can be abbreviated `port ena`.

| Key | Function |
|---|---|
| C-f / Right | Move cursor right |
| C-b / Left | Move cursor left |
| C-a | Move cursor to start of line |
| C-e | Move cursor to end of line |
| M-f | Move cursor to next word |
| M-b | Move cursor to previous word |
| C-p / Up | Retrieve the previous command |
| C-n / Down | Retrieve the next command |
| C-k | Kill text to end of line |
| C-y | Yank killed text into buffer |

**Figure 4.2.** Basic Readline Editing Keys.

### 4.4.2   The Location Syntax

One of Neo's strengths is its flexible location syntax. The location syntax is the format Neo uses to describe a device, a number of devices, or particular ports on a device. Generically, the location syntax takes the form *port@device*. That is, a port designator and a device designator separated by an at sign. In a simple example, this may be `5@switch.example.com`, representing port five on switch.example.com. However, either the port designator or the device designator may use more exotic options.

## The Device Designator

In the simplest case, a location may be just a single device with no associated ports. For this, use an at sign followed by the host name:

    @switch.example.com

Or in just this example alone, you can abbreviate it to the host name with no at sign:

    switch.example.com

Sometimes you will want a location to represent more than one device, which you can accomplish several different ways. First, you can list device names separated by commas:

    @switch1.example.com,switch2.example.com,router.example.com

Make sure there are no spaces in the location or Neo will interpret it as multiple arguments to a command instead of as a single location.

Often you will want to refer to so many devices that separating them all by commas would be cumbersome. One option is to reference a file that contains a list of host names and use the syntax @f:*filename*. For example, if you have a file `/var/tmp/switches` with a list of hosts, one per line, use the location syntax:

    @f:/var/tmp/switches

You can check yourself by asking Neo to describe which devices are present in a location using the `location print` command:

    neo: location print @f:/var/tmp/switches
    Devices (4) are:
      SWITCH1.EXAMPLE.COM
      SWITCH2.EXAMPLE.COM
      SWITCH3.EXAMPLE.COM
      SWITCH4.EXAMPLE.COM

On a large network, there may be so many devices that it's useful to divide them into smaller groups of devices. For example, you may wish to be able to refer to all the devices on one particular network or broadcast domain. Neo supports this through the use of a **keyfile**. The keyfile is a text file that looks something like this:

```
10.115|M5-201T-SWITCH-ENTRY.EXAMPLE.COM
10.115|M5-201T-SWITCH-1.EXAMPLE.COM
10.115|M5-201T-SWITCH-2.EXAMPLE.COM
10.115|M5-201T-SWITCH-3.EXAMPLE.COM
10.115|M5-201T-SWITCH-4.EXAMPLE.COM
10.115|M5-301T-SWITCH-1.EXAMPLE.COM
10.116|M6-332T-SWITCH-ENTRY.EXAMPLE.COM
10.116|M6-332T-SWITCH-1.EXAMPLE.COM
10.116|M6-332T-SWITCH-2.EXAMPLE.COM
10.116|M6-332T-SWITCH-3.EXAMPLE.COM
10.116|M6-432T-SWITCH-1.EXAMPLE.COM
10.116|M6-432T-SWITCH-2.EXAMPLE.COM
```

Each line contains a key string, followed a vertical bar, and then a value string. In Neo location syntax, we can refer to all of the devices whose key is 10.116 with the syntax:

```
@k:10.116
```

The k stands for key, of course. If you ask Neo for details on that location, you will find:

```
neo: location print @k:10.116
Devices (6) are:
  M6-332T-SWITCH-ENTRY.EXAMPLE.COM
  M6-332T-SWITCH-1.EXAMPLE.COM
  M6-332T-SWITCH-2.EXAMPLE.COM
  M6-332T-SWITCH-3.EXAMPLE.COM
  M6-432T-SWITCH-1.EXAMPLE.COM
  M6-432T-SWITCH-2.EXAMPLE.COM
```

At MIT we find it useful to organize the keyfile by network number because of the addressing scheme we use. But the key can really be any text string. You may choose to create a keyfile more like:

```
eastwing|SWITCH1.EXAMPLE.COM
eastwing|SWITCH2.EXAMPLE.COM
eastwing|SWITCH3.EXAMPLE.COM
```

```
northannex|SWITCH4.EXAMPLE.COM
northannex|SWITCH5.EXAMPLE.COM
northannex|SWITCH6.EXAMPLE.COM
core|SWITCH7.EXAMPLE.COM
core|SWITCH8.EXAMPLE.COM
core|SWITCH9.EXAMPLE.COM
```

and then refer to groups of devices as `@k:core` or `@k:northannex`.
There is also no rule that says the same device can't belong to multiple key groups if that suits your needs.

By default, Neo expects the keyfile to be named `/usr/local/etc/neo.keyfile`. You can modify this by changing one of Neo's built-in variables, described in Section 4.4.3, or by using the `-k` command line option, described in Section 4.4.11.

## The Port Syntax

A port designator, if present in a location, always precedes the at sign. If the location is to refer to an entire device, the port is left off entirely. If we do wish to specify a port, the format will depend on the design of the device.

Many devices have a simple notion of numbered ports; the first port on the device is port one, the next one is port two, and so on. The physical ports on the device may be labeled with this number. From a management point of view, there will typically be one or two more ports available via SNMP than are physically present on the device. These are loopback ports or ports otherwise intended for internal use. For a straightforward device like this, the port syntax is simply the number of the port. So port twelve on switch1.example.com would be:

```
12@switch1.example.com
```

Other devices, particularly devices with removable modules, have a notion of a port being numbered by a board number and port number on that board. For example, a Cisco Catalyst switch may have six slots, each one capable of holding a board with 24 ports. Instead of numbering each port on the device with a unique integer, we'd like to refer to a port as the board number the port is on and then the port number on that board. The notation for this is *board/port*. So port five on board three on switch5.example.com would be:

```
3/5@switch5.example.com
```

Note that this means the appropriate syntax depends on the type of device Neo is talking to. Most of the time, you will know the layout of the device before you wish to specify a particular port, but if you do use the wrong port syntax for a device, Neo will print a warning about the mistake. In Section 4.4.7, there is information on using the Neo `device` command to ask a device for its layout so that you will definitively know the correct syntax.

Also be aware that some devices that do not physically have boards do have an internal notion of boards. The Cisco Catalyst 2948 has 50 static, numbered ports with no modular components, but internally, the Cisco software considers these ports to be on board two, while a phantom board one is the management board.

Occasionally, you may wish to refer to a board itself with no particular port. You might want to ask a device about the status of board three, for example. The syntax for this is *board/@device*, as in:

```
3/@switch5.example.com
```

Just as you may wish to specify many devices in a single location, it is also useful to be able to specify many ports in a single location. You can use an asterisk in the port designator to represent multiple ports. By example:

```
*@switch1.example.com
```

refers to *all* ports on switch1.example.com, and this switch must be a switch without boards. If you wish to refer to all ports on a device that does have boards, use:

```
*/*@switch5.example.com
```

Similarly, you could refer to all ports on a particular board with:

```
4/*@switch5.example.com
```

Neo also allows you to use a period in place of an asterisk, for convenience in using wildcards on a shell command line. The following two examples are then identical:

```
*@switch1.example.com

.@switch1.example.com
```

Note that wildcards like these can be used on only the left side of the
at sign.

Figure 4.3 summarizes the different forms of location syntax.

| Location | Meaning |
|---|---|
| `@switch1` | The device switch1 |
| `switch1` | The device switch1 |
| `@switch1,switch5` | The devices switch1 and switch5 |
| `@f:/var/tmp/devicelist` | The devices listed in /var/tmp/devicelist |
| `@k:east` | Devices associated with "east" in the keyfile |
| `3/2@switch5` | Board 3, port 2 on switch5 |
| `10@switch1` | Port 10 on switch1 |
| `3/@switch5` | Board 3 on switch5 |
| `*@switch1` | All ports on switch1 |
| `.@switch1` | All ports on switch1 |
| `3/*@switch5` | All ports on board 3 on switch5 |
| `*/*@switch5` | All ports on switch5 |
| `*/@switch5` | All boards on switch5 |

**Figure 4.3.** Summary of Neo Location Syntax.

## 4.4.3   Variables

Neo has a number of built-in variables it uses for controlling user configuration options. Figure 4.4 lists the variables currently in use. You
can list the value of all variables by typing the `print` command with
no arguments:

```
neo: print
writecom = 'public'
readcom = 'public'
keyfile = '/usr/local/etc/neo.keyfile'
statsdelay = 5
```

```
timeout = 8
macmode = 'standard'
version = '1.2.12 (Atropine)'
burst = 1
```

You can change the value of a variable with the `set` command, and you can view the value with the `print` command:

```
neo: set writecom mysecret
neo: print writecom
writecom = 'mysecret'
```

The above example sets the SNMP community used for SNMP writes to `mysecret`. When setting the `writecom` and `readcom` variables only, you may leave off the final argument and Neo will prompt you to enter the community name without echoing the keystrokes you type to the terminal. This allows an operator to enter a secret string without others being able to see it.

The `timeout` variable controls how long Neo should wait for an SNMP response from a device. The value is in seconds and the default is eight seconds. If for some reason this is not a long enough timeout, you can change the value.

The `burst` variable can be used to force SNMP to send multiple copies of packets in the event that network conditions are degraded and packets are being dropped. This is discussed later in the chapter, as are the `statsdelay` and `macmode` variables.

| Variable | Function |
|----------|----------|
| readcom | SNMP read community |
| writecom | SNMP write community |
| keyfile | Filename of the keyfile |
| statsdelay | Delay for statics gathering |
| timeout | SNMP timeout |
| macmode | Format for MAC addresses |
| burst | The SNMP burst rate |

**Figure 4.4.** All Neo Variables.

### 4.4.4   The Arpfind Command

The `arpfind` command queries a device's ARP cache in order to translate an IP address to a hardware address. The syntax is simply: `arpfind` *hostname devicelocation.* For example:

```
neo: arpfind myhost.example.com router.example.com
router.example.com says 10.5.1.2 is 00:03:BA:09:1F:36
```

Or if you wish to search multiple devices, you can use a more interesting location syntax:

```
neo: arpfind otherhost.example.com @k:routers
router-east.example.com says 10.6.0.12 is 08:00:20:9A:D3:5F
```

### 4.4.5   The Locate Command

As described earlier, the `locate` command searches a switch's forwarding table for a particular hardware address. The syntax for the locate command is `locate [-v] [-u]` *address devicelocation.* Typical use would be:

```
neo: locate 00:03:BA:09:1F:36 @k:northannex
Found on 6@switch13.example.com
```

There is an important subtlety to notice here. If we run the locate command again with the `-v` option, it tells us about all the devices being searched:

```
neo: locate -v 00:03:BA:09:1F:36 @k:northannex
Probing devices ...
Searching switch11 ...
Searching switch12 ...
Searching switch13 ...
Found on 6@switch13 ...
Searching switch14 ...
Searching switch15 ...
Searching switch16 ...
1 locations found
```

In this particular example, all the switches are on the same physical network. But then why doesn't this MAC address appear on the other switches as well? The answer is that Neo employs some trickery to try

to ignore ports that are the uplink to the device. If you use the -u
option to the `locate` command, Neo will print every location found,
without filtering uplink ports:

```
neo: locate -u 00:03:BA:09:1F:36 @k:northannex
Found on 25@switch10
Found on 25@switch11
Found on 25@switch12
Found on 6@switch13
Found on 25@switch14
Found on 25@switch15
Found on 25@switch16
```

Here we see that port 25 is the uplink to these switches and that Neo
filtered those answers for us.

## 4.4.6   The Port Command

The port command has four different subcommands used to perform
functions on a port:

- `port enable`: Turn the port on

- `port disable`: Turn the port off

- `port status`: Report the administrative status of the port

- `port search`: Print the address of all devices on the port

These are all self-explanatory and examples follow. Do note that
the `port enable` and `port disable` commands use an SNMP write.
Assuming you do not have the write community for your devices set
to "public," you will need to set the Neo SNMP write community first
with the `set writecom` command.

```
neo: port disable 22@switch.example.com
22@switch.example.com disabled


neo: port enable 22@switch.example.com
22@switch.example.com enabled
```

```
neo: port status 22@switch.example.com
22@switch.example.com enabled

neo: port search 2/5@switch5.example.com
00:04:76:CB:B1:CD
00:05:02:4B:C6:50
00:06:5B:1D:68:43
00:06:5B:1D:68:46
00:50:8B:AD:FE:8E
00:E0:63:2B:D7:C4
00:E0:63:2B:D7:DC
```

When you use the `port search` command, the `macmode` variable controls the format of the hardware addresses returned. Figure 4.5 provides examples of the different settings for the `macmode` variable and the hardware address format that each setting corresponds to. You may wish to change the format to "cisco" if you will be feeding the results to a Cisco command prompt, thereby saving you the effort of converting each address format yourself.

| macmode | Example |
|---------|------------------------|
| standard | `00:04:76:CB:B1:CD` |
| cisco | `0004.76CB.B1CD` |
| dash | `00-04-76-CB-B1-CD` |

**Figure 4.5.** Settings for the `macmode` Variable.

## 4.4.7   The Device Summary Command

The `device` command has three subcommands:

- `device summary`

- `device info`

- `device type`

The first command, `device summary`, provides a useful summary of the layout of a device. For a simple device without boards, this prints a summary of all ports:

```
neo: dev sum switch1.example.com
Port summary:
 p type          u  lnk adm ap
------------------------------
 1 100TX            100  On
 2 100TX            100  On
 3 100TX             10  On
 4 100TX              -  On
 5 100TX              -  On
 6 100TX            100  On
 7 100TX             10  On
 8 100TX            100  On
 9 100TX            100  On
10 100TX              -  On
11 100TX            100  On
12 100TX            100  On
13 100TX            100  On
14 100TX            100  On
15 100TX            100  On
16 100TX            100  On
17 100TX            100  On
18 100TX              -  On
19 100TX            100  On
20 100TX              -  On
21 100TX              -  On
22 100TX            100  On
23 100TX              -  On
24 100TX              -  On
25 100?X         *  100  On
26 100?X         *    -  On
27 loop              10  On
```

The first column indicates the port number. The "type" column denotes
the media type of the port. The "u" column contains an asterisk if Neo
believes this port is an uplink. The "lnk" column is the link speed of
the port, or a hyphen if no link is present. Finally, the "adm" column
tells us whether the port is administratively on or off. The column
marked "ap" is not often used, but it can indicate that a port has been
automatically disabled by the device for some particular reason.

On a device with boards, the `device summary` command is particularly useful because it shows us the board layout of the device:

```
neo: dev sum switch5.example.com
Board summary:
 b type              sg  ul ultype
------------------------------------------
 1 Mgmt2 2 1000X        0
 2 24 10/100/1000T      0
 3 24 10/100/1000T      0
 4 Empty
 5 Empty
 6 24 100FX (mm)        0
```

The first column is the board number and the second is a description of the board. On this device, board three has 24 ports, each 10/100/1000T. The remaining columns are used occasionally for certain kinds of repeaters and indicate what segment the board is on and whether it has a modular uplink.

The most important aspect of the device summary command is that it can be used on a device without your knowing what the layout of the device is ahead of time. If you're starting cold with just a host name for a device, the device summary command is a good way to get your bearings before proceeding with commands that expect you to know its layout.

Once you do know that a device has boards, you can also use the **device summary** command to generate a port summary, just as for a device without boards. Simply use the location syntax for accessing all ports on a board:

```
neo: dev sum 3/*@switch5.example.com
Port summary:
 p type              u  lnk adm ap
------------------------------
 1 1000T              -  On
 2 1000T              -  On
 3 1000T              -  On
 4 1000T              -  On
 5 1000T              -  On
 6 1000T              -  On
 7 1000T              -  On
 8 1000T              -  On
 9 1000T              -  On
10 1000T              -  On
```

```
11 1000T                -  On
12 1000T                -  On
13 1000T                -  On
14 1000T                -  On
15 1000T                -  On
16 1000T                -  On
17 1000T                -  On
18 1000T             1000  On
19 1000T             1000  On
20 1000T             1000  On
21 1000T             1000  On
22 1000T              100  On
23 1000T             1000  On
24 1000T             1000  On
```

## 4.4.8   The Device Info Command

In its simplest form, the `device info` command prints the system information from a device:

```
neo: dev info switch.example.com
switch.example.com
  Device type: C2200
  Contact    : admin@example.com
  Name       : switch.example.com
  Location   : 5-142T
  Uptime     : 92 days 22:07:20
  ObjectID   : .1.3.6.1.4.1.52.3.9.3.4.84
  Descr      : Cabletron Systems, Inc. 2H253-25R Rev 04.00....
```

There are also subcommands that provide additional information. When possible, the `device weather` command will print information about the environmental conditions of the device:

```
neo: dev info weather router.example.com
Intake temp: 25C / 77F
Hotpoint   : 35C / 95F
Exhaust    : 32C / 89F
```

The power subcommand will print information about the power status of the device. This may be the status of the power supplies on a piece of network hardware or detailed information about the condition of a UPS:

```
neo: dev info power ups.example.com
  Type             : Symmetra
  Name             :
  # Alarms Present : <unsupported>
  Status           : Normal

  Battery Capacity : 100%
  Battery Run Time : 0 d 02:44:00
  Time On Battery  : 0 d 00:00:00
  Battery Voltage  : <unsupported>
  Battery Current  : <unsupported>

  Input 1 Voltage  : 199 V
  Input 1 Current  : <unsupported>
  Input 1 Freq.    : 60 Hz

  Output 1 Voltage : 213 V
  Output 1 Current : 13 A
  Output 1 Freq.   : 60 Hz
  Output 1 Load    : 20%

  (device specific section)

  Battery Status   : All batteries OK
  Last Fail Cause  : Self Test
```

If power or environmental information is not available for the device, Neo will print a warning message:

```
neo: dev info power switch3.example.com
Power info is not yet supported on this device
```

## 4.4.9   The Stats Command

The stats command is another extremely useful Neo command. It prints per-port traffic statistics:

```
neo: stats *@switch1.example.com
Probing devices ...
Getting first set of stats...
Getting second set of stats...
```

```
Port statistics:
 p type   u lnk adm ap kbs ikbs okbs  pps ipps opps ierps oerps
---------------------------------------------------------------
 1 100TX    100  On    20    0   20   26    0   26    0    0
 2 100TX    100  On    19    0   19   26    0   26    0    0
 3 100TX     10  On    20    0   20   27    0   27    0    0
 4 100TX      -  On     0    0    0    0    0    0    0    0
 5 100TX      -  On     0    0    0    0    0    0    0    0
 6 100TX    100  On   455   42  413  157   51  106    0    0
 7 100TX     10  On    19    0   19   26    0   26    0    0
 8 100TX    100  On    19    0   19   26    0   26    0    0
 9 100TX    100  On    19    0   19   26    0   26    0    0
10 100TX      -  On     0    0    0    0    0    0    0    0
11 100TX    100  On    19    0   19   26    0   26    0    0
12 100TX    100  On    19    0   19   27    0   27    0    0
13 100?X *  100  On   382  368   14   84   71   13    0    0
14 100?X *    -  On     0    0    0    0    0    0    0    0
15 loop      10  On    59   28   31   80   40   40    0    0
```

Note that this is a device without boards. If we wanted port statistics on a device with boards, we would use:

```
neo: stats 2/*@switch5.example.com
Probing devices ...
Getting device summary ...
Getting first set of stats...
Getting second set of stats...
Port statistics:
 p type   u  lnk adm ap kbs ikbs okbs  pps ipps  opps ierps oerps
----------------------------------------------------------------
 1 1000T   1000  On    11    0   11   13    0   13    0    0
 2 1000T   1000  On   235   78  157  191   90  101    0    0
 3 1000T   1000  On    13    1   12   14    2   12    0    0
 4 1000T   1000  On    36   12   24   43   15   28    0    0
 5 1000T    100  On   287  253   34   54   27   27    0    0
 6 1000T   1000  On    12    0   12   11    0   11    0    0
 7 1000T   1000  On    11    0   11   10    0   10    0    0
 8 1000T   1000  On    11    0   11   10    0   10    0    0
 9 1000T   1000  On    11    0   11   10    0   10    0    0
10 1000T   1000  On  2200 2126   74  288  176  112    0    0
11 1000T   1000  On  2276   68 2208  306  106  200    0    0
12 1000T   1000  On    24    5   19   21    4   17    0    0
13 1000T   1000  On    14    0   14   14    0   14    0    0
14 1000T   1000  On    13    0   13   15    1   14    0    0
15 1000T   1000  On    13    1   12   13    2   11    0    0
```

| 16 | 1000T | –    | On | 0  | 0 | 0  | 0  | 0 | 0  | 0 | 0 |
|----|-------|------|----|----|---|----|----|---|----|---|---|
| 17 | 1000T | –    | On | 0  | 0 | 0  | 0  | 0 | 0  | 0 | 0 |
| 18 | 1000T | –    | On | 0  | 0 | 0  | 0  | 0 | 0  | 0 | 0 |
| 19 | 1000T | –    | On | 0  | 0 | 0  | 0  | 0 | 0  | 0 | 0 |
| 20 | 1000T | –    | On | 0  | 0 | 0  | 0  | 0 | 0  | 0 | 0 |
| 21 | 1000T | 1000 | On | 13 | 1 | 12 | 12 | 1 | 11 | 0 | 0 |
| 22 | 1000T | 1000 | On | 12 | 1 | 11 | 10 | 0 | 10 | 0 | 0 |
| 23 | 1000T | 1000 | On | 13 | 0 | 13 | 11 | 0 | 11 | 0 | 0 |
| 24 | 1000T | 1000 | On | 12 | 0 | 12 | 10 | 0 | 10 | 0 | 0 |

which would give us port statistics for all ports on board two. Some devices support board statistics; that is, statistics on how much traffic is being handled by a particular board. If a device is capable of this, you can retrieve the information with `stats */@`*device* or just `stats` *device*.

In the above examples, the first few columns are labeled the same as for the `device summary` command. The latter columns denote, in order:

- **kbs**: Total kilobits per second of traffic through the port

- **ikbs**: Kilobits per second of traffic into the port

- **okbs**: Kilobits per second of traffic out of the port

- **pps**: Packets per second through the port

- **ipps**: Packets per second into the port

- **opps**: Packets per second out of the port

- **ierps**: Error packets per second into the port

- **oerps**: Error packets per second out of the port

In the last example, we can see 2.2Mb/s of traffic on board two, ports 10 and 11. Looking more closely, we can see that 2.1Mb/s of traffic is coming from port 10 (into the port) and 2.2Mb/s of traffic is being sent to port 11 (out of the port). Our intuition tells us this is probably data being sent from a machine on port 10 to a machine on port 11, though it is entirely possible that the two machines are independently speaking to other machines on a different board.

When running the `stats` command, you will usually notice a short delay between the text "Getting first set of stats..." and "Getting second set of stats...". This delay is present so that Neo can gather statistics over a reasonably average period of time. The default is five seconds, but you can change this by setting the `statsdelay` variable to another value. Note that Neo will allow there to be *more* time between data runs than the value specified in `statsdelay`, but it will always allow at least that much time. If for some reason Neo requires a long time to gather the first set of data, the second set may not begin until after the `statsdelay` time has elapsed.

## 4.4.10   Online Help

Neo has a complete online help system, which you can access by typing the `help` command with no arguments. Neo will print a list of help topics and the name of each command. If you give the topic or command name as an argument to the help command, Neo will print detailed information on the subject. For example, `help locate` will print information on using the locate command, and `help syntax` will print help on Neo's location syntax.

## 4.4.11   Command Line Arguments

You can use Neo in scripts by providing the commands you wish to execute as arguments to the program. For example:

```
Solaris% neo arpfind host.example.com router.example.com
10.5.0.1 says 10.5.1.2 is 00:03:BA:09:1F:36
```

For convenience, Neo has four command line options. From `help args`:

```
-k <keyfile>
    Set the kefyile to <keyfile>.

-w <community>
    Set the write community to <community>.

-r <community>
    Set the read community to <community>.

-c <community>
    Set both the read and write communities to <community>
```

This allows you to set private community names without requiring an extra command:

```
Solaris% neo -w mysecret port dis 10@switch1.example.com
10@switch1.example.com disabled
```

Be aware that this is a security risk. If you run Neo on a system that others can log into, and you place a secret community string on the command line, other users will be able to read it by looking at a list of running processes.

## 4.4.12   Other Commands

Neo has a few other commands that you may find useful. The `hostinfo` command performs DNS lookups, using built-in code:

```
neo: hostinfo host.example.com
Official name:  HOST.EXAMPLE.COM
Host address:   10.5.1.2
Host CPU:       SUN/ULTRA-10
Host OS:        SOLARIS
```

The `location print` command, as illustrated earlier, can be used to print information about the devices present in a Neo location. The `exec` command can be used to exec a shell command from the Neo prompt.

## 4.4.13   Using Neo in Degraded Network Conditions

One of the times we use Neo most is when a network is having an operational problem. Unfortunately, when a network is in trouble, it may be hard to get SNMP packets to the necessary devices on the network. Imagine a host on your network that has been broken into by a malicious cracker. The cracker runs a denial of service attack program that sends as much network traffic as possible to some distant host on another network. The traffic flooding the connection to your devices may make it difficult for your SNMP management packets to get through.

In an effort to remedy this situation Neo has a variable called `burst`, whose default value is one. In this state Neo will send out one SNMP packet when it needs to make a request. If no response is received and the SNMP timeout is close to expiring, Neo will try sending a second packet. If the burst value is set to two, however, Neo will send out two packets each time instead of one. If the burst value is 10 Neo will send

10 identical SNMP requests each time. The hope is that one or more of the packets will make it through the noise and reach the device and that one of the responses will make it back to your management station.

Use some care, even in very adverse network conditions, that you do not set the burst value too high. There is a tradeoff between ensuring reliability and adding to the congestion by sending multiple packets. Additionally, with a high burst rate, Neo has to work harder to process all the extra information sent and received. Generally, it's a good idea to try a burst setting between two and four before using anything higher. Larger values may be used, but they work better for queries that require only a few packets, such as disabling a port. Trying to gather statistics with a high burst rate can be difficult, for example. In general, there is probably never a reason to use a burst rate higher than 10 or 20, and those rates would be used only in the most extreme circumstances.

## 4.5   Examples of Use

How does it all come together in the day-to-day operation of a network? Here are a few examples that demonstrate common scenarios.

### Finding and Disabling a Host

Say you have the name of a host, `broken.example.com`, that you know has been compromised by a malicious cracker. You want to find the host and disable its network access.[1] First you ping the host in case it has been inactive and is no longer in the forwarding table of the relevant switches. When the device responds to your ping, any switches in the switching path that do not have the host in their forwarding table will add it:

```
Solaris% ping broken.example.com
broken.example.com is alive
```

You use the arpfind command to determine the hardware address of the host:

---

[1]This is one reason it is highly recommended you have only one machine attached to each managed port on the leaf switches in your network. If several machines were connected behind an unmanaged switch, you might be forced to disable network access to all of them.

```
neo: arpfind host.example.com router.example.com
10.5.0.1 says 10.5.1.2 is 00:03:BA:09:1F:36
```

Having that, you then locate the host on a collection of switches:

```
neo: locate 00:03:BA:09:1F:36 @k:northannex
Found on 6@switch13.example.com
```

Next, you may wish to see how much traffic is being generated by the host. Though this is optional, it may be of use:

```
neo: stats 6@switch13.example.com
Probing devices ...
Getting first set of stats...
Getting second set of stats...
Port statistics:
 p type    u lnk adm ap kbs  ikbs  okbs  pps ipps opps ierps oerps
 ------------------------------------------------------------------
 6 100TX    100 On    486   92   394  111  37   74    0     0
```

Before you turn it off, you also may wish to check how many devices are located on that port:

```
neo: port search 6@switch13.example.com
00:03:BA:09:1F:36
```

In this case, it is just the one machine, so you disable it:

```
neo: set writecom mysecret
neo: port dis 6@switch13.example.com
6@switch13.example.com disabled
```

## Locating a Problem and Disabling It

Now imagine a portion of your network is undergoing an active denial of service attack, sourced from a host within your own network. How can we find the problematic host? Start with the switch connected to the router:

```
neo: stats entry-switch.example.com
Probing devices ...
Getting first set of stats...
Getting second set of stats...
Port statistics:
```

| p | type | u | lnk | adm | ap | kbs | ikbs | okbs | pps | ipps | opps | ierps | oerps |
|---|------|---|-----|-----|----|----|------|------|-----|------|------|-------|-------|
| 1 | 100TX | | 100 | On | | 20 | 0 | 20 | 26 | 0 | 26 | 0 | 0 |
| 2 | 100TX | | 100 | On | | 19 | 0 | 19 | 26 | 0 | 26 | 0 | 0 |
| 3 | 100TX | | 10 | On | | 20 | 0 | 20 | 27 | 0 | 27 | 0 | 0 |
| 4 | 100TX | | - | On | | 0 | 0 | 0 | 0 | 0 | 0 | 0 | 0 |
| 5 | 100TX | | - | On | | 0 | 0 | 0 | 0 | 0 | 0 | 0 | 0 |
| 6 | 100TX | | 100 | On | | 50455 | 50042 | 413 | 7157 | 7051 | 106 | 0 | 0 |
| 7 | 100TX | | 10 | On | | 19 | 0 | 19 | 26 | 0 | 26 | 0 | 0 |
| 8 | 100TX | | 100 | On | | 19 | 0 | 19 | 26 | 0 | 26 | 0 | 0 |
| 9 | 100TX | | 100 | On | | 19 | 0 | 19 | 26 | 0 | 26 | 0 | 0 |
| 10 | 100TX | | - | On | | 0 | 0 | 0 | 0 | 0 | 0 | 0 | 0 |
| 11 | 100TX | | 100 | On | | 19 | 0 | 19 | 26 | 0 | 26 | 0 | 0 |
| 12 | 100TX | | 100 | On | | 19 | 0 | 19 | 27 | 0 | 27 | 0 | 0 |
| 13 | 100?X | * | 100 | On | | 382 | 368 | 14 | 84 | 71 | 13 | 0 | 0 |
| 14 | 100?X | * | - | On | | 0 | 0 | 0 | 0 | 0 | 0 | 0 | 0 |
| 15 | loop | | 10 | On | | 59 | 28 | 31 | 80 | 40 | 40 | 0 | 0 |

You can see that a suspiciously large amount of traffic is coming from port six, so you would then like to know what other network devices are connected to this port. There are several ways to do this. One method is to search the port for hardware addresses, then pick one of those hardware addresses and use the keyfile syntax to search for that address on the relevant network:

```
neo: port search 6@entry-switch.example.com
00:04:76:31:E5:78
00:06:5B:48:35:09
00:60:97:4D:FE:39
00:E0:29:05:85:66
00:E0:29:86:3D:0D
00:E0:63:C7:23:CB
00:E0:63:C7:23:E3
08:00:69:0E:AF:DD

neo: locate 00:04:76:31:E5:78 @k:northannex
Found on 6@entry-switch.example.com
Found on 5@switch4.example.com
```

You then know that switch4.example.com is a device behind port six. Another method would be to login to the router and ask it to translate each MAC address to an IP address, one of which will be that of the device in question.

Once you gather statistics on switch4.example.com, you again find one source of a significant amount of traffic and turn off the culprit just as in the previous example.

### Using Neo in a Script

Imagine you have a UPS and you would like to regularly track the battery capacity and input load. You might use Neo in a script like this one:

```
#!/bin/sh
ups=ups.example.com
log=/home/admin/upslog
while [ 1 ]; do
    date >> $log
    neo dev info power $ups | egrep "Capacity|Load" >> $log
    echo "" >> $log
    sleep 1800
done
```

This text is stored in a file and then the program is executed. More detail on writing and using scripts is presented in Chapter 10. This script runs Neo once every 30 minutes, saving the relevant information from the UPS into a logfile. Note that Neo commands are simply presented to Neo as arguments on the command line.

## 4.6   Maintaining Neo

Neo requires two maintenance tasks. The first is regularly updating the installed version of Neo simply because, as with any new piece of software, features and bug fixes are constantly being added. The latest version is always available on the Web site.

The second maintenance task is updating the keyfile, if you use one. Neo is an effective tool only if it knows which devices to contact. Make sure your keyfile reflects the current state of your network either by updating it manually or by using an automated process.

Neo does not require you to maintain SNMP MIBs; any necessary variable data is coded into the program itself. The upshot is that there is less complexity for the maintainer, though it also means that the software must be updated in order to include new functionality.

## 4.7   **References and Further Study**

Chapter 2 describes the SNMP protocol that Neo uses to perform its tasks and includes details on some of the relevant SNMP variables as well. The GNU readline library and other GNU tools are available from `http://www.gnu.org/`. Neo is available from `http://web.mit.edu/ktools/`, and bugs, problems, or suggestions for improvements should be sent to `bug-neo@mit.edu`.

There are many other SNMP-based management programs available. HP's OpenView (`http://www.openview.hp.com/`) is a widely used commercial example, and Scotty/Tkined (`http://wwwhome.cs.utwente.nl/~schoenw/scotty/`) is an open source example. This kind of program most often has a graphical user interface, and these two programs are no exception. This is a major disadvantage for accomplishing many administration tasks. One tool that does not have a graphical user interface is ND, written at Texas A&M University. A paper describing this system is available at `http://www.usenix.org/events/lisa00/mitchell.html`.

# Chapter 5

# NETFLOW

## 5.1   Overview of NetFlow and Flow-Tools

The traffic analysis tools described so far all produce quantitative information about network traffic: the amount of bandwidth used or the
number of transmitted packets per second, for example. However, it
is often necessary to have a more qualitative view of traffic. If your
network is attacked by a flood of packets, you would like to know something about the data in the packets. You need to know at least enough
to block the traffic from your network.

NetFlow is a feature available on some routers that will allow you
to view this information. It includes data such as the source and destination IP addresses, source and destination protocol port numbers,
number of packets transmitted, number of bytes transmitted, and much
more. Once NetFlow is enabled, the information can be viewed on the
router itself or it can be sent to another host on the network for more
detailed collection and analysis. NetFlow was originally implemented
by Cisco and therefore is available on Cisco routers as well as the Cisco
Catalyst 5000 switch if it is installed with a special board. Juniper
routers now also have the ability to export packet data in the same
NetFlow format as Cisco.

An excellent set of open source tools for collecting and processing
NetFlow data is the Flow-Tools package, written by Mark Fullmer and
available from Ohio State University. It includes utilities for collecting
flows on a server, storing the results, and printing and manipulating
flows as well as tools for producing reports based on the data.

## 5.2   What NetFlow Can Help You Do

Imagine your network is hit by a denial of service attack. The first thing you notice is that your network has degraded connectivity to the rest of the Internet. The interface counters on your border router indicate a very high rate of traffic, and when you examine the MRTG graph, you see a sudden, dramatic rise in traffic levels. This all points to a possible denial of service attack. Turning to NetFlow, you examine the traffic in real time and notice a large number of connections from a single host, all to sequentially increasing IP addresses inside your network:

```
srcIP            dstIP          prot  srcPort  dstPort  octets  packets
10.194.158.201  10.36.1.21     6     80       32966    466     1
10.54.59.138    10.209.0.60    17    32781    22       165     3
10.54.59.138    10.209.0.61    17    32781    22       165     3
10.54.59.138    10.209.0.62    17    32781    22       165     3
10.89.67.212    10.225.0.86    6     1751     1214     652     6
10.54.59.138    10.209.0.63    17    32781    22       165     3
10.54.59.138    10.209.0.64    17    32781    22       165     3
10.54.59.138    10.209.0.65    17    32781    22       165     3
10.54.59.138    10.209.0.66    17    32781    22       165     3
10.54.59.138    10.209.0.67    17    32781    22       165     3
10.54.59.138    10.209.0.68    17    32781    22       165     3
10.226.244.82   10.215.0.200   17    6257     6257     309     4
```

Realizing this is someone scanning your network, you can now block the traffic at the border router and notify the network administrators at the remote site.

## 5.3   How NetFlow Works

The following sections explore NetFlow in detail.

### 5.3.1   Flows

NetFlow is based on the idea of a **flow** of network traffic. What is a flow? It is what you would naturally think of as one full network conversation. The Transmission Control Protocol (TCP) connection a workstation opens to retrieve a Web page is a flow. The start of the TCP connection is the beginning of the flow, and when the connection is closed, the flow is complete. Another example of a flow would be the

series of ICMP packets that make up a ping test. The flow begins with
the first ICMP packet and ends with the last.

Every flow must have a unique set of the following:

- Source IP address

- Destination IP address

- Source port

- Destination port

- IP protocol number

- Type of service field

- Input interface

These values must remain the same for the entire flow. Retrieving
multiple Web pages over a single TCP connection, for example, is all
one flow. But if multiple TCP connections are made to the same Web
server, different port numbers will be used for each connection, so each
connection will be a different flow. Similarly, an attacker who is scanning destination IP addresses on your network will generate many flows:
one for each source/destination pair.

Also note that a flow is unidirectional. That is, one of the addresses
is only the source of traffic and the other is only the destination. This
means that a flow represents just the traffic moving in one direction. In
communications with a Web server there are really two flows present:
one is the traffic from the workstation to the server, and the other is
the traffic from the server to the workstation. The router will always
report flows for traffic that enters an interface, not traffic that leaves an
interface. So if NetFlow is enabled on the interface where your workstation resides, your workstation will be the source address in any flow
data. If NetFlow is also enabled on interfaces where another machine
is sending data to your workstation, the router will then report your
workstation as the destination address for those flows.

Of course, it is not always easy to determine what constitutes one
session's worth of traffic and therefore when a particular flow ends. For
a TCP connection, it is relatively easy; the session begins with a TCP

SYN and ends with a TCP FIN. For UDP or Internet Control Message Protocol (ICMP), it is more difficult, and the router must use heuristics to decide when the flow is complete.

Because the router has only a limited amount of memory available for holding flow data, it must occasionally remove flows from the cache in order to make room for new ones. For this reason, it is important to realize that when a router reports on a flow, it may not really be the entire conversation as expected. For example, one flow may represent the first part of a TCP connection, another two flows might be the middle, and yet another flow, the end. Or it is just as possible for an entire TCP connection to be reported in a single flow. It depends on whether the router needs to free up resources. By default, a Cisco router will expire a flow when one of the following occurs:

- The end of a TCP connection is found.

- No traffic has been present in the flow for 15 seconds.

- The flow has been running for over 30 minutes.

- The table of flows in the router is filled.

### 5.3.2   NetFlow and Switching Paths

NetFlow is sometimes called NetFlow Accounting or NetFlow Switching. Both are acceptable terms, but one very prevalent myth should be dispelled about the latter. NetFlow is *not* a switching path. That is, it is not a system the router uses to figure out which packets are sent to which interface. NetFlow always relies on one of the other switching paths, such as Cisco Express Forwarding (CEF) or optimum switching, to make these decisions. NetFlow does interact with the switching path, however. Decisions on whether a packet matches an access-list filter are optimized so that the decision is made only once per flow, instead of for every packet in the flow. This practice also has an impact on access-list counters, which will no longer represent the number of packets matched when used in conjunction with NetFlow.

### 5.3.3   Exporting NetFlow Data

Routers can export NetFlow data so that it can be received by a server and then processed in any way the network administrator wishes. The

host or software that receives the data is called a **flow collector**. The
NetFlow data is exported in UDP packets to an IP address and UDP
port number that are configured on the router. Because routers send the
exported data using UDP, it is possible for packets of NetFlow data to
be lost. As described below, version 5 of NetFlow introduces sequence
numbers so that if data is lost, the flow collector will at least be aware
of the loss. There is, however, no way to retrieve the lost data.

On a Cisco router, only one IP address can be specified as the recipient of exported flows, so if you need to send NetFlow data to more
than one collector, it will have to be forwarded from one collector to
the others. Note that one piece of data that is *not* included in a flow is
the router from which the flow was sent. Typically, a collector knows
which router the flow came from based on the source IP address of the
exported packets. However, if a flow is forwarded from one collector
to another, this data may be lost unless the forwarder either specially
includes the information via some other mechanism or forges the source
address of the forwarded packets to be that of the original router.

### 5.3.4   NetFlow Versions

There are several different version of NetFlow available. Version 1 was
the first, and each flow contained the following information:

- Source IP address

- Destination IP address

- Source port

- Destination port

- Next hop router address

- Input interface number

- Output interface number

- Number of packets sent

- Number of bytes sent

- sysUpTime when flow began

- sysUpTime when flow ended

- IP protocol number

- IP type of service

- Logical OR of all TCP flags seen

There are currently four other versions of NetFlow:

- **Version 5.** Includes Autonomous System (AS) numbers from Border Gateway Protocol (BGP) if available and also includes sequence numbers, which allows checking for lost packets.

- **Version 7.** Used only on the Cisco Catalyst 5000 product series, which also requires a special NetFlow Feature Card in order to perform NetFlow accounting.

- **Version 8.** Introduces Router-Based NetFlow Aggregation, a feature that can greatly reduce the amount of data sent when flows are exported from the router. By choosing an appropriate aggregation scheme, you can instruct the router to group flows with similar data into a single aggregate flow that is reported on behalf of all the others.

- **Version 9.** Introduces a template-based scheme for reporting flows, which allows a client receiving exported flow data to process the data without necessarily having prior knowledge of what kinds of data will be present.

## 5.4   Installing Flow-Tools

The OSU Flow-Tools package is available from `http://www.net.ohio-state.edu/software/`. Download the latest stable version (or an even later version if it suits you), then unpackage and build the software:

```
Linux% gunzip -c flow-tools-0.59.tar.gz | tar xvf -
Linux% cd flow-tools-0.59
Linux% ./configure
Linux% make
```

It should build without difficulty. Once it is built, you can install it on your system from a root account with:

```
Linux# make install
```

This will install everything in `/usr/local/netflow/`. The programs will be in `/usr/local/netflow/bin/`, which you can add to your path or you can run the programs with a full path name. For the examples in this chapter, it is assumed that the programs are in your path.

## 5.5   Configuring NetFlow on the Router

Before you can use the Flow-Tools programs to view flow data, you must configure the router to use NetFlow on at least one interface, and you must also configure the router to export flows to a host that will be running the Flow-Tools software. On a Cisco router, you can enable NetFlow on an interface with the interface configuration command `ip route-cache flow`. For example:

```
router#config term
Enter configuration commands, one per line.  End with CNTL/Z.
router(config)#int Ethernet1/2
router(config-if)#ip route-cache flow
router(config-if)#end
```

Remember that NetFlow will report on packets that enter an interface and not on packets that leave an interface. You can enable NetFlow on as many interfaces as you like, though be aware that if you export flow data, more interfaces means more reporting traffic that will be sent to the collector.

To instruct the router to export flows, use the `ip flow-export destination` configure command:

```
router(config)#ip flow-export destination 192.0.2.5 9995
router(config)#ip flow-export source Loopback0
```

This will send all flow data to the IP address 192.0.2.5 on UDP port 9995. In this case, we also specified an interface to be used as the source of the packets. This is optional; it is configured here to use a Loopback interface so that the source address of the flows will be consistent even if the other interface addresses on the router change.

Finally, you can specify which version of NetFlow the router should export. If you do not explicitly specify a version, it will default to version 1. To export version 5 instead, type:

```
router(config)#ip flow-export version 5
```

Remember to issue a **write mem** to save configuration changes. Now the router should be sending NetFlow packets to the address specified in the **ip flow-export destination** command, and you can use the Flow-Tools programs to receive them.

## 5.6  Using Flow-Tools

A number of programs make up the Flow-Tools software package. Figure 5.1 lists each program and its function. All major tools are described here, categorized into groups of tools that capture flows, tools that view flow data, and tools that manipulate flows.

### 5.6.1  Capturing Flows

There are two programs in the Flow-Tools distribution that receive flow data. One is **flow-capture**, which not only receives the flows, but also stores them to files on disk, rotates the files, and ensures that they do not grow larger than a limit you specify on the command line. The other program is **flow-receive** which sends the flow data to the standard output instead of storing flows on disk.

Note that the output from these commands, whether sent to the standard output or to a file on disk, is not a direct dump of NetFlow data in the format produced by the router. The Flow-Tools package stores flow data in its own format, which, among other things, allows it to easily store data from different versions of NetFlow in a single format.

In the following examples, both the flow-capture and the flow-receive programs will be run from the root account. This is not required; the tools can be run from a user level account instead, but with two caveats. First, if you wish to listen for flows on a port that is number 1024 or lower, you will not be able to do it from a user-level account. You must either modify your router configuration to send flows to a higher numbered port or run the tools from a root account. Second,

| Program | Function |
|---|---|
| flow-receive | Receive flows, send to stdout |
| flow-capture | Receive flows, store to disk |
| flow-print | Print flow data to the screen |
| flow-report | Produce flow reports for other programs |
| flow-stat | Print flow statistics to the screen |
| flow-dscan | Detect suspicious network traffic |
| flow-cat | Concatenate flow data files |
| flow-merge | Sort and concatenate flow data files |
| flow-expire | Remove old flow data files |
| flow-split | Split data files into smaller files |
| flow-header | Print meta data on a capture session |
| flow-fanout | Redistribute UDP exports to other addresses |
| flow-send | Send flow data in NetFlow format |
| flow-tag | Add user-defined tags to flows |
| flow-filter | Filter flows |
| flow-gen | Generate test flow data |
| flow-import | Import data from other NetFlow tools |
| flow-export | Export data to other NetFlow tools |
| flow-xlate | Translate flow data |

**Figure 5.1.** Programs Included with Flow-Tools.

flow-capture will attempt to write a file in /var/run containing the process ID of the program. If you are not root, you may not be able to write to this file, depending on your system configuration. However you can change this behavior with the -p option described below.

Try using the flow-receive program in conjunction with the flow-print program to check if flows are being received properly from the router:

```
Linux# flow-receive 0/0/9995 | flow-print
flow-receive: setsockopt(size=262144)
flow-receive: New exporter: time=1048976578 src_ip=10.255.255...
flow-receive: New exporter: time=1048976578 src_ip=10.255.255...
flow-receive: New exporter: time=1048976578 src_ip=10.255.255...
```

| srcIP          | dstIP          | prot | srcPort | dstPort | octets | packets |
|----------------|----------------|------|---------|---------|--------|---------|
| 10.26.196.41   | 10.221.0.157   | 17   | 2706    | 1497    | 35     | 1       |
| 10.175.106.3   | 10.221.0.157   | 6    | 4028    | 1497    | 81     | 2       |
| 10.132.140.22  | 10.253.1.161   | 17   | 1035    | 4665    | 46     | 1       |
| 10.253.1.161   | 10.132.140.22  | 1    | 0       | 771     | 74     | 1       |
| 10.67.8.175    | 10.203.0.180   | 6    | 47813   | 3150    | 81     | 2       |
| 10.253.1.191   | 10.246.38.98   | 17   | 65145   | 6671    | 138    | 3       |
| 10.24.233.164  | 10.221.0.157   | 17   | 1500    | 1497    | 35     | 1       |
| 10.119.5.60    | 10.243.0.64    | 17   | 33487   | 33487   | 53     | 1       |
| 10.181.135.108 | 10.236.0.107   | 6    | 80      | 2990    | 40     | 1       |
| 10.253.5.165   | 10.19.139.162  | 6    | 1680    | 80      | 647    | 4       |
| 10.88.171.11   | 10.235.0.166   | 17   | 1256    | 3813    | 35     | 1       |
| 10.253.1.191   | 10.213.33.193  | 17   | 65468   | 4665    | 46     | 1       |
| 10.61.67.199   | 10.253.2.21    | 17   | 6257    | 6257    | 317    | 4       |

This program will continue to run, filling your screen with output, until you break it with Control-C.

The three "new exporter" lines at the beginning are printed to the standard error by `flow-receive` and inform you every time the program detects a new device sending flows. The slash-delimited argument to `flow-receive` is a generic syntax that other Flow-Tools programs use as well. The format is *localip/remoteip/port*. In this case, *localip* is the local IP address that the program should listen on,[1] *remoteip* is the IP address that flows must be received from, and *port* is the local port the program will listen on to receive flows. In either of the address fields, a zero indicates that any address is acceptable. So in our example, 0/0/9995 means the program will accept flows to any local IP address, coming from any IP address, and destined for port 9995. Compare this with the following:

```
Linux# flow-receive 0/10.255.255.16/9995 | flow-print
flow-receive: setsockopt(size=262144)
flow-receive: Unexpected PDU: src_ip=10.255.255.15 not configured
flow-receive: New exporter: time=1048977556 src_ip=10.255.255...
flow-receive: Unexpected PDU: src_ip=10.255.255.15 not configured
flow-receive: Unexpected PDU: src_ip=10.255.255.22 not configured
```

---

[1]Some machines have more than one address. If a zero is used for the local address, any of the addresses can be used; otherwise, the program will use the specific address listed, and flows received at other IP addresses on the machine will be ignored.

| srcIP | dstIP | prot | srcPort | dstPort | octets | packets |
|---|---|---|---|---|---|---|
| 10.176.155.249 | 10.216.0.132 | 17 | 6257 | 6257 | 388 | 4 |
| 10.182.153.110 | 10.133.0.180 | 6 | 2164 | 3150 | 122 | 3 |
| 10.97.215.204 | 10.252.2.21 | 17 | 6257 | 6257 | 316 | 4 |
| 10.188.11.57 | 10.36.5.66 | 6 | 5190 | 1037 | 132 | 2 |
| 10.137.199.176 | 10.216.1.123 | 6 | 1594 | 1344 | 13132 | 316 |
| 10.188.11.236 | 10.221.0.105 | 6 | 5190 | 2428 | 489 | 4 |

Here flows must be received from a device with the IP address 10.255. 255.16. There is still a message to standard error when flows from this source are found, but there are also warnings about flows unexpectedly coming from other addresses. Flows from those other addresses are ignored. Note that the addresses checked here are those of the routers or other devices sending and collecting the flows, not the addresses contained within the flows.

It is convenient to use `flow-print` to visualize flows on the screen, and it can even be useful in diagnosing an ongoing network problem, but for typical use, you will want to store flow data on disk. This is the job of the `flow-capture` program. Not only will `flow-capture` store flow data in files, it will also compress it, make sure to separate it into reasonably sized files, and rotate the files to keep the total amount of used disk space under control.

There are many options to `flow-capture`, but a simple invocation would be:

```
Linux# mkdir /var/tmp/flows
Linux# flow-capture -w /var/tmp/flows 0/0/9995
```

This example demonstrates the only required options. The path following the `-w` flag is the name of the directory in which flow files are to be stored. The program will not create it for you, and if it does not exist, it will silently exit. The slash-delimited argument at the end is the port on which flows should be received, using the same syntax as the `flow-receive` program.

Once started, `flow-capture` will run in the background. Files will be named according to the date they are created. If a file is currently being created (data is still actively being added to it), the name will begin with `tmp-`; otherwise, the file name will begin with the prefix `ft-`.

By default, `flow-capture` will:

- Create a new file every 15 minutes

- Create a nested directory structure so that each year, month, and day of files has a separate directory

- Never remove files (the total amount of data will grow without bound)

- Compress files at a medium compression level

All of these settings can be changed, and they often are. The command line arguments for changing these settings are listed below, along with a few other important options. All of the options to `flow-capture` are listed in Figure 5.2.

## Bounding the Data Size

The `-E` argument allows you to specify the maximum size that data files may use in total. You can specify the size in bytes, kilobytes, megabytes, or gigabytes by using the letters b, K, M, or G, respectively. For example:

```
Linux# flow-capture -w /var/tmp/flows -E 1G 0/0/9995
```

would ensure that the data does not exceed 1 gigabyte of disk storage. Flow-capture accomplishes this by deleting the older data files. The program uses a time stamp stored in these files so that you need not worry about copied files being deleted or overlooked for deletion because the Unix time stamp is incorrect.

Also note that only files named with the Flow-Tools naming convention will be deleted. If you rename the file `ft-v01.2003-03-30.` `135300-0500` to `flow.save`, it will not be cleaned up as usual.

## Changing Directory Nesting

By default, the data files are nested into a hierarchical directory structure by year, month, and day. For example:

```
Linux# find /var/tmp/flows
/var/tmp/flows
/var/tmp/flows/2003
/var/tmp/flows/2003/2003-03
/var/tmp/flows/2003/2003-03/2003-03-29
/var/tmp/flows/2003/2003-03/2003-03-29/tmp-v01.2003-03-29.190000-0500
/var/tmp/flows/2003/2003-03/2003-03-29/ft-v01.2003-03-29.184647-0500
```

There is a directory for the year 2003, one below that for the month of March 2003, and one below that for the day March 29, 2003. In that directory are two flow files, one being created and one already completed. If this level of nesting does not suit you, there are six other options available, each represented by a number. From the flow-capture man page:

| Flag | Function |
|------|----------|
| -A | Replace 0 AS values |
| -b | Specify output byte order |
| -c | Enable TCP client connections |
| -C | Add a comment |
| -d | Turn on debugging |
| -e | Maximum number of files |
| -E | Maximum data size to store |
| -f | File name of filter list |
| -F | Specify active filter |
| -h | Display help |
| -m | Use a privacy mask |
| -n | Specify number of new files per day |
| -N | Set nesting level |
| -p | Specify PID file |
| -R | Execute a program after rotation |
| -S | Syslog timestamps at specified interval |
| -t | File to load tags from |
| -T | Tags to use |
| -V | Specify output format |
| -w | Specify directory to store data files in |
| -z | Set compression level |

**Figure 5.2.** Options to the Flow-Capture Program.

```
-3    YYYY/YYYY-MM/YYYY-MM-DD/flow-file
-2    YYYY-MM/YYYY-MM-DD/flow-file
-1    YYYY-MM-DD/flow-file
 0    flow-file
 1    YYYY/flow-file
 2    YYYY/YYYY-MM/flow-file
 3    YYYY/YYYY-MM/YYYY-MM-DD/flow-file
```

Though the documentation states that the default nesting level is 0, it is 3 in every version I have tested. The nesting depth is controlled with the -N flag. If you wish to run `flow-capture` so that no nesting is performed and all files are stored in a single, flat directory, type:

```
Linux# flow-capture -w /var/tmp/flows -N 0 0/0/9995
```

## Changing the File Rotation Rate

By default, `flow-capture` will write data into a file for 15 minutes and then close it and create a new file. This is a good way to break up the data into files that you can work with easily. There are also other programs in the Flow-Tools distribution that allow you to merge these files or separate them into even smaller files.

If you wish to change the interval at which new files are created, you can use the -n flag. The argument it takes is the number of times per day that `flow-capture` should create a new file. The default is 95. That is, 95 times a day it will create a new file, which is 96 files total. If you want to create a file for each hour, you need to ask for a new file to be created 23 times each day, as in:

```
Linux# flow-capture -w /var/tmp/flows -n 23 0/0/9995
```

## Changing the Process ID File

Because `flow-capture` runs as a daemon, it stores its process ID in a file for the convenience of administrators or other programs that may wish to send it a signal. By default, this file is `/var/run/flow-capture.pid`. You may not be able to write to this directory if you do not run the program from a root account. In this case, you may specify a different file with the -p option:

```
Linux# flow-capture -w /var/tmp/flows -p /var/tmp/pid 0/0/9995
```

If you use the filename "-", no PID file will be created.

## Using Compression

Flow-capture compresses flow data so that it takes up less space on disk. While taking up less disk space is an advantage, the trade-off is that it takes computational power to perform the compression. If your server is short on disk space but has lots of processing power, you may wish to use a higher level of compression than the default. On a server with lots of disk space and a slow CPU, you may want less compression or perhaps none at all. The compression level is a value from 0 to 9, where 0 is no compression and 9 is the highest level of compression. The default level is set by the zlib library, typically to 6. If you wish to disable compression, use:

```
Linux# flow-capture -w /var/tmp/flows -z0
```

## Killing Flow-Capture

If you need to stop flow-capture, you can send it a QUIT signal, as in:

```
Solaris# ps -ef | grep flow-capture
    root 10858    1  0 14:20:06 ?    0:00 flow-capture -w /var...
Solaris# kill -QUIT 10858
```

This will cause flow-capture to properly close and rename the data file that it is currently writing. If you kill flow-capture without specifying a signal (which defaults to the TERM signal), the file will be left with its temporary name. All of the Flow-Tools daemons write a file that contains the process ID of the running program. Instead of using ps to look up the process ID, we could have done:

```
Solaris# kill -QUIT `cat /var/run/flow-capture.pid.9995`
```

The 9995 on the end of the filename indicates that this flow-capture is running on port 9995, in case more than one copy of flow-capture is running at once.

Note that if a router is sending flow data to a port and there is no program like flow-capture, flow-receive, or flow-fanout listening on that port, the server will respond with ICMP port unreachable

messages back to the router. While there is no harm in sending or receiving a small number of these messages, a large number sent at a rapid
rate could have an operational impact either on network bandwidth or
on the CPU. If you plan to leave `flow-capture` down for a long time,
you may want to turn off the source of the flows or run `flow-receive`
and send the data to `/dev/null`.

If you would like to force `flow-capture` to stop writing to the current file, close it, and start a new file, you can send it a HUP signal:

```
Solaris# ps -ef | grep flow-capture
    root 10862    1  1 14:24:01 ?      0:00 flow-capture -w /var...
Solaris# kill -HUP 10862
```

## Allowing Remote Clients

The `-c` option to `flow-capture` will allow a remote client to make a
TCP connection to the program to receive flow data. Currently, the
implementation does not work very well; the connection is often closed
unexpectedly. With luck this will be fixed in a future release. Also
note that if you do not use an external wrapper, *any* client connecting
to the server can receive access to your NetFlow data. The number
listed after the `-c` simply specifies the maximum number of clients that
can connect at any one time:

```
Server# flow-capture -w /var/tmp/flows -c 10 0/0/9995
Client% nc server.example.com 9995 | flow-print
srcIP           dstIP           prot srcPort dstPort octets packets
10.254.70.105   10.61.171.218   6    3531    139     144    3
10.250.226.251  10.154.0.230    6    4662    1089    1218   24
10.50.61.48     10.91.178.156   17   1026    137     78     1
10.87.169.94    10.91.190.251   17   1025    137     78     1
```

The nc program is described in Chapter 9, Basic Tools. An alternative
to allowing remote clients to receive flow data via TCP is to forward
UDP flows to them using `flow-fanout`, as described in the section on
manipulating flow data.

## 5.6.2  Viewing Flow Data

Flow-Tools includes four programs for viewing flow data. They are:

- **Flow-print.** Prints flow data in ASCII. A number of predefined
  reporting formats are available.

- **Flow-report.** Generates reports with comma-separated field values, suitable for feeding into another program to produce graphs or to perform other data processing.

- **Flow-stat.** Available only in later versions of Flow-Tools. This program generates reports based on statistics of interest to the administrator, such as high bandwidth use by port.

- **Flow-dscan.** Analyzes flow data to find suspicious network traffic such as port scans. The program notifies the user if any are found.

## Flow-Print

Earlier we saw how `flow-print` could be used to examine data received in real time from `flow-receive`. Now you can feed it flow data stored in files from `flow-capture`:

```
Solaris# cat ft-v01.2003-03-30.133000-0500 | flow-print
srcIP          dstIP          prot srcPort dstPort octets packets
10.109.125.64 10.228.96.175 6    80      1862    35879  26
10.188.165.57 10.202.1.99   6    80      4633    695    4
10.73.86.70   10.243.41.92  6    80      1188    218    3
10.130.91.7   10.249.5.139  6    80      1458    596    5
10.210.86.68  10.226.112.52 6    3456    60263   40     1
10.17.247.8   10.252.25.243 6    80      33135   633    3
```

If you use the `-n` flag, `flow-print` will print symbolic names wherever possible:

```
Solaris# cat ft-v01.2003-03-30.133000-0500 | flow-print -n
srcIP          dstIP          prot srcPort dstPort octets packets
10.109.125.64 10.228.9.175  tcp  http    1862    35879  26
10.223.91.7   10.249.50.139 tcp  http    nrcabq- 596    5
10.141.51.240 10.153.55.151 tcp  Gnutell 3244    120    3
10.124.2.66   10.53.110.86  udp  3283    3283    33     1
10.143.66.23  10.53.212.40  udp  1297    ms-sql- 404    1
10.148.139.199 10.205.16.115 tcp  eDonkey 3913    144    3
10.85.4.150   10.205.12.92  tcp  imaps   49332   167    1
10.172.39.24  10.243.43.218 tcp  http    1310    11689  11
10.19.139.162 10.252.7.65   tcp  http    1307    40     1
10.73.86.70   10.243.0.92   tcp  http    1191    4505   5
```

Here you can see the IP protocol name has been printed, and when a port number is a well-known service, the name instead of the number is printed.

In addition to the simple output format above, the `flow-print` program has over 20 other formats available. The desired format can be specified with the `-f` option. For example:

```
Solaris# cat ft-v01.2003-03-30.133000-0500 | flow-print -n -f 5
Start               End             Sif  SrcIPaddress   SrcP  DIf  DstIPaddr...

0330.13:29:56.046 0330.13:29:56.398 3    10.109.125.64   80   40   10.228.0....
0330.13:29:56.046 0330.13:29:56.098 3    10.188.165.57   80   41   10.202.1....
0330.13:29:56.058 0330.13:29:56.198 3    10.73.86.70     80   30   10.243.0....
0330.13:29:56.082 0330.13:29:56.650 3    10.130.91.7     80    7   10.249.0....
0330.13:29:56.086 0330.13:29:56.086 3    10.210.86.68   3456  42   10.226.0....
0330.13:29:56.098 0330.13:29:57.846 3    10.17.247.8     80   10   10.252.2....
```

The formats, as described in the Flow-Tools documentation, are listed in Figure 5.3. Note that some formats print two lines per flow while others print only one.

## Flow-Report

While `flow-print` produces output that is easy to read on the screen, it is not particularly well suited for other use. If you wish to process the data in some automated way, be it performing a statistical analysis or simply importing the data into a graphing program, you will want to use the `flow-report` program to produce data in a simple comma-separated format.

In order to produce a flow report, you must first create a configuration file that specifies a few options. The following sample configuration file can be placed in `/var/tmp/report.conf`:

```
stat-report myreport
  type ip-source/destination-address/ip-source/destination-port
  output
    records 50
    sort +octets

stat-definition stat1
  report myreport
```

The first section defines a report called myreport. The next line specifies which general type of report it should be. This is a required line and

| No. | Format |
|-----|--------|
| 0 | 1 line, interfaces, hex ports |
| 1 | 2 line (includes timing and flags) |
| 2 | 2 line candidate TCP syn attack flows |
| 3 | 1 line, no interfaces, decimal ports |
| 4 | 1 line with AS number |
| 5 | 1 line, 132 column |
| 6 | show ip accounting emulation |
| 7 | 1 line, 132 column +router_id |
| 8 | 1 line, 132 column +encapsulation |
| 9 | 1 line with tag values |
| 10 | AS aggregation |
| 11 | Protocol Port aggregation |
| 12 | Source Prefix aggregation |
| 13 | Destination Prefix aggregation |
| 14 | Prefix aggregation |
| 15 | Destination aggregation (Catalyst) |
| 16 | Source Destination aggregation (Catalyst) |
| 17 | Full Flow (Catalyst) |
| 18 | ToS AS Aggregation |
| 19 | ToS Proto Port aggregation |
| 20 | ToS Source Prefix aggregation |
| 21 | ToS Destination Prefix aggregation |
| 22 | ToS Prefix Aggregation |
| 23 | ToS Prefix Port aggregation |

**Figure 5.3.** Formats for `Flow-Print`.

the value must be one of the 80 or so valid report types available. The names for all of them are listed in the `flow-report` Web page and man page that comes with the Flow-Tools distribution.

Next, the output section of the report lists options associated with the output. Here we have specified that a maximum of 50 records should be printed. After the first 50, the program will end the report. Next, the `sort +octets` line asks for the report to be sorted by octets, with the largest numbers first.

Run the report with:

```
Solaris# flow-report -s /var/tmp/report.conf \
   -Sstat1 < ft-v01.2003-03-30.153000...
# recn: ip-source-address,ip-destination-address,ip-source-po...
10.116.200.35,10.1.14.3,50100,50100,15,1544300277,1351782,3613224
10.116.200.34,10.1.14.1,50000,50000,14,1499274579,1244856,3612348
10.48.78.93,10.45.17.174,1058,5004,14,724389220,626401,3606776
10.252.12.21,10.96.1.28,445,1424,3,162981116,110004,905944
10.116.200.35,10.1.14.4,17100,17100,15,102237923,131847,3611996
10.116.200.34,10.1.14.2,17000,17000,15,102097558,131666,3611024
10.127.126.7,10.203.0.70,3519,59,3,78775788,74993,904048
10.240.64.63,10.2.213.188,32949,21088,18,74854576,57740,4514472
10.181.50.25,10.209.0.48,119,1038,4,74036545,70162,959184
```

The first line of output, beginning with a comment character, lists the order of the fields for the rest of the report. Here the first field is the source IP address of the flow, the second is the destination IP address, and so on. After that, each line is a line of data. Note that each line does not correspond to a single flow. For this report, each line corresponds to one unique combination of IP source address, IP destination address, source port, and destination port. This set of data objects is called the **key** for the report. The values for octets and packets listed on each line are the cumulative values for all flows matching a particular key.

There are a number of useful options to the **stat-report** and **output** commands in the configuration file. For example, you can display additional data such as the number of packets per second transmitted. You can also choose to view data such as the byte and packet counts as percentages of all observed data instead of viewing the raw numbers. All of the options are listed in the documentation.

## Flow-Stat

The **flow-stat** program is available only in later versions of Flow-Tools. It is a convenient way to produce the kind of data that **flow-report** generates, but it does not require a configuration file, and it prints the results in a readable format. Like **flow-print**, it uses a number of predefined formats. Here is an example of one of the many available reports. This one lists traffic by port number:

```
Solaris# flow-stat -f7 -w -P -S2 < ft-v01.2003-03-30.153000-0500
#   --- ---- ---- Report Information --- --- ---
#
# Fields:      Percent Total
# Symbols:     Disabled
# Sorting:     Descending Field 2
# Name:        UDP/TCP port
#
# Args:        flow-stat -f7 -w -P -S2
#
#
# port             flows     octets    packets   duration
#
50100              0.007     18.431    8.360     0.208
50000              0.007     17.893    7.695     0.159
5004               0.036     5.015     3.119     1.190
80                 6.637     4.421     2.939     3.105
1058               0.044     4.323     1.937     0.066
1214               2.690     3.438     1.775     3.560
4662               2.214     2.194     1.899     4.257
56464              0.226     2.178     12.750    6.706
17100              0.007     1.223     0.829     0.212
17000              0.005     1.220     0.821     0.160
445                0.253     1.037     0.924     0.188
1424               0.011     0.994     0.526     0.044
5005               0.075     0.989     3.856     2.385
```

The -f7 argument designates the format type. Other possible formats
are listed in Figure 5.4. The -w flag specifies that wide columns can be
used, -P asks for values to be reported as percentage of the total, and
-S2 causes the rows to be sorted by the second data column, in this
case the octets column. In this example, traffic to or from port 50100
or 50000 is taking up 36.3 percent of the total bandwidth in use.

## Flow-Dscan

The flow-dscan program attempts to detect unusual network traffic
like port scanning and host scanning. Before you run the program, you
will have to create two files in the current working directory:

```
Solaris# touch dscan.suppress.dst dscan.suppress.src
```

| No. | Format |
|-----|--------|
| 0 | Overall Summary |
| 1 | Average packet size distribution |
| 2 | Packets per flow distribution |
| 3 | Octets per flow distribution |
| 4 | Bandwidth per flow distribution |
| 5 | UDP/TCP destination port |
| 6 | UDP/TCP source port |
| 7 | UDP/TCP port |
| 8 | Destination IP |
| 9 | Source IP |
| 10 | Source/Destination IP |
| 11 | Source or Destination IP |
| 12 | IP protocol |
| 13 | Octets for flow duration plot data |
| 14 | Packets for flow duration plot data |
| 15 | short summary |
| 16 | IP Next Hop |
| 17 | Input interface |
| 18 | Output interface |
| 19 | Source AS |
| 20 | Destination AS |
| 21 | Source/Destination AS |
| 22 | IP ToS |
| 23 | Input/Output Interface |
| 24 | Source Prefix |
| 25 | Destination Prefix |
| 26 | Source/Destination Prefix |
| 27 | Exporter IP |
| 28 | Engine Id |
| 29 | Engine Type |
| 30 | Source Tag |
| 31 | Destination Tag |
| 32 | Source/Destination Tag |

**Figure 5.4.** Formats for `Flow-Stat`.

`flow-dscan` can use these files to suppress warnings about hosts that should not be reported. For now, the files can remain empty, but they must be present nonetheless.

You can instruct `flow-dscan` to run and print its warning messages to standard error with the `-b` flag:

```
Solaris# cat ft-v01.2003-03-30.153000-0500 | flow-dscan -b
flow-dscan: load_suppress 0
flow-dscan: load_suppress 1
flow-dscan: host scan: ip=10.124.2.66 ts=1049056190 start=0330...
flow-dscan: host scan: ip=10.3.21.106 ts=1049056204 start=0330...
flow-dscan: port scan: src=10.97.0.214 dst=10.8.15.1 ts=104906...
flow-dscan: host scan: ip=10.116.90.206 ts=1049056209 start=03...
flow-dscan: host scan: ip=10.57.101.250 ts=1049056215 start=03...
flow-dscan: host scan: ip=10.49.139.154 ts=1049056223 start=03...
flow-dscan: host scan: ip=10.186.240.211 ts=1049056226 start=0...
flow-dscan: host scan: ip=10.252.53.145 ts=1049056229 start=03...
```

If the `-b` flag is not used, `flow-dscan` will instead run in the background and send alert messages to syslog.

### 5.6.3   Manipulating Flow Data

The various methods for manipulating flow data are discussed in the following sections.

#### Flow-Cat and Flow-Merge

As seen earlier, the default behavior of `flow-capture` is to store 15 minutes' worth of flows in a single data file. What if you need to work with more than just 15 minutes? Perhaps you would like to produce a report on traffic from an entire day. Or maybe you wish to look for certain kinds of traffic over the entire month.

The `flow-cat` and `flow-merge` programs can be used in these circumstances. Both programs will combine flow data from separate files into a single set of flow data. This data can then be written to a single large data file or used directly in a pipeline. The difference between the two programs is that `flow-merge` will sort the data so that the new file contains all flows in their original chronological order. In contrast, `flow-cat` simply appends the data in the order the files are listed on the command line.

Here is a simple example using flow-merge to view data from multiple files:

```
Solaris# flow-merge ft-v01.2003-03-30.140900-0500 \
   ft-v01.2003-03-30.140937-0500 | flow-print
srcIP          dstIP         prot  srcPort  dstPort  octets  packets
10.124.25.66   10.53.9.94    17    3283     3283     33      1
10.124.25.66   10.53.9.96    17    3283     3283     33      1
10.53.1.135    10.0.0.251    17    5353     5353     116     1
10.124.25.66   10.53.12.101  17    3283     3283     33      1
10.124.25.66   10.53.12.102  17    3283     3283     33      1
```

You can also specify a directory name instead of a list of files, and the programs will include all flow data files beneath that directory. The following will concatenate all flows from March 29 and store them in a new file:

```
Solaris# flow-cat -o mar-29-flows \
   /var/tmp/flows/2003/2003-03/2003-03-29
```

Note that both programs are resource intensive and can take a long time to run when processing large amounts of data. `flow-merge` typically takes longer to complete than `flow-cat`, so if you do not need the flows merged by time, use `flow-cat` instead. Most of the time, the files you combine will be in chronological sequence anyway. Additionally, if you give the `-g` option to either program, it will ensure that the files on the command line are sorted by capture time before processing.

## Flow-Split

The `flow-split` program performs exactly the opposite operation of `flow-merge` and `flow-cat`: It takes flow data and splits it into separate smaller files, based on criteria you specify on the command line. For example, the `-T` flag instructs it to split flows after a given number of seconds:

```
Solaris# cat ft-v01.2003-03-29.231500-0500 | flow-split -T 300
```

Here the original data file happened to store 15 minutes' worth of flows. `flow-split` will create three files, each storing 5 minutes (300 seconds) of flow data. By default, the files will be named `split.0`, `split.1`, and so on. You can change the base name for the files with the `-o` option.

## Flow-Expire

flow-expire is a utility that will expire old flow data exactly as flow-capture does. It is useful in circumstances where you wish to store NetFlow data on a separate machine from where it is collected. The following will remove old data files in order to keep the total data size at less than 10 gigabytes:

```
Solaris# flow-expire -E 10G -w /var/tmp/flows
```

## Flow-Header

The flow-header program prints meta information that flow-capture stores in the header portion of a Flow-Tools data file. For example:

```
Solaris# cat ft-v01.2003-03-30.160000-0500 | flow-header
#
# mode:              normal
# capture hostname:  server.example.com
# capture start:     Sun Mar 30 16:00:00 2003
# capture end:       Sun Mar 30 16:15:00 2003
# capture period:    900 seconds
# compress:          on
# byte order:        big
# stream version:    3
# export version:    1
# lost flows:        0
# corrupt packets:   0
# sequencer resets:  0
# capture flows:     422712
#
```

Be aware that some programs, like flow-cat and flow-merge, require an additional argument in order to preserve header data between the input data and the output data.

## Flow-Fanout

Cisco routers can send exported NetFlow data to only a single host and port, which can be a serious limitation. In our environment, for example, there are two groups that need access to flow data: the Network Operations group and the Network Security group. Say that each group wants to use a different tool to capture flow data because different tools suit their different needs. The only practical solution is to send two feeds of NetFlow data, one to each group. Since the router cannot perform this task, `flow-fanout` will do it instead.

The `flow-fanout` program listens on a port, receives flow data packets, and then sends that data as is to as many other host/port pairs as you wish to configure. This is the only program in the Flow-Tools package that does not need to know anything about the flows themselves; it simply receives UDP packets and forwards them to other hosts.

The following will listen for NetFlow data on port 9995 and then send it on to two other hosts:

```
Solaris# ./flow-fanout 0/0/9995 0/192.0.2.3/9991 0/192.0.2.4/9992
```

Note that one piece of information is lost when flows are forwarded in this way. The NetFlow data packets do not contain a field indicating which router generated the flow. Typically, this can be determined from the source IP address of the exported UDP packets, but not if a flow is forwarded from one host to another. In the above example, the machines 192.0.2.3 and 192.0.2.4 will see flows coming from the IP address of the server that is forwarding them.

The `flow-fanout` program does have a trick for preserving the originating router information. If you use the `-s` flag on the command line, it will forge the source addresses of the outgoing UDP packets for each flow to be that of the original address that sent the flow. For example:

```
Solaris# ./flow-fanout -s 0/0/9995 0/192.0.2.3/9991 \
    0/192.0.2.4/9992
```

### Other Flow-Tools Programs

There are a few other useful tools in the Flow-Tools package. For example, the `flow-send` program will read flows from a data file and send them back in NetFlow format. The `flow-filter` command (and in later releases, `flow-nfilter`) allows you to filter flows based on ports, IP addresses, and more.

## 5.7   References and Further Study

In addition to the man pages and Web pages for each tool in the distribution, Flow-Tools includes pages called flow-tools and flow-tools-examples that give an overview of all of the tools and examples of specific use for each one.

The Cisco Web site at `http://www.cisco.com/` has detailed information on the NetFlow protocol and configuration examples on both routers and Catalyst 5000 series switches. Because NetFlow is a Cisco product, Cisco's Web site will have the most definitive information about the latest releases and protocol specifications.

# Chapter 6

# OAK

## 6.1 Overview of Oak

Machines that provide network services, and many network devices such as switches and routers, keep a log of messages about operational conditions. This message log is a useful tool for analyzing a problem after it has occurred. When an interface on a router stops functioning, you can login to the router and examine the error log for information about the problem.

There are drawbacks, however, to a system that requires you to login to a device in order to access its system logs. An outage of even a critical device may go unnoticed if it is off-hours and short in duration. But as an administrator, you need to know that it happened and why it happened so that you can prevent it from recurring. It is also difficult to monitor the log files via a login session if you have a large number of devices in your environment. With dozens of servers or network devices, you will not be able to check the log on each device every day.

For this reason, most devices that keep a local message log are also capable of sending notifications to a remote host using the **syslog** protocol. The syslog protocol was originally used to transport system log messages between Unix workstations but has since grown to become nearly ubiquitous for reporting error messages between devices. Using the syslog protocol, you can configure all of your servers and network devices to send error messages to a single machine, and from that machine, you can monitor the resulting error log. Depending on the device in question, you may even be able to select which kind of messages are forwarded and how severe a message has to be before it is forwarded.

Storing all the log messages on a central server is only half the battle. We would additionally like a system that can summarize and process the messages for us. If a critical problem is detected, an operator should be notified immediately. Less serious problems can be reported in an hourly or daily message. Oak is a program developed at MIT that will process messages and allow you to respond appropriately.

## 6.2  What Oak Can Help You Do

Oak examines a message log in syslog format and allows you to:

- Ignore unimportant messages

- Condense redundant information

- Produce reports of important messages

- Notify operators immediately of critical messages

Note that the term "syslog format" is a bit misleading. There is no standard format for the printed syslog messages themselves, only for the mechanism that transports them between machines. However, printed syslog messages are typically in one of a small number of formats, and Oak takes measures to correctly interpret the format of the message.

The Oak configuration file will specify which messages are important to you and how you wish to be notified in the event they should be received. For example, at MIT, we have Oak configured to send a daily report in email, an hourly report in an instant message[1] to the operational group, and an immediate instant message to the operational group if a critical problem is detected. One of the hourly messages might look like this:

```
Hourly message log

SERVER1.EXAMPLE.COM:
   2: login: ROOT LOGIN console
   1: syslogd: going down on signal 15
```

---

[1]Instant message here simply refers to a text message that is sent directly to the users; it is not delayed as email can be. At MIT, we use the Zephyr protocol and applications for this purpose.

```
   1: saslauthd[___]: Caught signal 15. Cleaning up $
   1: genunix: syncing file systems...
   1: genunix:   done
   1: genunix: ^MSunOS Release 5.9 Version Generic 64-bit
   1: genunix: Copyright 1983-2002 Sun Microsystems,$
   1: Use is subject to license terms.
   ** Too many messages found for host, truncating **

ROUTER.EXAMPLE.COM:
   6: ___:___ %LINEPROTO-5-UPDOWN: \
      Line protocol on Interface Ethernet9/4, change$
   5: ___:___ %LINEPROTO-5-UPDOWN: \
      Line protocol on Interface Ethernet9/4, change$
   2: ___:___ %LINEPROTO-5-UPDOWN: \
      Line protocol on Interface Ethernet9/2, change$
   1: ___:___ %LINEPROTO-5-UPDOWN: \
      Line protocol on Interface Ethernet9/2, change$

SERVER2.EXAMPLE.COM:
   9: named[___]: poll: Invalid argument

SERVER3.EXMPLE.COM:
   11: sshd[___]: ROOT LOGIN as 'root' from CLIENT.EXAMPLE.COM

   ** Message longer than 25 lines, message has been truncated **
```

The number to the left of each message indicates how many copies of the message were received. Note that in several places, Oak has replaced text with a series of underscores. These are examples of Oak's finding and removing information that may be redundant or unnecessary for reporting. If Oak did not remove the pieces of information to the left of the LINEPROTO-5-UPDOWN messages, each one would be reported on a line of its own. This would increase the size of your report and make it more difficult to understand.

Also notice that Oak truncates the message, both when there are too many messages for a particular host and when the message itself is too long. These are parameters set in the configuration file, and they can be set differently for different reports. The previous example was an instant message and as such was restricted to a relatively small amount of space. The daily email, however, is allowed to use many more lines.

A time-critical message might look like this:

```
**** CRITICAL MESSAGE LOG ****

SERVER4.EXAMPLE.COM:
   ufs: NOTICE: alloc: /var: file system full
```

Here we see a server with a full filesystem, which should be reported to an administrator right away.

## 6.3   Installing Oak

Oak is available from `http://web.mit.edu/ktools/`. Download the latest version and unpackage it:

```
Solaris% gunzip -c oak-1.3.5.tar.gz  | tar xvf -
Solaris% cd oak-1.3.5
```

Then configure and build it:

```
Solaris% ./configure
Solaris% make
```

Because Oak does not make use of any particularly nonstandard libraries, it should build without any problem. When it is complete, you will have a binary called `oak`, which you can install on your system from a root account:

```
Solaris# make install
```

This will place a copy of the `oak` binary in `/usr/local/bin/`.

## 6.4   Using Oak

Before configuring Oak to notify you of system events, you must first configure your servers and network devices to forward their syslogs to a central server, as described in the next section.

## 6.4.1   Configuring Syslog on Unix Workstations

Every syslog message has four basic parts:

- The system **facility**

- A **severity level**

- A time stamp

- The message content

The system facility refers to different services on a system so that messages can be sorted by the type of service. The valid service types for Solaris are listed in Figure 6.1. These are self-explanatory. The `mail` facility is used for messages about the mail system; the `kern` facility is used for messages from the kernel. There are eight facilities reserved for local admins to use as they please, named `local0` through `local7`. There is also a facility called `mark` which is used internally by syslog.

Some of these facilities, like the uucp facility, are a bit out of date, and you will notice that other modern services are not included. There is no `web` facility, for example. Some services, including the Apache Web server, choose to implement their own logging outside the syslog system.

| Facility |
|----------|
| user     |
| kern     |
| mail     |
| daemon   |
| auth     |
| lpr      |
| news     |
| uucp     |
| cron     |
| local0-7 |

**Figure 6.1.** Facility Types on Solaris.

| Facility |
| --- |
| emerg |
| alert |
| crit |
| err |
| warning |
| notice |
| info |
| debug |

**Figure 6.2.** Severity Level Values.

Along with the facility, each syslog message has a level of severity. Valid severity levels are listed in Figure 6.2. The `emerg` severity level is the most severe and `debug` is the least severe. The higher the severity level, the more immediate attention is required.

The purpose of designating each message with a facility and severity level is to allow operators to sort syslog messages by priority. As far as we're concerned, we need only to ensure that messages of sufficient importance are forwarded to the central logging machine. If important messages are not sent, Oak cannot alert us to problems. If too many messages are sent, the Oak configuration will become unnecessarily complicated in order to weed out the unnecessary messages.

The syslog configuration file on most systems is at `/etc/syslog.conf`. An ordinary `syslog.conf` might look like this:

```
*.err;kern.notice;auth.notice        /dev/console
*.err;kern.debug;daemon.notice       /var/adm/messages
*.emerg                              *
auth.info                            /var/log/auth
auth.notice                          /dev/console
mail.info                            /var/log/mailer
daemon.info                          /var/log/daemon
local2.notice                        /var/log/inetd
```

Each line begins with a list of facility/severity levels followed by a number of tab characters and then a file name. Note that on some systems, the separator between the first column and the second column must be tabs, not spaces.

The first column in each line of `syslog.conf` describes a set of messages to match, in the format *facility.severity*. The facility is simply the name of the facility to be used, or an asterisk, which matches all facilities. The severity works differently; the line will match all severities at the named severity level and higher. So the line that begins with `daemon.info` will match all messages in the daemon facility whose severity is `info` up through `emerg`. The only daemon messages not included will be those of severity level `debug` because `debug` is the only severity of less importance than `info`. Note also that you can specify several *facility.severity* tokens separated by semicolons.

The second column in `syslog.conf` specifies where the matching messages should be sent. Typically, this is a file name, as are all the examples above with one exception. On Solaris, you can send a syslog notice to a file, to logged in users, or to a remote machine. The syntax for each is listed in Figure 6.3.

Of particular interest to us is the syntax for sending a message to a remote host. Simply add a line like the following to `syslog.conf` on your servers:

```
*.warning;kern,user,auth.notice          @LOGGER.EXAMPLE.COM
```

This sends all messages of severity level warning or higher, plus kernel, user, and auth messages at the notice level or higher to the host logger.example.com. You may choose to use a more restrictive or less restrictive set of messages to be sent to the logging host, but it is wise to use the same configuration on all your servers. If you receive an error message from one machine, you will expect to receive the same kind of message from another machine encountering the same error.

| Action | Syntax |
|---|---|
| Append to file | *filename beginning with slash* |
| Send to logged-in user | *username* |
| Send to logged-in users | *user1,user2, ...* |
| Send to all logged-in users | * |
| Send to a remote host | *@hostname* |

**Figure 6.3.** Syslog Actions.

Once you have added the necessary line to your `syslog.conf`, remembering to use tabs as appropriate, you must send a SIGHUP to the syslog daemon so that it knows to reread the configuration file.[2] This must be done from a root account:

```
Solaris# ps -ef | grep syslog
root    211     1  0   Sep 19 ?        0:17 /usr/sbin/syslogd
Solaris# kill -HUP 211
```

You can now send a test syslog message using the `logger` program. By example:

```
Solaris% logger -pwarn "This is a test"
```

This will send a message to syslog at the user.warn level. As configured above, this message will be sent on to the host logger.example.com. Check the logs on that machine for the test message.

Of course, the host logger.example.com must also be configured to place messages it receives into a file. It is this file that Oak will monitor. An appropriate entry may already exist in the `syslog.conf`; if not, you can add one such as:

```
*.notice;kern.debug           /usr/adm/oaklog
```

Remember to create `/usr/adm/oaklog` and send syslogd a SIGHUP as before. For the remaining examples in this chapter, however, we assume messages are being logged to `/var/adm/messages`. Be aware that this is the default location for syslog messages on Solaris, but on Linux, the default is `/var/log/messages`. On either operating system, you should check that the default `syslog.conf` is configured to send all the messages you need to the file you are monitoring.

## 6.4.2   Configuring Syslog on Network Devices

Every device uses a different syntax for configuring remote logging. Cisco IOS uses the `logging` command from configure mode:

```
Router(config)#logging 10.7.21.88
```

---

[2]Also note that if you were adding a new file for syslog to log to, you must first create the new file before sending the SIGHUP to syslogd.

This will send log messages to the logging host 10.7.21.88, and by default, the facility will be local0. If you need to change the default logging facility (say it conflicts with a service you already depend on having as local0), use the `logging facility` command:

```
Router(config)#logging facility local3
```

Remember to issue a **write mem** to save your changes.

On Cisco devices running CatOS, you can configure remote logging from enable mode with:

```
switch18> (enable) set logging server 10.7.21.88
switch18> (enable) set logging server enable
```

## 6.4.3  An Introduction to Regular Expressions

The last thing we must understand before configuring Oak is the **regular expression**, an integral part of the Oak configuration language. A regular expression is syntax used to represent a pattern that a text string can either match or not match. For example, the first argument to the **grep** command is a kind of regular expression:

```
Solaris% grep domain /etc/resolv.conf
domain EXAMPLE.COM
```

Grep checks every line of the file `resolve.conf` to see if the string "domain" is present. In this simple case, the regular expression is "domain"; if that text is found on any line of the file, the line is printed to the screen. Here's a grep command with a slightly more interesting regular expression:

```
Solaris% grep do..in /etc/resolv.conf
domain EXAMPLE.COM
```

A period in a regular expression signifies that *any* character (other than a newline) can take its spot. In this case, the "m" and the "a" fill those roles. If, however, we had tried:

```
Solaris% grep do.in /etc/resolv.conf
```

there would be no matching line. Each period has to be replaced by exactly one character.

The regular expressions used in `grep` are somewhat limited unless we use special options with the program. The regular expressions in Oak are more full featured. The most common features are listed below, but a full listing of features is available in the regex man page.

Unless a character is otherwise designated for a special purpose the regular expression will match that character exactly. That is, an "e" in a regular expression simply means that an "e" must be present in the text.

## The . Character

As described above, a single period will match any character except a newline character.

## The + and * Modifiers

A character followed by an asterisk means the character can be present zero or more times. For example, the regular expression:

```
fo*bar
```

will match "foobar" as well as "fbar" and "foooobar." Likewise, the expression:

```
foo.*bar
```

will match all of "foobar," "fooqbar," and "fooqqqbar."

A character followed by a plus sign means the character must be present one or more times. So the regular expression:

```
foo.+bar
```

will match "fooabar" and "fooaaabar" but *not* "foobar."

## The [ ] Operator

When a number of characters are enclosed in square brackets, the regular expression will match on any one of those characters. The expression:

```
foo[123]bar
```

will match on "foo1bar," "foo2bar," but not "foo4bar." This expression can be combined with the previous + and * modifiers, so that:

```
foo[123]+bar
```

will match any string that starts with "foo," ends with "bar," and contains one or more of the characters "1," "2," or "3" in the middle, such as "foo1332bar."

If the first character inside the square brackets is a circumflex, the character in the text must be anything *other* than those listed. Thus:

```
foo[^123]bar
```

will match "foo5bar," but not "foo1bar."

Additionally, a hyphen used within square brackets can denote a range of characters. The regular expression:

```
[0-9]+
```

is extremely useful because it matches a series of one or more digits.

## The ^ and $ and Anchors

The ^ and $ characters are called anchors because they force the expression to be interpreted at a particular place on the text line. The circumflex denotes the beginning of the line. When placed at the beginning of a regular expression, it indicates that the next character must be the first character of the line being matched. Using grep as an example again:

```
Solaris% grep omain /etc/resolv.conf
domain EXAMPLE.COM
Solaris% grep ^omain /etc/resolv.conf
Solaris% grep ^domain /etc/resolv.conf
domain EXAMPLE.COM
```

Similarly, a dollar sign denotes the end of a line. So:

```
foobar$
```

will match a line that ends with "foobar" but not a line that ends with "foobarbaz."

## Quoting with \

Any special character preceded by a backslash indicates the actual character should be matched. Using \.+ matches one or more periods, not one or more of any character except newline.

The backslash itself is no exception; if you wish to match on a real backslash, use \\ in your regular expression.

## Substitution with ( )

Ordinarily parentheses can be used in a regular expression to grab a section of text for later use. In Perl, for example, the regular expression:

```
foo(.+)bar
```

will match the text foo52bar, and furthermore, the string "52" will be stored in a variable that can be used later.

Oak also allows parentheses to be used in regular expressions but for a different purpose. Anything found in parentheses is replaced with underscores. This is how you will inform Oak which information in a message is redundant or private and should not be included in notifications. For example:

```
^sendmail\[(.+)\]: (.+): SYSERR.*: Cannot open btree database .+
```

We see two sections enclosed in parentheses. The second one is the sendmail queue ID number. If this message is a problem that will occur on every piece of mail processed, we do not wish to see a different log message for every piece of mail, just a single message indicating the problem. When we tell Oak that the sendmail queue ID is unimportant, it will condense many messages into one.

## 6.4.4   Configuring Oak

The Oak configuration is centered on the idea of a message **queue**. Each queue is defined to take a certain action at a specified time interval. One queue may send an email every morning. Another may send an instant message each hour. After the queues are defined, you will define regular expressions that control which messages are sent to which queues. For convenience, there is a built-in "trash" queue for messages that can be discarded.

The typical Oak configuration follows this order:

- Set global options

- Define queues

- Define regular expressions for critical messages

- Define regular expressions for trash messages

- Define regular expressions for summarizing other messages

- Define a catch-all regular expression for everything else

It is important to understand that when a message is processed by Oak, it will be matched against the list of regular expressions in order from top to bottom, and when a match is found, the message will not be checked against any further expressions. This explains the ordering above.  First, we look for critical messages.  If the message doesn't match any critical messages, check if it should be thrown away, and if not, try to summarize it.

## Global Options

Oak has 10 global options available, listed in Figure 6.4.  Each line in the configuration file that sets a global option begins with the key word "set."

The `infile` option defaults to `/var/adm/messages`, but it is good practice to define it explicitly.  It is also the case that the `nukepid`, `nukeciscoid` and `nukesmqid` options are all on by default.  The beginning of a Oak configuration file might look like:

```
set infile /var/adm/messages
set nukepid
set nukeciscoid
set nukesmqid
```

## Defining Queues

Every queue definition begins with a line in the form "define queue *queuename*" and is followed by options for that queue. For example:

```
define queue network-gazette
  prescan
  action mail admin@example.com devnull@example.com "Daily Report"
    action-limits 1000 100 100 100
  fire 09:00
  header Daily message log
```

This defines a queue called "network-gazette" that sends an email message every day at 9:00 a.m.

The `action` command defines what action the queue should take when it's ready to send a message. There are currently three built-in options: `mail`, `zephyr`, and `exec`. Mail is for email, and zephyr is an instant messaging system in use at MIT and a number of other universities. The `exec` option can be used to run any external program. This can be a program that pages your operations staff or sends some other kind of immediate message. A queue can have as many actions as you like; simply list each one on a separate line, each beginning with the `action` command.

The arguments to the `mail` action are *to from subject*. In the example above, mail is sent to admin@example.com from the address devnull@example.com with the subject line Daily Report.

| Option | Function |
|---|---|
| set infile *file* | Define the file to be monitored |
| set nukepid | Automatically remove process IDs |
| set no nuke pid | Do not automatically remove PIDs |
| set nukeciscoid | Remove log IDs from cisco syslogs |
| set no nukeciscoid | Do not remove Cisco log IDs |
| set nukesmqid | Remove Sendmail queue IDs |
| set no nukesmqid | Do not remove Sendmail queue IDs |
| set ignorehosts *host* [ *host* ... ] | Ignore logs from the listed hosts |
| set onlyhosts *host* [ *host* ... ] | Process logs only from the listed hosts |
| set replacestr *string* | Replace text with *string* instead of underscores |

**Figure 6.4.** Facility Types on Solaris.

When the `exec` action command is used, the first argument is the name of the program to be run, and the following arguments are arguments to be passed to that program. The messages in the queue are sent to the standard input of the program being executed.

After an `action` statement, you may define `action-limits` specifying the limitaions on the size of messages sent through the action. The four arguments, in order, are:

- Maximum number of lines

- Maximum number of characters on a line

- Maximum number of hosts to report on

- Maximum number of logs per host

If no action limits are specified, the message size will be set to default values coded into Oak.

Next, the `fire` statement defines how often Oak should report messages for this queue. A number in the form *hh:mm*, using a 24-hour clock, will report every day at the given time. A number in the form *`*`num`h|m|s`*, will repeat at regular intervals. For example, `*25m` will be triggered once every 25 minutes, and `*1h` will be triggered once an hour. The time can also be the string `now`, which instructs Oak to report immediately on messages placed in this queue. More information about using `now` follows. The `header` command simply specifies a header to be prepended to the outgoing message.

There are two special commands that can be included in the definition of a queue. One is used above: It is the `prescan` command. This instructs Oak that upon startup, any messages already in the logfile should be included in the first notification. If, in this example, we had to kill and restart the Oak daemon, we would still like earlier messages in the log to be included in the next morning's email. However, we do not want the instant messaging queue to send an IM including all the errors that took place already today, so the `prescan` option is not defined for the IM queue.

The other special command is the `locking` command, which tells Oak to suppress repeated notifications from this queue for a certain period of time. For example:

```
define queue network-now
     action exec /usr/local/bin/page network-admins
       action-limits 25 30 100 10
     fire now
     locking 30m
     header **** CRITICAL MESSAGE LOG ****
```

This is a queue that fires immediately. It is used to send a message
to the pagers of the network administrators when a critical message
arrives. Because many such messages may be logged, and because you
do not want the administrators to be paged repeatedly, this `locking`
statement will cause Oak to suppress pages matching a given line for
30 minutes. If a different message comes in, Oak will page about it, so
use a queue like this carefully; make sure that redundant information is
removed from log messages or you will be bombarded with notifications.

Notice that the `prescan` option is not set for this queue; when starting up Oak, we wish for only newly arriving messages to page the operational staff.

For completeness we will also define the following queue used in
later examples:

```
define queue network-zephyr
     action zwrite network-admins oak *
       action-limits 25 100 100 10
     fire *1hr
     header Hourly message log
```

This queue sends an instant message every hour, if there is something
to report.

## Defining Regular Expressions

Each regular expression begins with the keyword on followed by the
regular expression and then a newline. On the next line we list the
queues that should receive any matching messages. Usually, we start
with the critical messages section first:

```
on ^sendmail\[(.+)\]: (.+): SYSERR.*: (.+): cannot fork:
     queues network-now network-zephyr network-gazette
```

```
on ^sendmail\[(.+)\]: WorkList for .+ maxed out at .+
    queues network-now network-zephyr network-gazette
on ^unix: WARNING: Sorry, no swap space to grow stack for pid (.+)
    queues network-now network-zephyr network-gazette
on ^(.+): %SYS-2-MALLOCFAIL: Memory allocation of (.+) bytes \
    failed from (.+), pool Processor, alignment (.+)
    queues network-now network-zephyr network-gazette
on file system full
    queues network-now network-zephyr network-gazette
```

The line matching MALLOCFAIL is split for readability but must be on only one line in the config and does not include the backslash.

Let's examine the first regular expression above. It matches messages from sendmail when it complains about being unable to fork. The part of the regular expression just after the string sendmail is used to ignore the process ID of the sendmail program. Because we have automatic process ID removal enabled, this isn't strictly necessary, but we can do it anyway. Note that we have chosen to match on any character between real brackets (the backslashes are necessary to indicate the brackets are present in the syslog message and are not used as special regular expression characters). We could have been more exacting and required the characters between the brackets to be digits, but that would have failed to match the underscores that Oak will automatically substitute for the process ID. The (.+) instructs Oak to replace the characters between the brackets because it is redundant information.

When Oak encounters a message that fits the criteria of this first regular expression, it will replace any of the sections within parentheses, and then add the message to the "network-now," "network-zephyr," and "network-gazette" queues, as defined on the next line. This way, it is sent out for immediate notification but is also included in the hourly and daily reports.

After all the critical messages are out of the way, you may list messages that never need to be viewed by putting them into the trash queue. Here are a few examples of messages we do not care to see. The last one discards root login messages, which can be a nuisance if administrators are often logging into servers. You may choose to configure this differently, or you may wish to ignore only login messages from particular users or machines:

```
on ^(.+):(.*)%SYS-5-CONFIG_I: Configured from console
    queues trash
on ^imapd\[(.+)\]: PROTERR: Connection reset by peer
    queues trash
on ^eklogind\[(.+)\]: ROOT login by (.+) \((.+)\)
    queues trash
```

Note that you do not need to define a trash queue; it exists for you by default. You may wonder if there is any point to using substitutions in these regular expressions if the messages are just going to be thrown away. They have been included only because the redundancy information was easy to encode at the time, and if we should want to move the messages out of the trash queue at a later point, we will already have the appropriate formatting.

Next, you can include all the messages that should be in the regular reports but need to have redundant information removed. Here is an excerpt from this part of the configuration:

```
on ^sendmail\[(.+)\]: (.+): SYSERR.*: Cannot open btree databas
    queues network-zephyr network-gazette
on ^sendmail\[(.+)\]: (.+): (.+): SMTP DATA-2 protocol error: 5
    queues network-zephyr network-gazette
on ^sendmail\[(.+)\]: (.+): SYSERR(.*): (.+) config error: mail
    queues network-zephyr network-gazette
```

Finally, at the very end, you may include a statement catching anything that has not already been matched:

```
on .*
    queues network-zephyr network-gazette
```

If a line like this is not included at the end, messages that do not match any of the earlier lines will simply be ignored.

Of course, the above style of organizing the Oak configuration is optional. You do not have to place critical messages first, followed by trash, other messages, and then the catch-all. You can use any method you like as long as you keep in mind the rule that Oak will match on the first line it finds and that if it does not find a maching line, it will ignore the message.

## Running Oak

Oak runs as a daemon and is invoked simply as **oak** -c *configfile*. If necessary, you can kill the program at any point and restart it. Remember that only queues defined with the `prescan` option will pick up messages already in the system log. If you change the Oak configuration file, you will need to stop and restart the program in order for it to notice the change.

If your system is set up to rotate log files, you do not need to take any special action to make Oak recognize a new file. Oak will automatically detect if the filename originally used no longer points to the file that Oak is actively monitoring. When this happens, Oak will open the new file and begin monitoring it instead, without any operator intervention.

Oak does not necessarily need to be run with root privileges. It does need to have access to read the syslog file it monitors, however. On some systems, the log file is readable only by root, and on others, it is readable by everyone. Check that the account you will run Oak from has access to read the syslog file.

## A Small Sample Configuration

Here is a small, sample Oak configuration. It is just enough to get you started working with the program.

```
# global options
set infile /var/adm/messages

# define queues
define queue testqueue
    action mail admin@example.com devnull@example.com Report
      action-limits 1000 100 100 100
    fire *5m
    header 5 Minute Test Report

# critical messages
on ^sendmail\[(.+)\]: (.+): SYSERR.*: (.+): cannot fork:
    queues testqueue

# trash
on ^(.+):(.*)%SYS-5-CONFIG_I: Configured from console
    queues trash
```

```
# other
on ^(.+): %SYS-3-CPUHOG: Task ran for (.+) msec \((.+)\),
    queues network-zephyr network-gazette
on .*
    queues network-zephyr network-gazette
```

## 6.5   Maintaining Oak

The bulk of the maintenance required for Oak is creating and updating
the configuration file. As you change other components of your system,
such as upgrading router software or deploying new servers, you can expect to see new and different syslog messages. The Oak configuration
must be updated to reflect these changes. The risk of a stale configuration is that notifications will become long and less compact, which
may make it easy to overlook important warning messages.

It is good practice to update the configuration every few weeks by
looking over earlier reports and determining which information can be
safely ignored or made more compact.

## 6.6   References and Further Study

There are a number of other free programs available that perform system log monitoring. For example, the `logwatch` program, available
from `http://www.logwatch.org/`, is free and now comes installed with
many Linux systems. Unlike Oak, it allows you to write customized filters that condense information into any kind of message you desire.
However, the notification options are limited and the configuration is a
bit tricky.

A very popular log monitoring tool is Swatch, available from `http:`
`//swatch.sourceforge.net/`. Swatch is similar to Oak in that it uses
a simple configuration language based on regular expressions, and each
regular expression can trigger a notification. The advantage Swatch has
over Oak is that it is much more widely used and has been around a lot
longer, making it a more stable and reliable tool. Oak allows for much
more flexibility in notification options than Swatch does, and it has a
few more features, but as a younger piece of software, it is not nearly
as tried and true. If you encounter bugs or other problems with Oak,
send a detailed description of the problem to `bug-ktools@mit.edu`.

The remote syslog protocol that allows syslogs to be sent between machines is described in RFC 3164. The options for the `syslogd` program and the `syslog.conf` file can be found in the Unix man pages for `syslogd` and `syslog.conf`, respectively. Regular expression syntax is described in the Unix man pages `regex` and `regexp`, and there are books available on regular expressions, such as *Mastering Regular Expressions* (O'Reilly and Associates, 2002) by Jeffrey Friedl.

# Chapter 7

# SERVICE MONITORING

## 7.1  Overview of Service Monitoring

The most common type of problem that network administrators deal with is something that spontaneously stops working: A network link fails, a Web server refuses connections, or a switch stops passing traffic. Often, failures like these do not result in any kind of notification to administrators. A switch that loses power or suffers a software failure does not have any way of sending a message indicating that it is no longer functioning. It is is vital, however, for administrators to be notified of failures like this when they occur.

The solution is to use some kind of monitoring or polling software. This is a program running on one or more servers that sends out probes at regular intervals in order to test network connectivity and service functionality. This software may ping all of your switches and routers. If a device does not respond, the failure is reported to the appropriate administrators. The software might also attempt to retrieve Web pages, make SNMP requests, or perform other kinds of service level testing. Any failure to respond as expected can similarly be reported to an appropriate administrator.

There are some subtleties to performing this task effectively. Imagine the scenario depicted in Figure 7.1. Switch B is connected to a large number of servers. Each one is important, and if any one of them should fall off the network, an administrator needs to be paged. The polling server pings each one, and if any one server does not respond, a notification is sent. What happens if switch B itself fails? Not only can the polling server not contact switch B, but it can also no longer contact any of the servers behind the switch. If the polling software were not

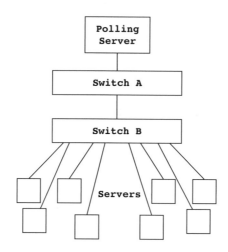

**Figure 7.1.** Many Servers Behind a Single Failed Device.

intelligent, it would send notifications about every service behind switch B. If all these messages were sent to a network administrator's pager, they would overwhelm the recipient and also obscure the real problem. For this reason, intelligent polling software includes a mechanism for describing which services depend on which others. If the software knows that switch B has to be operating in order for the servers behind it to respond, it can ignore the failed tests for the servers and simply report that switch B is not responding.

Note that system polling can have an impact on the performance of the network or the devices being monitored. If, for example, ping tests are performed at an excessively fast rate, the polling software itself can cause network congestion. Additionally, a network device with a relatively slow CPU can be easily overwhelmed by rapid ping tests or SNMP queries. Even devices with a fast CPU, such as high-end routers, can experience degraded service if asked to participate in an excessively large number of SNMP transactions. By default, system polling software will usually place an appropriate delay between tests. If you choose to change the testing interval or find that your network is experiencing degraded service after you deploy monitoring software, check to make sure the monitoring software itself is not causing an unnecessarily high load on the system.

There are two pieces of free, open source software that make good service monitors. One is called Sysmon, available from `http://www.sysmon.org/`. This is a relatively simple program that is easy to configure and get running. It does not have many advanced features, but for a small to medium-sized network, it will get the job done. The other tool is called Nagios and is available from `http://www.nagios.org/`. This is a better tool for large networks. It is a much more complicated program, but it includes advanced functionality that may be required at a larger installation. This chapter focuses almost exclusively on Sysmon, except for a discussion at the end that lists the additional features available in Nagios.

## 7.2 What Service Monitoring Can Help You Do

The most obvious benefit to running a service monitor is that it gives you early warning of failures. Practically speaking, this allows you to fix a problem before it becomes an even larger problem. If a piece of hardware fails in the middle of the night, you have the chance to repair or replace it before the start of business the next day. Or say you have a piece of network hardware whose sole purpose is to provide redundancy for another piece of hardware. When the primary device fails, the backup is configured to take over gracefully. If the primary fails and it goes unnoticed for months, what happens if the backup hardware fails as well?

Monitoring software can also help determine where in your network a problem resides. Users typically report problems only from their own point of view. If a connection serving hundreds of users goes down and you rely on user reports to notify administrators when something is wrong, by the time reports come in, there may be an overwhelming number of cases to deal with and it may not be immediately clear where the problem really is.

Additionally, it is always in your best interest to know about problems before either your customers or your superiors do, regardless of how quickly you intend to take action. There is nothing more embarrassing than hearing that a core service is down from one of them first.

In daily use, you will typically ignore the system polling software until it pages you or otherwise notifies you of a problem condition. You may also view the status of monitored services on a Web page such as the one in Figure 7.2. Here, the darker line indicates a service that is not responding, and the lighter lines are servers that are functioning without any problem.

| | | | | | | | | | | | |
|---|---|---|---|---|---|---|---|---|---|---|---|

Last Updated:
04/08/03 11:15:50

| HostName | Description | Type | Port | Down N | Up N | Notified | Status | Time Up | Time Failed | Last Outage | Uptime |
|---|---|---|---|---|---|---|---|---|---|---|---|
| server2.example.com | Server2 | www | 80 | 948 | 0 | Yes | Conn Ref | Never | Apr 7 18:51:22 | Never | 0.00% |
| www.example.com | Web Server | www | 80 | 0 | 945 | No | up | Never | Never | Never | 100.00% |
| www.example.com | Web Ping | ping | 0 | 0 | 938 | No | up | Never | Never | Never | 100.00% |
| 192.0.2.6 | Router1-ServerNet1 | ping | 0 | 0 | 938 | No | up | Never | Never | Never | 100.00% |
| 192.0.2.7 | Router1-ServerNet2 | ping | 0 | 0 | 938 | No | up | Never | Never | Never | 100.00% |
| server1.example.com | Monitoring Host | ping | 0 | 0 | 938 | No | up | Never | Never | Never | 100.00% |

**Figure 7.2.** Sample Sysmon Status Web Page.

## 7.3   Installing Sysmon

The following sections provide specifics on installing Sysmon.

### 7.3.1   Where to Place the Server

Because Sysmon will suppress notifications for any failed devices behind a single failed device, it is important to run the monitoring program somewhere that has a good view of the network. It would be a mistake to place the server four devices removed from the core of the network, especially if one of those devices tends to fail often. When one does fail, Sysmon will lose its view of the rest of the network. You would rather have the Sysmon server located as close to the core as possible, if not directly on the backbone. This way Sysmon will be able to give the most accurate report possible when something fails.

### 7.3.2   How to Install Sysmon

The installation for Sysmon is mostly straightforward. Download the latest version from `http://www.sysmon.org/`, then unpackage and build the software. There is one step that is out of the ordinary; you must change to the `src` directory before typing `make`:

```
Solaris# gunzip -c sysmon-0.91.17.tar.gz | tar xvf -
Solaris# cd sysmon-0.91.17
Solaris# ./configure
Solaris# cd src
Solaris# make
```

On Solaris, you may see a list of warnings for every file that is built. This is not a serious problem; it is the compiler complaining about the curses library. Sysmon uses curses to build a program that will display a nice list of unreachable hosts. As long as the files `sysmon` and `sysmond` are present, the build was successful:

```
Solaris# file sysmon
sysmon:          ELF 32-bit MSB executable SPARC Version 1, dyn...
Solaris# file sysmond
sysmond:         ELF 32-bit MSB executable SPARC Version 1, dyn...
```

At this point, you can install the software from a root account. By default, it will place the `sysmon` and `sysmond` programs in `/usr/local/bin/`:

```
Solaris# make install
```

## 7.4  Using Sysmon

The following sections discuss the details of running Sysmon.

### Starting the Sysmon Daemon

While Sysmon does not strictly have to be run from a root account, any account that does not have root privileges will be unable to run ping tests. So practically speaking, you will probably want to run the daemon as root. If you are concerned about security and do not need to use ping tests, you may run Sysmon from a user-level account.

Before starting the Sysmon daemon, you will need to create a configuration file. A short sample config will be sufficient for now. Place the following in `/usr/local/etc/sysmon.conf`, which is the default location for the configuration file:

```
root="server";
config showupalso;
config statusfile text "/var/tmp/status.txt";
```

```
object server {
   ip "server.example.com";
   type ping;
   contact "admin@example.com";
};
```

Replace "server" and "server.example.com" with the name of the machine you are running Sysmon on and replace "admin@example.com" with your email address. Now you can start the daemon with:

```
Solaris# /usr/local/bin/sysmond
sysmond: 15:25:36 Starting System Monitor version v0.91.17
System Monitor version v0.91.17
/usr/local/bin/sysmond started on server.example.com
forked process as pid 7467
```

If you are running Sysmon from a user-level account and do not have access to write the configuration file to /usr/local/etc, you may place it in another file and start sysmond with the -f option:

```
Solaris% /usr/local/bin/sysmond -f /var/tmp/sysmon.conf
```

If the configuration has an error, it will be reported at startup time. Some errors are considered only warnings, and sysmond will start with the new config regardless. For example, if no description had been set for the "server" object:

```
Solaris# /usr/local/bin/sysmond
sysmond: 15:30:57 WARNING: object has no descripton near line 10
sysmond: 15:30:57 Starting System Monitor version v0.91.17
System Monitor version v0.91.17
/usr/local/bin/sysmond started on server.example.com
forked process as pid 7476
```

If Sysmon detects an error in an object definition, it may choose to exclude that object from the configuration and start without it.

Once Sysmon is up and running, you can check the status of monitored devices by looking at /var/tmp/status.txt, whose path was specified in the configuration file:

```
Solaris# cat /var/tmp/status.txt
Network Summary     System Monitor version v0.91.14
Hostname     Type  Port DownN UpN   NotifiedStat     Time Failed
server       ping  0    0    220   No    up          Never
```

This file is periodically written by Sysmon, and it will contain the latest status information as long as the Sysmon daemon is running.

## Stopping the Sysmon Daemon

Though you can kill Sysmon by sending it a signal, it is more convenient to use the `sysmond` program instead:

```
Solaris# /usr/local/bin/sysmond stop
sysmond: 15:35:33 sending signal 15 to sysmond process 7467

sysmond: 15:35:33 Please remain seated as your ride comes to a...
```

As the output indicates, this is equivalent to sending a TERM signal to the sysmond process.

## Pausing Sysmon

You can also instruct Sysmon to temporarily stop functioning and then resume later with the `pause` and `resume` commands:

```
Solaris# /usr/local/bin/sysmond pause
sysmond: 15:37:15 sending signal 17 to sysmond process 7486

Solaris# /usr/local/bin/sysmond resume
sysmond: 15:37:19 sending signal 17 to sysmond process 7486
```

Both commands send a USR2 signal to the `sysmond` process, which toggles between the paused and running states.

## Reloading the Configuration

After changes are made to the configuration file, Sysmon has to either be restarted or be instructed to reload the configuration. Otherwise, the changes will not take effect. The `reload` command is executed as:

```
Solaris# /usr/local/bin/sysmond reload
sysmond: 19:07:23 sending signal 1 to sysmond process 7486

sysmond: 19:07:23 Done reloading new config file
```

The reload command sends a HUP signal to `sysmond`. If the configuration is not valid, the process will continue to run with the old configuration. Otherwise, the new configuration will take effect.

## Connecting with a Remote Client

Sysmon runs a TCP service on port 1345 where it provides data about monitored services. You can connect to it using the curses client that was built and installed as /usr/local/bin/sysmon:

```
Solaris% /usr/local/bin/sysmon server.example.com
```

The screen will clear and a display like the following will come up:

```
Server: server              Current Time:  Apr  7 18:22:57 2003
Hostname          Type  Port Count Notif Stat       Time Failed
----------------------------------------------------------------
www.example.com   www   80   66    Yes   Conn Ref   Never


----------------------------------------------------------------
 q = quit    space = refresh   h = help
```

Only services that are down or have failed tests will be present. You can exit this application by pressing press the "q" key.

## Other Runtime Options

Running the sysmond program with the -help argument will produce a listing of all the options that can be used on the command line:

```
Solaris# /usr/local/bin/sysmond -help
Usage: /usr/local/bin/sysmond [ -f config-file ] [ -n ] [ -d ]
   [ -v ] [ -t ] [ -p port ] [ reload ]
  -b             : IP Address to listen on
  -f config-file : Alternate config file location
         DEFAULT: /usr/local/etc/sysmon.conf
  -n             : Don't do notifies
  -d             : Don't fork
  -i             : Disable ICMP
  -v             : Print version then exit
  -w             : Toggle warning messages
  -D             : Toggle debug messages
  -M             : Toggle memory debugging
  -t             : Test/check config file then exit
  -p #           : Change port number listening on (0 to disable)
  -q             : Quiet
  -l             : do not syslog
  reload         : Test/check config file, and if it passes ...
```

```
pause              : Suspend/resume monitoring (SIGUSR2)
resume             : Suspend/resume monitoring (SIGUSR2)
stop               : End monitoring and quit (SIGTERM)
```

## 7.5   Configuring Sysmon

Once you have verified that `sysmond` is up and running, you can begin
to fill out the configuration with the devices you wish to monitor. The
Sysmon configuration is made up of a list of objects to be monitored,
along with a section of global configuration options. Within each object
definition, you must specify the IP address of the device to be tested,
the kind of test that should be performed, and any objects the device
depends on. When object A is configured to depend on object B, notifications will not be sent about the status of object A if object B is
also unreachable.

Note that each line of the configuration ends with a semicolon, except for lines that end with an open curly brace. Additionally, lines
beginning with a pound sign (#) are ignored and can be used for com-
ments.

### 7.5.1   The Root Node

Sysmon requires one object to be defined as the root of the device
hierarchy. This is the object that all others depend upon to be up. A
good choice for this is the server that Sysmon runs on itself, as was
configured in the earlier example. Note that in defining the root node,
the name of the object must be in quotation marks:

```
root="server";
```

### 7.5.2   Objects and Dependencies

Now you can add to the configuration other objects to be monitored.
Start by adding a simple ping test for the router that server.example.com
is connected to:

```
object router1 {
  ip "192.0.2.5";
  type ping;
  desc "Router1";
```

```
    dep "server";
    contact "admin@example.com";
};
```

## The Object Name

First note the name of the object, here "router1." The name does not need to correspond to the hostname of the device, though having it correspond may keep the configuration easy to maintain. The object name is used solely for referencing the object later in the configuration. It can be any text string you like, as long each object has a unique name.

## Setting the IP Address

The first object option listed above is the `ip` option, which specifies the IP address of the device to be tested. This field can really contain either the hostname or the IP address of the device. There are advantages and disadvantages to both. If an IP address is used, Sysmon will have no dependence on DNS's working properly, and the test will be performed appropriately even if DNS has failed. However, if you have many pieces of equipment to keep track of and the hardware being monitored may be replaced by a device with a different IP address that later takes over the older hostname, it would be highly preferable to use hostnames instead of IP addresses. This way, your Sysmon configuration does not become a second place where DNS information must be maintained. Sysmon does keep its own DNS cache, which gives you some ability to control the interaction between Sysmon and the DNS independent of the software running on the server. The options that control this behavior are described in the section on Global Options.

## Setting the Test Type

The next line in the object added above directs Sysmon to perform a ping test on the device in question. There are 10 other possible values for the the test type, all of which are listed in Figure 7.3. Most of these tests are configured just like the ping test: Simply declare the test type, and you're done. For a few of them, there are extra options you must use. For example, in configuring an object to test Web service, using the `www` test type, you must include the `url` and `urltext` options:

```
object web-server {
  ip "www.example.com";
  type www;
  desc "Main Web Server";
  dep "router1";
  url "http://www.example.com/";
  urltext "<TITLE>";
  contact "admin@example.com";
};
```

This tests the URL `http://www.example.com/`. If the page is not loadable or does not contain the text <TITLE>, the test will fail.

The `tcp` and `udp` tests must have a port number specified so that Sysmon knows which port to test. The `pop3` test requires a valid username and password, and the `radius` test requires the same, along with a radius secret string.

### Setting the Object Description

The object description, set with `desc`, is simply text you add to help identify the object in reports. Sysmon will run if you do not include this option, but because of the way the configuration file is parsed, if the `desc` option is not present, the description from the previous object

| Test | Function | Options |
|------|----------|---------|
| `ping` | standard ping test | |
| `pop3` | working POP3 server | `username`, `password` |
| `tcp` | generic listening TCP port | `port` |
| `udp` | generic listening UDP port | `port` |
| `radius` | working radius server | `username`, `password`, `secret` |
| `nntp` | listening news server | |
| `smtp` | listening mail server | |
| `imap` | listening IMAP server | |
| `x500` | listening x500 directory server | |
| `www` | listening web server | `url`, `urltext` |
| `sysmon` | running remote sysmon server | |

**Figure 7.3.** Sysmon Test Types.

will be used. This is probably not the desired behavior. If you explicitly want to set no description for a device, you can do it with:

```
desc "";
```

## Specifying Dependencies

An object's dependencies are set with the dep command. Every object must depend on at least one other object, with the exception of the root node, which has no dependencies. An object may depend on more than one other object by including multiple dep lines:

```
object server1 {
  ip "server1.example.com";
  type ping;
  desc "Server 1";
  dep "router1-servernet";
  dep "router2-servernet";
  contact "admin@example.com";
};
```

In this example, server1.example.com has a connection to two different routers, which are objects defined elsewhere in the config. If either router is functioning, there will be connectivity to the server. By listing two dependencies, you can direct Sysmon to ignore the server's status only if both routers are down.

Also notice that the address listed for each router is the address of the relevant interface. It is good practice to use separate dependencies for each interface instead of using just one of the router's addresses for every dependency. This way, if a particular interface goes down, you will ignore only services behind that interface instead of the services behind the entire router.

## Setting the Contact

The contact command specifies the email address that should be no-tified if an object fails its tests. You can list multiple email addresses by separating them with commas:

```
contact "admin@example.com,joe-pager@example.com";
```

## Using the Spawn Option

Email is not always the best way to notify an administrator of a critical problem. To begin with, email is not guaranteed to be a timely service. Though abnormal, it is possible for an email message to be queued for hours, or even days. Additionally, email notifications will be useless if the mail system itself is unavailable. It is preferable to send critical notifications via some other mechanism, such as a direct message to a pager or cell phone.

Sysmon does not yet have support for sending pages by itself, but there is a hook that will let you do it. The `spawn` command will execute a program of your choosing when notification needs to be sent for an object. The argument to `spawn` is the name of the program to execute and the arguments that should be passed to that program. In those arguments, you must specify the format of the message to be sent. Sysmon has a number of "replacement" variables that will translate to different pieces of Sysmon information. For example, `%H` is replaced with the DNS name of the host being monitored, `%s` is the name of the service, and `%U` is the state of the service, either "up" or "down." So the spawn line might look like:

```
spawn "/var/tmp/notify.sh %H %s %U";
```

Then you can create a simple program `/var/tmp/notify.sh`:

```
#!/bin/sh
echo "$*" | /usr/lib/sendmail admin@example.com 2> /dev/null
```

Of course, it would be silly for your notification script to send email like this since you could accomplish your goal just as well with the `contact` command. It is used here simply as an example. In your own environment, you would instead send the text to a program that would send a page, such as QuickPage.[1]

The result of the above `spawn` command, if a service goes down, would be text that looks like:

```
WWW.EXAMPLE.COM www down
```

---

[1] The QuickPage program is available from `http://www.qpage.org/`.

There are many more replacement variables available, and you can use them to create as detailed a message as you would like. They are all listed in Figure 7.4, which is taken from the Sysmon documentation.

| Var | Replacement |
| --- | --- |
| %m | local host name |
| %H | DNS name of host being monitored |
| %s | service |
| %p | port number (numeric) |
| %T | Current Time hh:mm:ss |
| %t | Current Time mm dd hh:mm:ss |
| %d | Downtime dd:hh:mm |
| %D | Downtime with seconds dd:hh:mm:ss |
| %i | Unique ID for outage |
| %I | IP of host down |
| %w | warning/what |
| %u | error-type converted into string describing it |
| %h | hostname with failure |
| %r | reliability percentage |
| %V | Verbose History (not implemented) |
| %c | Failure iteration count (since last success) |
| %C | Success iteration count (since last failure) |
| %U | Service state (as 'up' or 'down') |

**Figure 7.4.** Sysmon Replacement Variables.
From Sysmon online documentation at `www.sysmon.org/config.html`.

## Other Object Options

A couple of other options can be used in an object definition. In particular, the `contact_on` option can direct Sysmon to send notifications only when a service goes up or when it goes down, instead of on both occasions, as is the default behavior. There is also an option called `reverse` that swaps the meaning of "up" and "down" for service status. This is useful if you use Sysmon to monitor another Sysmon server.

The use of these and other object options is listed in the documentation that comes with the Sysmon package and on the Sysmon Web page.

## 7.5.3   Global Options

Most of the global options in the Sysmon configuration start with the word `config`, followed by the option name. While global options can be listed anywhere in the configuration, they are usually placed at the beginning of the file, before any objects are defined.

### The Status File

When the Sysmon daemon is running, it will periodically write a file with the status of services that it is monitoring. This can either be in HTML to produce a Web page or in a raw text format suitable for viewing from a terminal. By default, only services that are down are listed, but you can change this by using the `showupalso` option described below. Use the `config statusfile` option to direct Sysmon to write the file:

```
config statusfile html "/usr/local/apache/htdocs/sysmon.html";
```

Or if you want a text file:

```
config statusfile text "/var/tmp/status.txt";
```

The time interval that Sysmon waits between refreshing these files is 60 seconds by default, but you can change it with the `html refresh` option. For example:

```
config html refresh 30;
```

would cause the file to be rewritten every 30 seconds.

### Viewing Both Up and Down Services

The status file will print a list of services that are not responding, but if you would like it to also include those services that are responding, use the `showupalso` option:

```
config showupalso;
```

In the HTML version of the status file, hosts that are up are printed in green, hosts that are down are in red, and hosts that are failing tests and may go down are yellow. These colors can be changed with the `upcolor`, `downcolor`, and `recentcolor` options, respectively.

## Mail Header Options

Ordinarily, Sysmon sends mail messages with a from address of "root" at the server the software is running on. You can change this and other mail headers in the global configuration:

```
config from "admin@example.com";
config replyto "admin@example.com";
config errorsto "errors@example.com";
```

You can also change the format of the subject line, using the same replacement variables as before:

```
config subject "Sysmon: %H %s %U";
```

Or you can disable subject lines entirely with:

```
config nosubject;
```

This can be advantageous if you use email to send messages to a phone or pager that does not handle subject lines gracefully.

## Test Queuing Options

There are a few options available that control how Sysmon processes service tests and notifications. First, the `numfailures` option controls how many tests a service must fail before a notification message is sent. By default, a service must fail four tests in a row, but if you wanted notification after only three failures:

```
config numfailures 3;
```

Normally, Sysmon schedules a test to be run 60 seconds after the last time the same test was completed. If you are monitoring a very large number of services, you can reduce the load on the server by increasing this interval. If you need tests run faster, thereby making Sysmon more sensitive, you can decrease it. The following would set the interval to 90 seconds:

```
config queuetime 90;
```

Though it is tempting to lower the queue time in order to make Sysmon detect problems quickly, anything lower than 60 seconds is probably excessive.

Sysmon will happily run more than one test at a time; by default, it will run up to 100 tests simultaneously. You can raise or lower this value with the `maxqueued` option:

```
config maxqueued 50;
```

A server that has limited resources and many tests to run may need to run fewer tests at once, while a fast server can benefit by taking advantage of the ability to run more tests at a time.

Usually Sysmon sends only one notification when a service changes status. If you would like it to send repeated messages when a service is down, you can use the `pageinterval` option. Unlike with the other options, the units are in minutes:

```
config pageinterval 20;
```

This would send a reminder notification every 20 minutes when a service is down.

## DNS Options

As mentioned earlier, Sysmon keeps its own DNS cache separate from the one the server's operating system uses. By default, entries from the cache are expired every 15 minutes, but you can change this with the `dnsexpire` option, which takes an argument in seconds:

```
config dnsexpire 300;
```

This would expire entries from the cache every 5 minutes.

Every 10 minutes, Sysmon also sends information about the cache to syslog. This interval can be changed with the `dnslog` option, in seconds:

```
config dnslog 900;
```

## Message Formatting Options

If you do not like the message format that Sysmon uses by default, you can change it by using the replacement variables described earlier, in conjunction with the **pmesg** global configuration option. For example:

```
config pmesg "%H %s %U";
```

would produce the simple text just as before, but this time, it would be the body of all mail notifications. The default message format is:

```
%H (%I) %w is %u %d
```

## Using Variables

If you have an even moderately sized installation, you may have many objects configured with the same information again and again, and worse yet, some of that information may need to change over time. Say you have a couple of different groups of people that should receive notifications when different services go down. One group is responsible for a certain set of hardware, another is responsible for a different set. You can list all the email addresses with every object, but then when an address needs to be added or removed, you will need to reconfigure every object. Instead, you can use a global variable to store information once, and that information will be used as is throughout the rest of the file. When you wish to make a change, you will have to do it in only one place. The following example demonstrates the use of variables to store lists of contacts:

```
set network-group = "netops@example.com, joe-pager@example.com";
set network-group-nopage = "netops@example.com";
set web-group = "frank@example.com, jill@example.com;

object router5 {
  ip "router5-backbone.example.com";
  type ping;
  desc "Router 5 Backbone";
  dep "server";
  contact "$network-group";
};

object web-ping {
  ip "www.example.com";
```

```
    type ping;
    desc "Web Server Ping";
    dep "server";
    contact "$network-group-nopage";
};

object web-server {
  ip "www.example.com";
  type www;
  desc "Main Web Server";
  dep "web-ping";
  url "http://www.example.com";
  urltext "<TITLE>";
  contact "$web-group";
};
```

The variables defined at the beginning are referenced later with a dollar sign in front of the variable name. Notice that quotation marks still need to be used, even when a variable is referenced.

## Using Includes

Another problem for large installations is that the configuration file can quickly become large and unwieldy. It will be easier to maintain if you break it down into smaller files by whatever grouping makes the most sense for you. Sysmon will let you do this with the `include` option:

```
include "/usr/local/etc/sysmon.webservers.conf";
```

The named file will have its contents included wherever the statement is placed in the configuration.

There are a number of different ways to organize groups of configuration files. You may wish to have different files for different services: one for Web servers, one for ping tests, and so on. Or perhaps it would work better in your environment to organize into different files for different physical parts of the network.

## Other Global Options

Other global configuration options available include an option to change the file to which the process ID is written, an option to turn off registration messages sent to the Sysmon registration server, and an option to

change the facility to which the program sends syslog messages. These
are all described in the documentation that comes with Sysmon.

## 7.6   Maintaining Sysmon

The toughest part of maintaining Sysmon is keeping your configuration
in check with reality, especially if you have a large installation or if the
people who are deploying equipment are not the same ones who will
be updating the config. However, if you wish to have your notification
system consistently alert you to trouble, you must keep the configuration accurate. This requires some discipline. Because failures do not
occur often, it is easy to forget about the importance of updating the
files. If the data becomes stale, with many devices marked as failed
that really have been taken out of service, it will become hard to trust
Sysmon when it reports that a device has failed. It becomes the server
that "cried wolf."

## 7.7   Nagios

While Sysmon is a good package that takes care of the needs of the
average network administrator, it does have a few limitations that can
be serious drawbacks for very large networks. Nagios,[2] available from
http://www.nagios.org/, is better suited to these installations. Some
of the major advantages of Nagios are:

- **Escalation.** Nagios can be configured to take one action when
  a service first fails and then different actions if it continues to
  fail. This way, you can receive an email or instant message when
  a device is first encountering a problem but a message to your
  pager only if the problem persists for long enough. The actions
  and delays are all configurable.

- **Configuration templates.** Because Nagios has many more configurable options, the config file can grow even larger than Sysmon's. However, Nagios allows you to use templates to reduce the

---

[2]According to the Nagios Web site, the name is pronounced *nah-ghee-ose* and
has nothing to do with the fact that the service nags you when it detects system
failures.

size and complexity of the configuration. You specify information that will remain the same for a large number of objects, give that information a name, and then reference it from any objects where it applies. Thus, the only information configured for a particular object is the information that makes it different from others.

- **Monitoring time periods.** Nagios has the ability to send notifications for objects during only certain time periods that you specify. For example, you can direct it to send pages for a particular object only during business hours. You can also inform Nagios about scheduled down time. This way, you can avoid paging the entire operations staff in the middle of the night while you are upgrading a piece of equipment.

- **Modular test plugins.** The tests that Nagios performs are all executed from a set of plugin modules. Each plugin is simply an external program that tests a service, but it follows a specific contract with Nagios so that the results can be processed appropriately. This means that it is easy to write your own tests to complement the suite of tests that comes with the Nagios plugin package.

- **Passive tests.** Some information that you wish to monitor cannot be sent to the monitoring server by means of the server requesting the data. SNMP traps, for example, can be sent from a device at any time. Nagios can receive and monitor such data and report on it just as it would for an ordinary service test.

- **Host and contact groups.** Both hosts and people can be categorized into generic groups. These groups make it easier to change the configuration for a large, similar set of devices all at once. For example, you could change the escalation procedure for all core routers by changing only one line in the config.

- **Flap detection.** Occasionally, you will find that a test repeatedly fails and succeeds, causing a large number of up and down notifications. In this state, the service is said to be flapping. Nagios has the ability to detect flapping and automatically disable notifications for the service until the flapping has stopped.

- **Optional dependencies.** Dependencies are considered optional in Nagios but are required in Sysmon. Having optional dependencies is the equivalent of allowing as many root notes as you would like. While it is the case that every device ought to have at least one parent, it is sometimes practical and convenient to add a few tests that have no dependencies.

The downside to Nagios is that it is a much more complicated program than Sysmon. As a result, it will take a significant amount of time to install and configure. Whereas Sysmon can be set up in an afternoon, setting up Nagios may take several days or longer. If you need the functionality, however, it is well worth the time spent.

## 7.8   References and Further Study

Both Sysmon and Nagios have documentation within their respective packages, and both have documentation online as well. Sysmon is at `http://www.sysmon.org/` and Nagios is at `http://www.nagios.org/`.

Both packages also currently require you to use external software for paging. A popular program for this is QuickPage, available from `http://www.qpage.org/`. QuickPage uses the TAP/IXO protocol and the Simple Network Paging Protocol (SNPP), which is described in RFC 1861.

# Chapter 8

# TCPDUMP

## 8.1 Overview of Tcpdump

Most network administration tools are not based directly on the data being transmitted on a network, but rather on information related to that data. MRTG, for example, uses network bandwidth values. Other tools make use of system logs on network equipment or they test for system availability. It is sometimes necessary, however, to examine the packets themselves. Doing so will allow you to diagnose some particularly tricky network problems and can also serve as a hands-on approach to learning more about network protocols.

The most widely used open source tool for directly analyzing packets is a program called tcpdump, originally written by Van Jacobson. The standard tcpdump, through version 3.4, is maintained and distributed by the Lawrence Berkeley National Laboratory. Additional work has produced a second train of tcpdump releases as high as version 3.7.2 available from `http://www.tcpdump.org/`. The tcpdump that ships with most Linux distributions comes from this source. Both versions of tcpdump rely on the pcap library, a system for capturing packets across different operating systems. The pcap library is available from both the LBL and `www.tcpdump.org`.

One word of caution is necessary before you use tcpdump and other packet analyzers. Even though encryption is becoming more and more common in network protocols, there are still many protocols that transport data unencrypted. When using a packet analyzer to monitor network traffic, you will be able to view private data sent by users on the network—data that they may believe is not visible to others. There are serious legal implications to monitoring such data because it can be considered a form of wire tapping. Be sure to research relevant state and federal law before using a program such as tcpdump in an environment where user data will be present. When do you use a packet analyzer in this manner, remember to respect the privacy of other users as fully as possible and also ensure that you adhere to any privacy policies in place at your facility.

## 8.2   What Tcpdump Can Help You Do

Tcpdump will allow you to view the entire data portion of an Ethernet frame or other link layer protocol and can optionally print the frame header as well (see Figure 8.1). In common use this means tcpdump will allow you to view the entirety of an IP packet, an ARP packet, or any protocol at a higher layer than Ethernet. By default, tcpdump prints packets at the IP layer.

An example of typical tcpdump output looks like this:

```
11:51:46.637811 10.25.71.241.80 > 10.18.0.100.61965: . ack 415 ...
11:51:46.643077 10.25.71.241.80 > 10.18.0.100.61966: . ack 415 ...
11:51:46.644830 10.209.29.151.80 > 10.18.0.100.61961: . ack 458...
11:51:46.653025 10.18.0.100 > 10.7.14.114: icmp: echo request (DF)
11:51:46.653226 10.7.14.114 > 10.18.0.100: icmp: echo reply (DF)
11:51:46.658675 10.209.29.137.53 > 10.18.0.100.53454: 46268*- 2...
11:51:46.659970 10.18.0.100.53454 > 10.70.10.79.53: 23134 A? sn...
11:52:24.306670 arp who-has 10.18.1.80 tell 10.18.0.1
```

Each line represents one packet. Details on how to read each field are presented later in the chapter, but at first glance, we can see an ARP request, a DNS query and response, and access to a web server.

In another mode, we can ask tcpdump to print all the data within each packet. The output is obviously much longer:

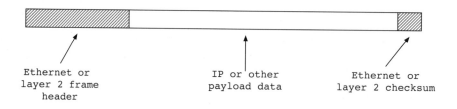

**Figure 8.1.** An Ethernet or Layer 2 Frame.

```
16:05:52.209620 10.7.21.77.80 > 10.18.0.100.62532: P 1:236(235)...
                    4500 0113 27a4 4000 3f06 d977 0a07 154d
                    0a12 0064 0050 f444 dec4 4cd8 5894 b1d4
                    5018 f82f c99a 0000 4854 5450 2f31 2e31
                    2033 3034 204e 6f74 204d 6f64 6966 6965
                    640d 0a44 6174 653a 2046 7269 2c20 3033
                    204a 616e 2032 3030 3320 3231 3a30 353a
                    3532 2047 4d54 0d0a 5365 7276 6572 3a20
                    4d49 5420 5765 6220 5365 7276 6572 2041
                    7061 6368 652f 312e 332e 3236 204d 6172
                    6b2f 312e 3420 2855 6e69 7829 206d 6f64
                    5f73 736c 2f32 2e38 2e39 204f 7065 6e53
                    534c 2f30 2e39 2e36 670d 0a43 6f6e 6e65
                    6374 696f 6e3a 204b 6565 702d 416c 6976
                    650d 0a4b 6565 702d 416c 6976 653a 2074
                    696d 656f 7574 3d31 352c 206d 6178 3d39
                    390d 0a45 5461 673a 2022 3236 3166 3932
                    6265 2d32 342d 3365 3135 6662 3164 220d
                    0a0d 0a
```

This is one entire IP packet, beginning with the IP version number (4) and the IP header length (5, representing the number of 32-bit words in the header).

The number of problems that can be solved with the help of tcpdump is limitless. Because it prints such detailed information about network traffic, tcpdump is to a network administrator what the microscope is to a biologist. It will not give you a feel for large trends as Neo or MRTG will, but it will give you a very clear picture of a specific part of your network. For this reason, it is an excellent tool to use when the problem is simply that something is not working properly.

Imagine a Web browser that is unable to load pages from a particular server; the Web browser just hangs. Is it a problem with the client, the server, or something in between? If you run tcpdump while loading the Web page, you can watch every stage of the transaction. You can make sure the DNS query for the Web server's hostname is completed, watch the client make the HTTP request to the server, and check to see if the server responds. Regardless of whether the server responds or not, you are now one step closer to understanding the problem.

Tcpdump can also help debug denial of service attacks. If a network is flooded and all other attempts to determine the source or destination of the traffic fail, tcpdump will show you the source address, destination address, and type of traffic involved. Even when other methods can pinpoint the traffic for you, tcpdump is often useful for examining the contents of the traffic should you wish to learn more about the nature of the attack.

There is one catch that can make tcpdump difficult to use: The machine running it must be connected to the network in such a way that it can view the traffic you wish to monitor. This means both that the machine must be connected to the same physical network as the one in question and that the physical network must allow your machine to view the traffic. Both issues are discussed in the section on using tcpdump.

## 8.2.1   Limitations of Tcpdump

Although tcpdump will display very detailed information about the packets on a network, its view is in some ways limited by the network hardware. For example, a typical Ethernet card will discard packets with an invalid checksum. Therefore, tcpdump will not be a helpful tool for detecting this kind of broken packet on your network. For that, you will need specialized hardware.

Tcpdump is also able to report on only what it finds in the packet. If an IP address is forged in the packet, tcpdump has no ability to report anything else. Be aware that tcpdump is showing you only what the data is, not what it ought to be.

## 8.3   Installing Tcpdump

The sections that follow provide specifics on tcpdump installation.

## 8.3.1   You May Already Be a Winner

Modern Linux systems and some other operating systems now come with tcpdump already installed. If your Linux system has tcpdump installed, it can usually be found as /usr/sbin/tcpdump. If you do not know if your system has tcpdump installed, try logging in as root and typing:

```
Solaris# type tcpdump
```

If this returns "`tcpdump not found`," tcpdump probably is not installed on your system. You may also check for the existence of `/usr/local/bin/tcpdump` if it is possible another administrator installed the program before you. If you find tcpdump is already present on your system, you can skip the entire section on installing it.

Solaris does not come installed with tcpdump, but does come with a packet capturing program called snoop, installed as `/usr/sbin/snoop`. While snoop has a few features that tcpdump does not, it is to your advantage to install tcpdump as well. Tcpdump is widely used, and as a result, a number of programs can use its output to produce other reports. Tcpdump is also a better tool in some circumstances, including gathering packets over a long period of time.

## 8.3.2 Which Version to Build

As mentioned before, there are two trains of tcpdump software: the older and more standard version at the LBL and the newer version at `http://www.tcpdump.org/`. The latter version contains features that the older version does not, of course. You may choose to download and build either one; the installation process for both is fairly straightforward. In the following examples, the LBL version is used.

## 8.3.3 The Pcap Library

As mentioned earlier, tcpdump requires the pcap library, which can be downloaded from `ftp://ftp.ee.lbl.gov/libpcap.tar.Z`. On a Linux system, you will likely find that `/usr/lib/libpcap.a` or `/usr/lib/libpcap.so` already exists. If so, you do not need to build the pcap library on your own. If you are on a system where it does not already exist, you will have to build it. Begin by uncompressing and unpackaging the file:

```
Solaris% uncompress libpcap.tar.Z
Solaris% tar xvf libpcap.tar
Solaris% cd libpcap-0.4
```

Then configure and build the package:

```
Solaris% ./configure
Solaris% make
```

When you are done, there will be a file named `libpcap.a` in the current directory. If you wish to install the pcap library on your system, you may do so by logging in to a root account and typing `make install`. However, you can also point the tcpdump build at the file you just created without installing it on your system.

### 8.3.4   Tcpdump

Retrieve the source for tcpdump from `ftp://ftp.ee.lbl.gov/tcpdump.tar.Z`. If you did not choose to install the pcap library on your system, you will want to place the tcpdump source so that its parent directory and the pcap source parent directory are the same. That is, from one directory you would like to see:

```
libpcap-0.4/  libpcap.tar   tcpdump.tar.Z
```

This will allow tcpdump to find the pcap library automatically. Now uncompress and unpackage the tcpdump source:

```
Solaris% uncompress tcpdump.tar.Z
Solaris% tar xvf tcpdump.tar
Solaris% cd tcpdump-3.4
```

Of course, the directory you change to will depend on the latest version number of tcpdump. Now build the package:

```
Solaris% ./configure
Solaris% make
```

And then you may install tcpdump from a root account:

```
Solaris# make install
Soalris# make install-man
```

The directory in which tcpdump is installed will depend on your system; on Solaris it will be `/usr/local/sbin`.

## 8.4   Using Tcpdump

Details on using tcpdump are presented in the following sections.

## 8.4.1  Running as Root

Ordinarily, a network interface is not configured to capture every packet it sees on the network. It collects only packets that are addressed to that particular interface, or broadcast packets that are addressed to every interface.[1] In order to capture packets that are not addressed to the interface itself, tcpdump must put the interface into *promiscuous mode*. In promiscuous mode, all packets are collected regardless of their layer 2 destination address. On Unix-based operating systems, root privileges are required to put an interface into promiscuous mode; therefore, you will typically want to run tcpdump as root.[2] Occasionally, you may come across a version of tcpdump that requires a special flag to be set in order to enable promiscuous mode, but typically, tcpdump will attempt to enable it by default.

Do note that in certain extreme circumstances, enabling promiscuous mode can lead to degraded performance of the operating system. For example, a system with high-speed interfaces, or simply a very large number of interfaces in promiscuous mode, will place a heavy burden on the kernel. Under more typical conditions, such as a machine with one or two interfaces running 10 or 100Mb/s Ethernet, there should be little problem, however.

## 8.4.2  Command Line Options

Tcpdump has a number of command line options available, all of which are documented in the tcpdump man page. Some of the most common options are listed here.

As you experiment with the options below, note that your network topology may not allow you to view all of the traffic on your network. The reasons for this and possible solutions to this problem are described in detail in Section 8.4.7.

---

[1]Some Ethernet addresses are also available for "group" addressing. Packets addressed to one of these *multicast* addresses may be collected by a network card as well.

[2]Be aware that different systems deal with promiscuous mode differently. On some systems, for example, once an interface has been placed in promiscuous mode by the root account, other accounts will also have access to all packets. This is the exceptional case, however.

**-n**

By default, tcpdump performs a DNS query to look up the hostname associated with an IP address and uses the hostname in the output. For example:

```
12:54:07.594427 server.example.com.telnet > client.example.com...
12:54:07.686828 client.example.com.37580 > server.example.com...
```

Here, tcpdump read the source and destination IP addresses from the packet, looked up the hostnames associated with those addresses, and printed those names instead of the numeric IP addresses.

Though this is a convenient feature, it can have a serious impact on the performance of the program. If many different hosts are present, some with name servers on distant networks, tcpdump may experience delays while waiting for DNS queries to complete. Allowing tcpdump to look up hostnames is perfectly acceptable for short-term viewing when network conditions are favorable. But for long-term packet monitoring, or if you suspect tcpdump will have trouble performing DNS queries, it is preferable to disable hostname lookups. This is the function of the -n flag, as you can see below:

```
Linux# tcpdump -n
13:00:46.335152 10.18.0.100.23 > 10.56.0.43.37580: P 1:29(28) ...
13:00:46.435029 10.56.0.43.37580 > 10.18.0.100.23: . ack 29 ...
```

Also notice that instead of printing "telnet" as the port on the server, tcpdump used the numeric port number 23.

**-s** *snaplen*

One counterintuitive default of tcpdump is that the amount of data captured is only the first 68 bytes of the packet. This is usually enough to grab the protocol headers, but it is not the entire packet. The *snaplen* option allows you to set the number of bytes tcpdump will grab from the packet. If you wish to view the entire packet (as with the -x option) or if you wish for the verbose options (-v and -vv) to have access to all of the data present in the packet, specify a snaplen size of 1500:

```
Linux# tcpdump -s 1500
```

We choose 1500 because it is the maximum size of the payload of an Ethernet frame. If we were using tcpdump on a network that is not Ethernet, we might need to set the snaplen size to an even larger value.

## -x

The -x option instructs tcpdump to print the packet contents, which it does in hexadecimal notation:

```
13:11:44.459933 client.example.com.48630 > server.example.com...
                        4510 0028 7b8e 4000 fc06 dcc4 1265 0192
                        0a12 0064 bdf6 0017 b6e8 5b3c 2fdc c055
                        5010 210c a7f7 0000 0000 0000 0000
```

Note that if the snaplen, as described above, is smaller than the size of a packet, only the snaplen number of bytes will be printed in the output.

Later we will use a program to convert the hexadecimal output into a more readable format.

## -v and -vv

As the previous examples have demonstrated, tcpdump understands some of the protocol information in the data it captures. In fact, it actually understands quite a bit more protocol information than it prints by default. If you add the -v option to the command line, tcpdump will print more information than usual about the protocols present, and if you instead use the -vv option, it will print even more detailed information. For example:

```
Linux# tcpdump -vv
...client.example.com.53454 > dns.example.com.domain: 15279 (38...
...dns.example.com.domain > client.example.com.53454: 15279* q:...
```

With the -vv option present, tcpdump now prints information about a DNS query being performed, including the name being looked up (server.example.com).

## -q

The opposite of the -v and -vv options is the -q option, which instructs tcpdump to be more quiet; that is, to print less information on each line.

## -i *interface*

If your system has more than one interface, you can specify which one tcpdump should listen on with the -i option, as in:

```
Linux# tcpdump -i eth1
```

If you do not specify an interface, tcpdump will choose the lowest numbered interface that is up and is not the loopback interface.

## -e

If the -e option is supplied on the command line, tcpdump will include
the Ethernet (or other layer 2) header information in the output:

```
Linux# tcpdump -e
23:48:28.556873 0:3:ba:9:1f:36 0:5:dc:95:d0:a ip 76: client.exa...
```

The first hardware address (0:3:ba:9:1f:36) is the source Ethernet
address, and the second is the destination address. The text "ip" indicates that the protocol is IP, and 76 is the length of the payload data.

## -l

In some circumstances, you may wish to force tcpdump output to be
line buffered. For example, if you are sending the output to a file but
wish to view the results at the same time, run tcpdump as:

```
Linux# tcpdump -l | tee tcpdump.out
```

This will allow packets to be displayed as soon as tcpdump detects
them, instead of waiting for a large amount of data to be present.

## -w *file* and -r

In the preceding example, the output from tcpdump is stored directly
in a file. While this is a reasonable way to capture and store data for
later analysis, it is not very efficient and it can be difficult to work with
because the format is not conducive to automated processing.

As an alternative, you can use the -w option to store packet data in
a binary format:

```
Linux# tcpdump -w tcpdump.data
```

Tcpdump can later play back the data exactly as if it were being read
from the wire, using the -r option:

```
Linux# tcpdump -r tcpdump.data
11:51:46.637811 10.25.71.241.80 > 10.18.0.100.61965: . ack 415...
11:51:46.643077 10.25.71.241.80 > 10.18.0.100.61966: . ack 415...
```

When you replay the data, you can change the options to tcpdump in order to view the data differently. There are also a number of programs available that can use the tcpdump data file format to process packets for other kinds of analysis.

### 8.4.3 Filters

Everything on the tcpdump command line following the above options is an expression used to dictate exactly which packets should be captured and which should be ignored. Typically, you are interested in only a small number of the packets on the network. The filtering expression allows you to ignore anything you do not need to examine. A simple example is the best way to begin understanding how filters work:

```
Linux# tcpdump src client.example.com and dst server.example.com
```

In this example, tcpdump will print only those packets whose source address is that of client.example.com and whose destination address is that of server.example.com. The keywords **src** and **dst** are known as *primitives*. Another primitive is **host**, which specifies all traffic to or from a named host:

```
Linux# tcpdump host client.example.com
```

Here we view all traffic sent to or received from client.example.com. Some other useful tcpdump primitives are listed in Figure 8.2.

Primitives can be combined with the boolean operators **and**, **or** and **not**, along with parentheses, to construct specialized filters. For example:

```
Linux# tcpdump "host client and not ( port telnet or port domain )"
```

will capture all packets sent to or from the host client.example.com but not those whose destination or source port is either telnet (port 25) or domain (port 53). We add the double quotes so that the parentheses will be passed directly to tcpdump instead of being interpreted by the shell.

| Primitive | Function |
|---|---|
| src *addr* | Source IP address matches *addr* |
| dst *addr* | Destination IP address matches *addr* |
| host *addr* | Source or destination IP address matches *addr* |
| ether \<src/dst/host\> *addr* | Ethernet address matches *addr* |
| [src/dst] net *net* | IP address is on network *net* |
| net *net* | Source or destination IP addr is on network *net* |
| net *net* mask *mask* | As above but network range defined by *mask* |
| [src/dst] port *port* | Port is *port* |
| port *port* | Source or destination port is *port* |
| less *octets* | Packet size is less than or equal to *octets* |
| greater *octets* | Packet size is greater than or equal to *octets* |
| icmp | Packet is an ICMP packet |
| tcp | Packet is a TCP packet |
| udp | Packet is a UDP packet |
| ip | Packet is an IP packet |
| arp | Packet is an ARP packet |
| broadcast | Packet is addressed to a broadcast address |

**Figure 8.2.** Some Tcpdump Packet Matching Primitives.

## 8.4.4  Command Line Examples

Using the above knowledge, we can put together a number of useful tcpdump command lines. To display quick information on all traffic to or from the host broken.example.com:

```
Linux# tcpdump -q host broken.example.com
```

To view the entire packet for all bootp traffic:

```
Linux# tcpdump -xs 1500 port bootps or port bootpc
```

To leave tcpdump running for a long time, gathering data about ssh connections to client.example.com:

```
Linux# tcpdump -nxs 1500 -w tcpdump.data port 22 and host client
```

## 8.4.5   Understanding the Output

Some of the information printed by tcpdump is a bit cryptic, especially since the format is different for each protocol. The tcpdump man page lists the output format for each protocol, and the common ones are presented here as well.

### UDP Output Format

In the case of a simple UDP packet, the output format is:

> *time source > destination*: udp *datalen*

So in the following line:

```
13:45:20.364930 10.7.15.82.2103 > 10.18.0.100.47028: udp 342 (DF)
```

we see that 10.7.15.82 on port 2103 sent 342 bytes to 10.18.0.100 on port 47028. The 342 bytes of data refers to the data portion of the UDP packet. The (DF) at the end indicates that the IP "don't fragment" bit is set.

### TCP Output Format

For TCP packets, the output format is:

> *time source > dest flags sequence* [ack *ack*] win *window* [*urgent*] [*options*]

For example:

```
...10.7.21.70.80 > 10.18.0.100.34639: P 1461:2921(1460) \
   ack 973 win 63268 (DF)
```

indicates that 10.7.21.70 on port 80 sent data to 10.18.0.100 on port 34639. The TCP PUSH flag was set, indicated by the "P." The string 1461:2921(1460) gives us information about the TCP sequence number. It indicates that the packet is starting 1461 octets (eight-bit bytes) from the first sequence number tcpdump observed. This is called a relative sequence number. If you would rather view the actual sequence number used in the TCP packet, you can supply the −S argument on the tcpdump command line. The number after the colon is one more than the sequence number of the last byte in the packet, though this number is not really in the TCP header. The number in parentheses, 1460, is the length of the data sent.

The text "`ack 973`" indicates a TCP ACK was present and that the next expected sequence number in the other direction (data sent from 10.18.0.100 to 10.7.21.70) will be 973. This is also a relative sequence number if the −S flag is not used.

Finally, "`win 63268`" indicates that 10.7.21.70 will accept a TCP window size of 63268 octets. As in the UDP example, the (DF) represents the presence of the IP don't fragment option. In this example, the urgent TCP flag is not used and there are no extra options to report.

### 8.4.6  Viewing Packet Data

As described earlier, the −x option, when used in conjunction with the −s 1500 setting, will instruct tcpdump to print the entire contents of a packet in hexadecimal. Because the hexadecimal output can be difficult to read, we can use an additional program to print character representations of each byte as well. Save the following into a file called `tpcdump-data-filter.pl`:

```perl
#!/usr/bin/perl
# This code is hereby placed in the public domain by its author,
# Marc Horowitz . If you use it, it would be polite if you left
# my name on it, but there's no requirement.
$| = 1;
while(<>) {
    if (/^\s/) {
        ($nospc = $_) =~ s/\s+//g;
        ($spc = $nospc) =~ s/(....)/$1 /g;
        ($bin = pack("H*",$nospc)) =~ tr/\000-\037\177-\377/./;
        printf("%16s%-45s%s\n","",$spc,$bin);
    } else {
        print;
    }
}
```

and give it execute permissions:

```
Linux# chmod u+x tcpdump-data-filter.pl
```

We can now pipe the tcpdump output through this program:

```
Linux# tcpdump -xls 1500 | ./tcpdump-data-filter.pl
tcpdump: listening on eth0
20:11:35.686269 host.example.com.53454 > c.gtld-servers.net.dom...
        4500 003d 9f2a 4000 ff11 add6 0a12 0064        E..=.*@........d
        c01a 5c1e d0ce 0035 0029 3674 8930 0000        ..\....5.)6t.0..
        0001 0000 0000 0000 0364 6e73 0765 7861        .........dns.exa
        6d70 6c65 0363 6f6d 0000 0100 01               mple.com.....
20:11:35.740531 host.example.com.34243 > web.example.com.80: P ...
        4500 03f4 a6f9 4000 4006 5641 0a12 0064        E.....@.@.VA...d
        0a07 154d 85c3 0050 f0b0 2504 41bc a72f        ...M...P..%.A../
        5018 60f4 3db0 0000 4745 5420 2f20 4854        P.`.=...GET / HT
        5450 2f31 2e30 0d0a 486f 7374 3a20 7765        TP/1.0..Host: we
        ...
```

The character representation does not add much meaning to the packet header data, but it makes it much easier to understand the the protocol data. In the first packet, we can see host.example.com perform a DNS query for dns.example.com. In the second packet, we can see host.example.com performing a "GET / HTTP/1.0" in an HTTP transaction with web.example.com.

## 8.4.7   Seeing It All

Before the arrival of the modern network switch, it was easy to view all of the traffic on an Ethernet network. Every packet on the network arrived at every network card, and as long as the card was in promiscuous mode, the operating system could capture every packet. On a switched network, this is no longer the case. Traffic patterns are optimized so that a link carries only the traffic destined for hosts connected to that link.[3] On a fully switched network this means tcpdump will be able to view only:

---

[3]Actually, this is not strictly true. Before a switch has figured out where a host resides, it sends traffic to every port. As a result, you may see occasional traffic for hosts on other links. This is one reason you should not rely on switching for data privacy.

- Traffic destined for your host

- Traffic originating from your host

- Broadcast traffic

- Small random amounts of traffic for other hosts (see the footnote)

This is a real setback if the point of using tcpdump is to help us
monitor the packets sent by some other host. There are two ways to
solve this problem. One is to connect the host in question and your
monitoring host to a true repeater, as in Figure 8.3. This is a simple
and effective solution if you can easily travel to the machine and attach
another host appropriately. If not, an alternative solution is to configure
your network hardware to forward the packets you are interested in to a
port you can monitor them from. Not all network hardware is capable
of doing this, however.

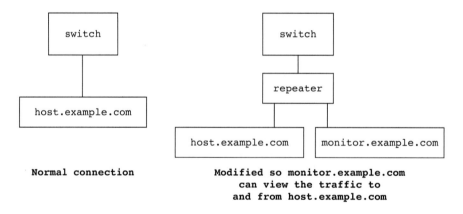

**Figure 8.3.** Using a Repeater to Monitor Traffic.

## Monitoring on Cisco CatOS Devices

Cisco switches are capable of sending packets to additional ports for
monitoring, though the syntax depends on which generation of switch
software you are using. On the older CatOS systems, use the "`set
span`" command (SPAN stands for switch port analyzer). From en-
able mode:

```
switch15> (enable) set span 2/49 2/9 both inpkts enable
```

In this example, all the traffic that would ordinarily be transmitted to port 2/49 or received from port 2/49 will also be sent to port 2/9. Now a host attached to port 2/9 can run tcpdump and monitor any packets that would be sent or received by a host attached to port 2/49 (see Figure 8.4).

On this particular switch, port 2/49 happens to be the uplink to the rest of the network, so monitoring its traffic allows us to monitor traffic of every device on the switch. Use caution when redirecting a large amount of traffic like this; if the destination link is not as large as the source link, you may flood the monitoring host.

The keyword `both` in the example above indicates that both transmitted and received traffic should be sent. The `inpkts enable` option is important; it tells the switch that it should process incoming packets to port 2/9 normally. The default behavior for a port with SPAN enabled is to ignore incoming packets. If you do not care about having your monitoring host able to talk to the rest of the network, you may leave the inpkts option out, but if you do wish to have the monitoring host accessible, be sure to include it. Note that some early versions of the CatOS software do not have the ability to use the `inpkts enable` option.

The `set span` syntax also allows you to specify multiple source ports and ranges of ports. For example, `2/1-8` would represent port 2/1 through port 2/8. Using `2/1-8,2/10-50` would mean ports 2/1 through 2/8 and 2/10 through 2/50.

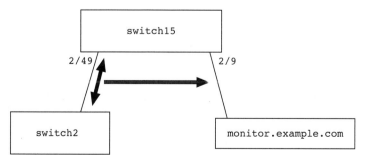

**Figure 8.4.** Forwarding Traffic to an Additional Port for Monitoring.

You can view the status of SPAN sessions with the `show span` command:

```
switch15> (enable) show span
Status          : enabled
Admin Source    : Port 2/49
Oper Source     : Port 2/49
Destination     : Port 2/9
Direction       : transmit/receive
Incoming Packets: enabled
```

### Monitoring on Cisco IOS Devices

On Cisco devices running IOS (either switches or routers), port monitoring is configured with *monitoring sessions*. From configure mode:

```
switch18(config)#monitor session 1 source interface Gi1/1
switch18(config)#monitor session 1 destination interface Gi1/2
```

This would direct packets on port Gi1/1 to be copied to port Gi1/2. Remember to issue a `write mem` so that the configuration will still be in effect the next time the device is rebooted.

You can view monitoring sessions with the `show monitor` command:

```
switch18>show monitor

Session 1
---------
Source Ports:
    RX Only:        None
    TX Only:        None
    Both:           Gi1/1
Source VLANs:
    RX Only:        None
    TX Only:        None
    Both:           None
Destination Ports: Gi1/2
Filter VLANs:      None
```

## 8.5   Examples of Debugging with Tcpdump

The following sections provide specific examples of debugging with tcpdump.

## 8.5.1   Packet Flooding

Using tcpdump to find the source of a traffic flood is usually straight-forward. Start by connecting a machine in a place where it will be able to monitor network traffic. If it is necessary to configure a switch so that packets will be sent to an additional port for monitoring, make sure to do so. Then run tcpdump and look for high talkers. Be sure to disable domain name lookups:

```
Linux# tcpdump -n
17:36:16.265220 10.255.255.27.1221 > 10.18.0.100.9995: udp 1168 (DF)
17:36:16.269171 10.255.255.27.1221 > 10.18.0.100.9995: udp 1168 (DF)
17:36:16.273130 10.255.255.23.1221 > 10.18.0.100.9995: udp 1168 (DF)
17:36:16.285228 10.255.255.27.1221 > 10.18.0.100.9995: udp 1168 (DF)
17:36:16.302173 10.255.255.27.1221 > 10.18.0.100.9995: udp 1168 (DF)
17:36:16.319372 10.255.255.27.1221 > 10.18.0.100.9995: udp 1168 (DF)
17:36:16.334600 10.7.15.65.7000 > 10.18.1.140.7001: rx ack (66) (DF)
17:36:16.334975 10.7.15.65.7000 > 10.18.1.140.7001: rx data (36) (DF
17:36:16.336606 10.255.255.27.1221 > 10.18.0.100.9995: udp 1168 (DF)
17:36:16.336623 10.7.1.70.7000 > 10.18.1.140.7001: rx ack (66) (DF)
17:36:16.336939 10.7.1.70.7000 > 10.18.1.140.7001: rx data (36) (DF)
17:36:16.352253 10.255.255.27.1221 > 10.18.0.100.9995: udp 1168 (DF)
17:36:16.356199 10.255.255.27.1221 > 10.18.0.100.9995: udp 1168 (DF)
17:36:16.396921 10.255.255.27.1221 > 10.18.0.100.9995: udp 1168 (DF)
17:36:16.398427 10.155.0.153.57195 > 239.255.255.253.427: udp 49
17:36:16.400831 10.255.255.27.1221 > 10.18.0.100.9995: udp 1168 (DF)
17:36:16.404805 10.255.255.27.1221 > 10.18.0.100.9995: udp 1168 (DF)
17:36:16.408749 10.255.255.27.1221 > 10.18.0.100.9995: udp 1168 (DF)
17:36:16.412705 10.255.255.27.1221 > 10.18.0.100.9995: udp 1168 (DF)
17:36:16.416750 10.255.255.27.1221 > 10.18.0.100.9995: udp 1168 (DF)
```

From this short sample of output, we can see that there is a suspiciously large amount of traffic coming from 10.255.255.27 port 1221, directed at 10.18.0.100. Each packet is a UDP datagram with 1168 bytes of UDP payload data. The small difference in time stamps between packets helps convince us of the speed with which they are being sent.

Frequently, there is so much traffic on the network that it will not be so easy to determine who the high talker is. If that is the case, you may wish to rule out certain network traffic or include only certain network traffic in an attempt to focus in on the problem. For example, if you happen to know the flooding is directed at a particular host, use a filter to view traffic destined for that host:

```
Linux# tcpdump -n dst victim.example.com
```

## 8.5.2    A More Complicated Example

Imagine several workstations are having trouble accessing your Web
server. The Web browser just hangs. Oddly, other machines on the
same network have no problem reaching the server in a timely manner,
and tests from your own workstation indicate there is no problem in
connectivity. So you use a machine running tcpdump to examine the
problem. First you may choose to look at the Web traffic originating
from a workstation exhibiting the problem. You start tcpdump, instructing it to monitor port 80 (the port used for HTTP transactions)
and then try to open the page in a Web browser:

```
Linux# tcpdump host client.example.com and port 80
```

But you see no traffic. Immediately, you can rule out the Web sever as
the problem. If no traffic is sent to the Web server in the first place, the
problem is probably not the fault of the server. So you decide to look at
more traffic than just Web traffic by removing the port 80 restriction:

```
Linux# tcpdump host client.example.com
18:06:11.162372 client.example.com.45600 > dns.example.com.doma...
```

What is of interest is what you did *not* see. Although client.example.com
makes a DNS request to dns.example.com, there is no response. If you
look closer:

```
Linux# tcpdump -xls 1500 host client | ./tcpdump-data-filter.pl
18:14:12.842409 brokenclient.example.com.55313 > dns.example.co...
     4500 0048 058b 4000 ff11 9d80 0a12 0064     E..H..@........d
     0a05 061e d811 0035 0034 8a44 e4ca 0010     .......5.4.D....
     0001 0000 0000 0001 0377 7777 0765 7861     .........www.exa
     6d70 6c65 0363 6f6d 0000 0f00 0100 0029     mple.com.......)
     0800 0000 8000 0000                         ........
```

In the body of the request, you can see the DNS lookup is for www.
example.com. Now the problem is clear: The clients are attempting to
look up the IP address of www.example.com before connecting to the
Web server, but the DNS server is not responding. This explains why
some workstations can connect without difficulty; they already have the
IP address of the Web server cached from an earlier transaction.

## 8.6   Maintaining Tcpdump

Tcpdump requires essentially no maintenance. You may wish to upgrade the program on occasion, but it does not change very often. The most recent LBL version, 3.4, was released in 1998.

## 8.7   Other Packet Analyzers

Though tcpdump is the old, reliable standard for analyzing packet data, some newer tools offer attractive new features. For example, the Ethereal program, included with modern Linux distributions as `ethereal`, breaks down protocol data and displays it in a convenient graphical interface. It can capture live data or it can be run on a tcpdump datafile created with the `-w` option. This is a useful tool for digging deeply into the guts of a particular network protocol. More information on Ethereal is available at `http://www.ethereal.com/`.

Another popular tool is Snort, which is an intrusion detection system. Snort grabs data like tcpdump does but then analyzes it at a much higher level. It attempts to detect suspicious network traffic of all sorts, including various forms of attacks and probes. It is available from `http://www.snort.org/`.

## 8.8   References and Further Study

The man page installed with tcpdump includes information on features of the program not covered here. In particular, tcpdump understands a number of additional protocols, and the filter syntax is capable of more advanced expressions for specifying which packets should be captured.

RFC 791 describes the Internet Protocol (IP), including details of the header format. This explains the significance of the first 20 bytes viewed with the `-x` option. Further, the UDP protocol is described in RFC 768 and TCP, in RFC 793. ICMP is described in RFC 791. The books *Internetworking with TCP/IP* (Prentice Hall, 2000) by Douglas Comer and *TCP/IP Illustrated* (Addison-Wesley, 1994) by W. Richard Stevens both have descriptions and diagrams of all of these protocols, and both are easier reads than the RFCs.

There is a useful page of links to information about other packet analyzers at `http://www.tcpdump.org/`, under the Related Projects section. This includes pointers to programs such as Ethereal, TCPslice, and Snort.

# Chapter 9

# BASIC TOOLS

This chapter presents a number of tools that do not warrant a full chapter of their own. While these tools are not as complicated as the others listed in this book, they are the the tools most frequently used in network administration. When something goes awry, they will likely be the first tools you use, even if only to rule out certain problems before continuing with a more detailed examination.

The tools listed here include the ping program, which performs basic tests for network reachability to a host; the telnet and Netcat programs, which allow you to test application level protocol problems; traceroute and MTR, which determine network routing paths; and netstat, which prints information about network connections to a workstation.

## 9.1   Ping

Perhaps the first tool that most administrators reach for when debugging a network problem is the ping program. It can tell you if a machine is alive on the network, and it can print statistics on the network conditions from your machine to another. Though the ping program is relatively simple, it has a few subtleties that are often overlooked.

Ping comes installed with every Unix operating system, so there is no need to build it yourself unless you wish to use a different version than the one you have installed. Be aware that the program tends to use different options and has different default behavior on different systems.

## 9.1.1   How Ping Works

The ping program operates by sending an Internet Control Message Protocol (ICMP)[1] echo message (an ICMP message whose type is **echo**) to a remote host. When a networked device, such as the remote host, receives the ICMP echo message, it responds with an ICMP **echo reply** to the sending host. The ping program waits to receive this ICMP echo reply message and uses the fact that it has arrived, the amount of time it took to arrive, and other data to report statistics back to the user.

Using a ping test on a device is similar to using sonar on a submarine. Your submarine sends out a loud ping and then waits to hear the response from the sound bouncing off other objects. You want to know if the sound returned at all (otherwise there's nothing out there), and if it does, you want to know how long it took to make the trip.

In the simplest case, the ping program can be used as a test to see if a machine is reachable on the network. One or more ICMP echo messages are sent, and if the device responds within a reasonable amount of time, the ping program will indicate that the machine is alive:

```
Solaris% ping workstation.example.com
workstation.example.com is alive
Solaris% ping client.example.com
no answer from client.example.com
```

Note that one difference in the ping program behavior on different platforms is already relevant. The Solaris version of ping performs this simple alive-or-dead test by default, while the Linux version will send continuous echo requests unless you specifically ask it not to.

If the test is successful, what have you learned? You know that the ICMP packet was sent from your workstation to the remote host and that the remote host was able to send an ICMP packet back to your workstation. If the test fails, however, you do not know exactly where the problem is. It may be that your ICMP echo packets are not reaching the remote machine, or it may be that the remote machine is receiving the packets but the responses are not reaching your workstation. This may be or may not be expected behavior. Some sites administratively block ICMP traffic so that even if a host is on the network, you will not be able to ping it. On rare occasion, you may find

---

[1]ICMP is a part of the Internet Protocol and is used for sending messages about errors and other control information at the IP layer.

a host where the operating system has been modified to ignore ICMP echo messages while other parts of the system will respond normally to network requests. Typically, however, you can expect a host operating under normal conditions to respond to pings, especially if you know it did at some point in the past.

One common problem that can be diagnosed with the ping program is a machine whose netmask or gateway is misconfigured. If either of these pieces of information is incorrect, you may not be able to successfully ping the machine from a different network, but you *can* ping it from a host (or router) that is on the same network.[2] Details on using a router to ping a host are presented later in this section.

You can diagnose other problems by running ping in a different mode. By repeatedly sending ICMP echo request packets, a continuous ping test can report results as they change in real time. Linux will use this behavior by default; on Solaris you must use the -s option:

```
Solaris% ping -s server1.example.com
PING server1.example.com: 56 data bytes
64 bytes from server1.example.com (192.0.2.3): icmp_seq=0. time=14. ms
64 bytes from server1.example.com (192.0.2.3): icmp_seq=1. time=14. ms
64 bytes from server1.example.com (192.0.2.3): icmp_seq=2. time=14. ms
64 bytes from server1.example.com (192.0.2.3): icmp_seq=3. time=13. ms
64 bytes from server1.example.com (192.0.2.3): icmp_seq=4. time=13. ms
64 bytes from server1.example.com (192.0.2.3): icmp_seq=5. time=13. ms
64 bytes from server1.example.com (192.0.2.3): icmp_seq=6. time=13. ms
64 bytes from server1.example.com (192.0.2.3): icmp_seq=7. time=14. ms
64 bytes from server1.example.com (192.0.2.3): icmp_seq=8. time=14. ms
64 bytes from server1.example.com (192.0.2.3): icmp_seq=9. time=13. ms
64 bytes from server1.example.com (192.0.2.3): icmp_seq=10. time=14. ms
^C
----server1.example.com PING Statistics----
11 packets transmitted, 11 packets received, 0% packet loss
round-trip (ms)  min/avg/max = 13/13/14
```

Once every second, the ping program sends an ICMP echo packet. For each ICMP echo reply the program receives, a single line of output is printed. When the user sends a break (by typing <ctrl>-C), the program terminates and reports the cumulative statistics. Included in the statistics is the **packet loss** rate, which is the percentage of ICMP packets sent for which there was never a corresponding response. Though applications will tolerate low levels of packet loss, any amount

---

[2]The definition of "network" is a little fuzzy here, and "subnet" might be a better word. It is essentially any set of machines that can communicate directly without going through an IP router.

of packet loss indicates a network problem. A solid local network should have 0% packet loss.

The last field on each line printed in a continuous ping test indicates the time period from when an ICMP echo packet was sent and the corresponding ICMP echo reply was received. This is called the **round-trip-time (RTT)**. In this case, the average RTT is 13 milliseconds, as you can see from the last line of the output. What is a normal value for the RTT? The answer depends on what you are testing. If the remote host is next door on the same physical network, you would expect a low RTT, say 0–3 ms. If instead the remote host is across many networks and on the other side of the world, you should not be surprised to see 150 ms or larger RTTs.

Because the RTT is a very high-level measurement of latency, a large RTT value can be the result of any number of factors and it does not immediately indicate that something is broken. For example, some transmission media such as satellite links are expected to have a high latency.[3] One common condition that causes high RTT times is when the CPU of the host being pinged is too busy to respond quickly to ICMP requests. Many routers will prioritize other tasks over responding to ICMP when the CPU becomes bogged down with tasks. If this happens, the RTTs to the router will be much higher than normal but not because of any problem with the network itself.

You will also want to note whether the RTT values are consistent or erratic. Very large and erratic changes in RTTs can be a sign of congestion, high collision rate, route flapping, or other network problems.

## Options for Ping

Though each ping program is different, most will let you change the default options to facilitate more interesting testing. The most important option is the size of the ICMP packets sent. The default size of the data portion sent by most ping programs is 56 bytes. With 28 bytes added for the IP and ICMP headers, the full IP packet ends up being

---

[3]It takes light a little while to make it all the way up to the satellite and back, of course.

84 bytes long, which is still a relatively small packet.[4] Since a number
of network problems will not present themselves unless larger packets
are used, you will frequently want to instruct the ping program to send
more data in a single packet. On Solaris, the packet size is specified
as an additional argument after the hostname; on Linux, you must use
the -s option (not to be confused with the Solaris -s option, which
requests a continuous ping).

```
Solaris% ping -s client.example.com 1450
PING client.example.com: 1450 data bytes
1458 bytes from CLIENT.EXAMPLE.COM (192.0.2.114): icmp_seq=0. time=1. ms
1458 bytes from CLIENT.EXAMPLE.COM (192.0.2.114): icmp_seq=1. time=1. ms
1458 bytes from CLIENT.EXAMPLE.COM (192.0.2.114): icmp_seq=2. time=1. ms
1458 bytes from CLIENT.EXAMPLE.COM (192.0.2.114): icmp_seq=3. time=1. ms
1458 bytes from CLIENT.EXAMPLE.COM (192.0.2.114): icmp_seq=4. time=1. ms
1458 bytes from CLIENT.EXAMPLE.COM (192.0.2.114): icmp_seq=5. time=1. ms
1458 bytes from CLIENT.EXAMPLE.COM (192.0.2.114): icmp_seq=6. time=1. ms
1458 bytes from CLIENT.EXAMPLE.COM (192.0.2.114): icmp_seq=7. time=1. ms
1458 bytes from CLIENT.EXAMPLE.COM (192.0.2.114): icmp_seq=8. time=1. ms
1458 bytes from CLIENT.EXAMPLE.COM (192.0.2.114): icmp_seq=9. time=1. ms
^C
----client.example.com PING Statistics----
10 packets transmitted, 10 packets received, 0% packet loss
round-trip (ms)  min/avg/max = 1/1/1
```

Because Ethernet can support packets as large as 1500 bytes, we
choose to send packets with 1450 bytes of data, which leaves a little room for protocol headers. Note that if one of the links between
us and client.example.com has a smaller maximum transmission unit
(MTU) than 1500 bytes, the packets will need to be fragmented before
transmission, which may have unexpected results on your test. If the
problem you are debugging is possibly an MTU problem, the results
will be relevant, but if it is not an MTU problem, they may confuse the
issue. A thorough ping test will test each link at a variety of packet
sizes.

Other options that many ping programs will allow include changing
the time interval between pings, the IP time-to-live (TTL) value, the
IP source address and the IP type of service field. While these are
occasionally useful options, they are not often needed to help diagnose
network problems.

---

[4]You will notice that the ping program reports 64 bytes received; this is referring
to the combined ICMP header and data, but not the IP header. The IP header adds
20 bytes, for a total packet length of 84 bytes.

## Pinging from Network Devices

Most managed network devices have ping software built in, which allows you to run a ping test from many different places on your network. The IOS ping that runs on Cisco routers, for example, is illustrated here:

```
router# ping client
Translating "client"...domain server (192.0.2.160) [OK]

Type escape sequence to abort.
Sending 5, 100-byte ICMP Echos to 192.0.2.114, timeoout is 2 se...
!!!!!
Success rate is 100 percent (5/5), round-trip min/avg/maz = 1/1...
```

As with the other ping programs, the Cisco IOS ping will allow you to set more interesting options. If you run the ping command with no arguments, you will be prompted for the more advanced features:

```
router# ping
Protocol [ip]:
Target IP address: 192.0.2.114
Repeat count [5]: 50
Datagram size [100]: 1450
Timeout in seconds [2]:
Extended commands [n]: y
Source address or interface:
Type of service [0]:
Set DF bit in IP header? [no]:
Validate reply data? [no]: yes
Data pattern [0xABCD]:
Loose, Strict, Record, Timestamp, Verbose[none]:
Sweep range of sizes [n]:
Type escape sequence to abort.
Sending 50, 1450-byte ICMP Echos to 192.0.2.114, timeoout is 2 ...
!!!!!!!!!!!!!!!!!!!!!!!!!!!!!!!!!!!!!!!!!!!!!!!!!!!
Success rate is 100 percent (50/50), round-trip min/avg/max = 1...
```

Setting the don't-fragment (DF) bit in the IP header can help debug MTU and fragmentation problems. Validating that the ICMP data field is returned as sent can help detect data corruption on the wire. These and all of the other extended options are available only from enable mode on the router.

## Running an Effective Ping Test

Using the ping program to effectively diagnose a problem frequently requires more thought than simply running the program once against a problematic host. A good ping test will explore different possible problems and attempt to eliminate anything unrelated to the true problem. If ping performance is poor to a particular host, is it also as bad to other hosts on the same network? What about hosts on networks between yours and that of the remote host? Does the problem exhibit itself for large packets only? Is the problem transient or consistent? Use these questions as a guide to begin your debugging.

## 9.2 Telnet

Telnet is another program that comes installed with every Unix operating system. Ordinarily, it is used to login to remote hosts, but it can also be a valuable tool for network administration. Many networking protocols are designed so that you can participate in the protocol using the telnet program. HTTP (for loading Web pages), IMAP (for retrieving email), and SMTP (for sending email) are a few services that fit into this category. For example, the following will retrieve the root Web page from www.example.com:

```
Solaris% telnet www.example.com 80
Trying 192.0.34.166...
Connected to www.example.com (192.0.34.166).
Escape character is '^]'.
GET / HTTP/1.0

HTTP/1.1 200 OK
Date: Wed, 26 Feb 2003 13:47:13 GMT
Server: Apache/1.3.27 (Unix)  (Red-Hat/Linux)
Last-Modified: Wed, 08 Jan 2003 23:11:55 GMT
ETag: "3f80f-1b6-3e1cb03b"
Accept-Ranges: bytes
Content-Length: 438
Connection: close
Content-Type: text/html

<HTML>
...
```

The only lines typed by the user are the telnet command and the GET
/ HTTP/1.0 line, which must be followed by an extra blank line; that
is, press enter a second time. The text after that is the response from
the server, most of which has been removed here for the sake of brevity.

The 80 on the end of the telnet line informs the program to connect
to port 80 on the remote host, which is the port that Web servers listen
on. The GET command is the HTTP command for retrieving a Web
page; we ask it for the Web page named / and specify the version of
HTTP we speak as version 1.0. If you replace the word GET with the
word HEAD, the Web server will print only the HTTP headers, leaving
off the actual HTML content.

In this example, everything worked as it should. But what kind of
problems would telnet have alerted you to? First, it would have told
you if it was not possible to contact the service:

```
Solaris% telnet www.example.com 80
Trying 192.0.34.166...
telnet: Unable to connect to remote host: Connection refused
```

This means that www.example.com is on the network,[5] but for some
reason, it will not respond to requests on port 80. The most likely
reason is that the Web server software is not running. However, you
do know that the server is alive on the network because the operating
system received our packet destined for port 80 and sent a response
indicating that it will not accept connections on that port.

Under different circumstances, telnet might hang waiting for a response instead of coming back immediately with the connection refused
message:

```
Solaris% telnet www.example.com 80
Trying 192.0.34.166...
```

Your prompt does not return until you break the process with <ctrl>-
C. This means either that www.example.com is not on the network at
all or that packets on port 80 are not making it to or from the machine,
likely because of a filter or a firewall between you and the server.

If telnet makes it as far as the "Connected to ..." line but stalls
after that, the problem is likely on the server. It could, for example, be

---

[5]As you can test with ping.

experiencing an abnormally heavy load. However, this could also be an indication of a network problem such as a path MTU mismatch, so further debugging is required before the blame can be placed immediately on the server.

The telnet program can connect to only text-based TCP services and then only if the service is appropriately line oriented. The exact specifications for many of these protocols are listed in RFCs available from `http://www.ietf.org/`. HTTP version 1.1 is described in RFC 2068, SMTP is described in RFC 2821, and the base IMAP protocol is described in RFC 1730.

## 9.3 Netcat

Netcat is the next logical step up from telnet. Like telnet, it lets you send data to and from text-based TCP protocols, but it also has the following additional features:

- It can send and receive binary data.

- It can handle UDP protocols.

- It can be set up as a listener for incoming connections.

- Data can be piped to or from a file.

### 9.3.1 Installing Netcat

Netcat sometimes comes installed with operating systems, but most often it does not. If you do have it, it will likely be called nc and may live at /usr/bin/nc. If you do not have it, it can be retrieved from `http://www.atstake.com/research/tools/network_utilities/`. Be sure to unpackage it in its own separate directory because it will not create one for you. For example:

```
Solaris% mkdir nc
Solaris% mv nc110.tgz nc
Solaris% cd nc
Solaris% gunzip -c nc110.tgz | tar xvf -
```

The build system for Netcat is somewhat nontraditional. There is no configure script, but instead, you supply the name of the operating system to the make command line:

```
Solaris% make solaris
```

or

```
Linux% make linux
```

You can find the names used for other systems by reading the `Makefile` in the distribution. When the build is complete, there will be a file called `nc`, which is the Netcat program.

## 9.3.2  Using Netcat

Running Netcat with the `-h` option will produce a help listing:

```
Solaris% nc -h
[v1.10]
connect to somewhere:   nc [-options] hostname port[s] [ports] ...
listen for inbound:     nc -l -p port [-options] [hostname] [port]
options:
        -g gateway      source-routing hop point[s], up to 8
        -G num          source-routing pointer: 4, 8, 12, ...
        -h              this cruft
        -i secs         delay interval for lines sent, ports scanned
        -l              listen mode, for inbound connects
        -n              numeric-only IP addresses, no DNS
        -o file         hex dump of traffic
        -p port         local port number
        -r              randomize local and remote ports
        -s addr         local source address
        -u              UDP mode
        -v              verbose [use twice to be more verbose]
        -w secs         timeout for connects and final net reads
        -z              zero-I/O mode [used for scanning]
    port numbers can be individual or ranges: lo-hi [inclusive]
```

If you wish to test a Web server, just as you did with telnet:

```
Solaris% nc www.example.com 80
HEAD / HTTP/1.0

HTTP/1.1 200 OK
Date: Wed, 26 Feb 2003 13:58:14 GMT
Server: Apache/1.3.27 (Unix)  (Red-Hat/Linux)
Last-Modified: Wed, 08 Jan 2003 23:11:55 GMT
ETag: ''3f80f-1b6-3e1cb03b''
```

```
Accept-Ranges: bytes
Content-Length: 438
Connection: close
Content-Type: text/html
```

Remember to type an extra newline after the request, regardless of whether it is a GET or a HEAD request.

Netcat behaves somewhat differently than telnet. For one thing, it does not print a message indicating that the connection was established unless you use the -v option on the command line, indicating that you want verbose output. In a similar manner, you will need to use -v to ask Netcat to explicitly inform you if the connection is refused.

Here is an example of how Netcat can be used to pipe data to or from a file:

```
Solaris% (echo "GET / HTTP/1.0" ; echo ) | nc www.example.com \
    80 > /var/tmp/out
```

This is something that could not easily be done with telnet. In this example, Netcat is both reading input from a pipe and redirecting its output to a file. Of course, you do not have to do both; you may choose to pipe input from a file and view the results on the screen, or you may send the results to a file while typing the input to Netcat yourself. Here the entire output is sent to the file /var/tmp/out. For the input, we use the trick of placing two echo statements in parenthesis so that the extra newline character will be sent.

Netcat can also store a hexadecimal dump of traffic using the -o option:

```
Solaris% nc -o /var/tmp/hexout www.example.com 80
GET / HTTP/1.0
```

You will still be able view the text traffic on the screen, but an additional copy will be stored in /var/tmp/hexout that contains both the hexadecimal and text representations of the data. Data sent from the client to the server will be preceded by a right angle bracket; data sent from the server to the client will be preceded by a left angle bracket:

```
Solaris% head /var/tmp/hexout
> 00000000 47 45 54 20 2f 20 48 54 54 50 2f 31 2e 30 0a    # GET / HTTP/1.0.
> 0000000f 0a                                              # .
< 00000000 48 54 54 50 2f 31 2e 31 20 32 30 30 20 4f 4b 0d # HTTP/1.1 200 OK.
```

```
< 00000010 0a 44 61 74 65 3a 20 54 75 65 2c 20 32 35 20 46 # .Date: Tue, 25 F
< 00000020 65 62 20 32 30 30 33 20 32 32 3a 31 31 3a 31 31 # eb 2003 22:11:11
< 00000030 20 47 4d 54 0d 0a 53 65 72 76 65 72 3a 20 41 70 #  GMT..Server: Ap
< 00000040 61 63 68 65 2f 31 2e 33 2e 32 37 20 28 55 6e 69 # ache/1.3.27 (Uni
< 00000050 78 29 20 20 28 52 65 64 2d 48 61 74 2f 4c 69 6e # x)  (Red-Hat/Lin
< 00000060 75 78 29 0d 0a 4c 61 73 74 2d 4d 6f 64 69 66 69 # ux)..Last-Modifi
< 00000070 65 64 3a 20 57 65 64 2c 20 30 38 20 4a 61 6e 20 # ed: Wed, 08 Jan
```

Constructing a UDP example is slightly harder because most UDP protocols are not encoded in a simple text format. However, if you place the appropriate binary data for a UDP service into a file, Netcat will happily send it.

The following Perl script will create a valid DNS query in a binary format:

```
#!/usr/bin/perl
print pack("H*", "f5bc"."0100"."0001"."0000");
print pack("H*", "0000"."0000"."0377"."7777");
print pack("H*", "0765"."7861"."6d70"."6c65");
print pack("H*", "0363"."6f6d"."0000"."0100");
print pack("H*", "01");
```

Place the program in a file called make-packet.pl and give it execute permission with:

```
Solaris% chmod u+x make-packet.pl
```

You can then use it to place the packet data in a file:

```
Solaris% ./make-packet.pl > /var/tmp/packet
```

Now you can pipe that packet data to Netcat and have Netcat send it to a root name server while capturing the response in /var/tmp/hexout. If you wish, you can also run tcpdump at the same time to watch for the response.

```
Solaris1% cat /var/tmp/packet | nc -o /var/tmp/hexout -u \
    198.41.0.4 53 > /dev/null
```

You will have to type <ctrl>-C to break the Netcat process. Since it is not making a TCP connection, it has no way of knowing when the conversation is over. Now examine the results in /var/tmp/hexout. You will see the packet you constructed sent to the server and the response from the server, which should list the address for www.example.com and the addresses of other top-level name servers as well.

Finally, Netcat can be directed to listen on a port and accept incoming connections. This is useful for all sorts of things, including examination of client behavior. Say you have a Web browser that is not behaving properly and you suspect it may be sending strange options to the Web servers it tries to contact. You can instruct Netcat to listen on a port while the user attempts to load a Web page from your workstation:

```
Solaris# nc -l -p 80
```

After you have started the program, it will sit and wait for a connection. Note that you must run Netcat from a root account if you wish to listen on port 80 or any other port below 1024. If you do not have root access to a machine, you can always use a higher numbered port and point the Web browser at that instead.

Now you, or the user whose Web browser is misbehaving, can attempt to open a Web page using your workstation as the serving host. If the name of your workstation is `workstation1.example.com`, the URL would be `http://workstation1.example.com/`. Once it is accessed, output like the following will appear from Netcat:

```
GET / HTTP/1.0
Connection: Keep-Alive
User-Agent: Mozilla/4.78 [en] (X11; U; SunOS 5.8 sun4u)
Host: client1.example.com
Accept: image/gif, image/x-xbitmap, image/jpeg, image/pjpeg, ima...
Accept-Encoding: gzip
Accept-Language: en
Accept-Charset: iso-8859-1,*,utf-8
```

If necessary, you can continue the HTTP transaction by typing text into Netcat. Otherwise, if you have all the information you need, you can break the session with <ctrl>-C.

## 9.4  Traceroute

The traceroute program is a very useful tool that prints a list of the routers an IP packet travels through on its way to a particular destination. If there is trouble communicating with a machine and you suspect the problem may be due to misrouted packets or an intermediate network that is off the air, traceroute will help identify the problem.

## 9.4.1  How Traceroute Works

The specification for IP includes a mechanism for recording the path taken by a packet. Each router can add its address directly to a packet that has the appropriate option set. However, this mechanism is not commonly used for two reasons. One is that the design allows for a only a very small number of routers to store their addresses in the packet. The other is that routers may treat packets differently if they have special options set. Since the goal is to determine what the router would do with *ordinary* traffic, it may defeat the purpose to have these packets given special treatment.

Instead of using the IP feature for recording route paths, traceroute uses an extremely clever hack[6] to figure things out. It does not rely on any special options at all but instead takes advantage of an unexpectedly useful but required behavior of IP.

Every IP packet contains a field in its header called the TTL field. This is a number that can range from 0 to 255. When a packet is sent out from a machine, it starts with a relatively high TTL, usually 255, and each router the packet passes through along the way to its destination decrements the TTL value by one.[7] If in the course of decrementing the TTL value the router finds the new value will be zero, the packet is discarded and an ICMP error message is sent back to the original sender. The idea is that no packet should be able to live on the network forever. This helps keep a routing loop or other misconfiguration from becoming a catastrophic problem. Eventually, after being forwarded 255 times, a packet will just disappear from the network.

So how does this help determine the route to a particular destination? Say we want to know the path to www.example.com from client.example.com. Instead of sending out the first packet with the usual TTL value of 255, we send it with the TTL set to one. The first router that receives our packet will decrement the TTL value to zero, and as a result, it will send an ICMP error message back to

---

[6]Here the word hack does not refer to anything malicious but is instead used in its older and more traditional sense of a clever and unexpected solution to a problem.

[7]Actually, the router may decrement the value by more than one but must always decrement the value by at least one. In practice, each router will decrement the value by one.

client.example.com indicating the problem. So now we know the IP address of the first router: It is the source address of the ICMP error message! The router gives away its identity when it reports the problem. Next, we send a packet to www.example.com with the TTL value set to two. The packet will make it through the first router, which decrements the TTL to one, but the second router will decrement the TTL to zero and send an ICMP error message back to client.example.com. Now we have the address of the second hop router. We continue in this way, sending out packets with successively higher TTLs until we can reach the final destination host.

Traceroute uses this algorithm to collect information, as you can see from the sample output that follows. Each line represents one router, beginning with the nearest hop and ending with the destination host. Instead of sending one packet for each test, traceroute sends three; the numbers at the end of each line tell you how much time elapsed after the packet was sent and before the ICMP response for the attempt was received.

```
Solaris% traceroute server.example.com
traceroute to SERVER.EXAMPLE.COM (192.0.2.50), 30 hops max, 40...
 1  ROUTER-1.EXAMPLE.COM (192.0.2.1)  0.379 ms  0.273 ms  0.316 ms
 2  ROUTER-2.EXAMPLE.COM (192.0.2.2)  0.335 ms  0.365 ms  0.320 ms
 3  SERVER.EXAMPLE.COM (192.0.2.50)  69.641 ms  38.169 ms  39.9...
```

## 9.4.2  Installing Traceroute

Most modern versions of Unix come with traceroute installed by default. On Linux and Solaris, it lives in **/usr/sbin/traceroute**, which might be in your path only if you are logged in to a root account. If your system does not have traceroute installed, you can download it from **ftp://ftp.ee.lbl.gov/traceroute.tar.gz**. It will build easily on most systems:

```
Solaris% ./configure
Solaris% make
```

If you have a particularly old system, you may run into problems building traceroute. Read the **INSTALL** file in the distribution for additional help.

Traceroute needs to be run with root privileges. Typically, it is installed with root as the owner and the setuid bit enabled, which allows non-root users to run it with root privileges. If for some reason it is not installed this way on your system, you will either need to run the program from a root account or turn the setuid bit on yourself:

```
Solaris# chown root /usr/local/bin/traceroute
Solaris# chmod u+s /usr/local/bin/traceroute
```

Of course, you must execute these commands from a root account. Do note that if someone else is maintaining your system, that person may have disabled the setuid bit on traceroute on purpose. Since bugs in setuid programs can occasionally let an attacker gain root access to the system from a user-level account, some administrators will disable the setuid bit from all non-essential programs.

## 9.4.3   Using Traceroute

Most of the time, the only argument given to traceroute is the name of the destination to which you wish to learn the path, though occasionally you may wish to use the -n flag to turn off DNS lookups for the router names. The traceroute man page lists a number of more fancy options that control the behavior of the program.

Traceroute will sometimes print special characters designating that a particular kind of unexpected response was received. The meaning of these characters is listed in Figure 9.1.

As with any diagnostic tool, it is important to consider what the tool is actually testing because the output is not always a direct representa-

| Character | Meaning |
|-----------|---------|
| * | No response received |
| !H | Host unreachable |
| !N | Network unreachable |
| !P | Protocol unreachable |
| !S | Source route failed |
| !F | Fragmentation needed |
| !X | Administratively unreachable |
| !*number* | Other ICMP unreachable |
| ! | Response TTL < 1 |

**Figure 9.1.** Special Traceroute Characters.

tion of reality. Under abnormal conditions, for example, traceroute may present unexpected results. If your site or a site that you are probing is blocking ICMP traffic, traceroute will not work. The routers will send ICMP error messages when the TTL is decremented to zero, but when those messages are blocked from reaching your workstation, traceroute cannot collect the information.

Also remember that on the Internet, every packet sent from machine A to machine B does not have to take the same path. In Figure 9.2, there are many different paths available between the two hosts, and each packet may take a different path, even in the middle of downloading a single Web page. If traceroute finds that more than one router responds to different probes of the same TTL value, it will print the responses from each router. But this does not guarantee that the paths listed by traceroute are the same as those that other traffic took. Perhaps traceroute was unlucky and did not happen to find the same path. Or perhaps an operator administratively changed the path between the time you experienced the problem you are attempting to debug and your attempts to run traceroute. This should not dissuade you from using traceroute as a diagnostic tool; in most cases, traceroute will display the same path other traffic would have taken. But do be aware that it is possible for the path to be different.

The traceroute man page discusses a number of other interesting cases in which the output is unexpectedly affected by bugs in software, such as the destination host's operating system. Most of these bugs were corrected long ago, but reading these examples is a good way to understand how seemingly unrelated problems can affect traceroute's behavior.

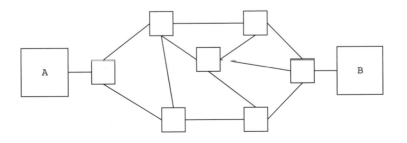

**Figure 9.2.** Different Paths Between Two Hosts.

## 9.5　MTR

Matt's traceroute (MTR) is a newer version of traceroute that combines the functionality of traceroute and ping in a single interactive session. If your system will support it, it will even use a fancy graphical interface to display its results.

### 9.5.1　Installing MTR

MTR is available from `http://www.bitwizard.nl/mtr/`. It will build easily on Linux:

```
Linux% gunzip -c mtr-0.53.tar.gz | tar xvf -
Linux% cd mtr-0.53
Linux% ./configure
Linux% make
```

But Solaris will be a bit more trouble. First, Solaris does not come installed with the ncurses package, which is required by MTR. You can download it from `http://www.gnu.org/` and it should build cleanly:

```
Solaris% gunzip -c ncurses-5.3.tar.gz | tar xvf -
Solaris% cd ncurses-5.3
Solaris% ./configure
Solaris% make
```

Then set the **CFLAGS** and **LDFLAGS** environment variables appropriately before configuring MTR. If you use the bash, Korn, or Bourne shell,[8] it will be something like:

```
Solaris% CFLAGS=-I/var/tmp/ncurses-5.3/include export CFLAGS
Solaris% LDFLAGS=-L/var/tmp/ncurses-5.3/lib export LDFLAGS
```

But if you use csh or tcsh it will be:

```
Solaris% setenv CFLAGS -I/var/tmp/ncurses-5.3/include
Solaris% setenv LDFLAGS -L/var/tmp/ncurses-5.3/lib
```

In either case, the path should correspond to wherever you built the ncurses package.

---

[8]The Bourne shell is `/bin/sh`.

Now you may configure and build MTR:

```
Solaris% gunzip -c mtr-0.53.tar.gz | tar xvf -
Solaris% cd mtr-0.53
Solaris% ./configure
Solaris% make
```

But it will likely fail at the last step because of a bug in the way MTR configures for Solaris. You can work around the problem as follows. Type:

```
Solaris% make >! /var/tmp/buildlog
```

Then open the file **/var/tmp/buildlog** in an editor. There will be a few lines, one much longer than the rest:

```
make  all-recursive
Making all in img
cc  -I/var/tmp/ncurses-5.3/include/ -L/var/tmp/ncurses-5.3/lib/...
*** Error code 1
*** Error code 1
*** Error code 1
```

Remove every line except for the one long line. Then, at the very end of that line, leave a space and append the text **-lncurses** so that the end of the line looks something like:

```
...-lm -ltermcap -lncurses
```

Now save the file, and execute:

```
Solaris% source /var/tmp/buildlog
```

When it is complete, there should be an executable file named `mtr` in the directory, indicating that the build was successful.

## 9.5.2   Using MTR

Just like traceroute, MTR requires root privileges to run correctly. You can either install MTR with setuid root privileges or simply run MTR from a root account.

Here is a capture of a text-based interactive session, which was started with the command `mtr -t` **www.example.com** on workstation1. mit.edu:

```
                              Matt's traceroute  [v0.52]
      workstation1.mit.edu                          Tue Feb 25 18:41:58 2003

      Keys:  D - Display mode    R - Restart s     Packets              Pings
      Hostname                               %Loss  Rcv  Snt  Last Best  Avg  Worst
       1. ROUTER1.MIT.EDU                      0%    5    5     0    0    0     0
       2. EXTERNAL-RTR-2-BACKBONE.MIT.EDU      0%    5    5     0    0    0     0
       3. p4-0.bstnma1-cr5.bbnplanet.net       0%    4    4     0    0    0     0
       4. so-4-3-0.bstnma1-nbr2.bbnplanet.net  0%    4    4     0    0    0     0
       5. p9-0.nycmny1-nbr2.bbnplanet.net      0%    4    4     6    6    6     6
       6. p15-0.nycmny1-nbr1.bbnplanet.net     0%    4    4     6    6    7     7
       7. p1-0.nycmny1-cr11.bbnplanet.net      0%    4    4     6    6    6     6
       8. pos2-1.pr1.lga1.us.mfnx.net          0%    4    4     6    6    6     6
       9. so-3-0-0.cr2.lga1.us.mfnx.net        0%    4    4     7    7    7     7
      10. so-1-0-0.cr2.iad1.us.mfnx.net        0%    4    4    11   11   11    11
      11. so-1-0-0.cr2.dca2.us.mfnx.net        0%    4    4    11   11   11    11
      12. so-5-3-0.mpr4.sjc2.us.mfnx.net       0%    4    4    73   73   76    81
      13. pos8-0.mpr1.sjc2.us.mfnx.net         0%    4    4    73   73   73    74
      14. pos0-0.mpr2.lax2.us.mfnx.net         0%    4    4    82   82   82    82
      15. pos11-0-0.mpr1.lax1.us.mfnx.net      0%    4    4    83   83   83    83
      16. 208.184.95.130.mdr-icann.zoo.icann.o 0%    4    4    83   83   83    83
      17. www.example.com                      0%    4    4    83   83   83    83
```

The session continues to send packets and update the display until we break out of it by typing Q or <ctrl>-C. MTR uses essentially the same kind of traceroute algorithm as above to determine the path between you and the destination host but then uses pings (ICMP echo requests) to gather statistics about the reachability of each router. Remember that many routers will treat ICMP traffic differently from other traffic. As mentioned earlier, a busy router may decide that ICMP requests destined for the router itself are a lower priority than traffic passing through the router. For this reason, the statistics presented by MTR sometimes will not represent the same conditions that normal user traffic would encounter.

The MTR man page lists a number of options; those most commonly used are listed in Figure 9.3. As noted at the top of the display, you

| Option | Meaning |
|--------|---------|
| -n | Do not perform DNS lookups |
| -g | Force use of the graphical interface |
| -t | Force use of the terminal interface |
| -h | Print help |

**Figure 9.3.** Commonly Used MTR Options.

can also use the R key to reset the statistics and the D key to toggle into two other display modes for viewing packet statistics.

Aside from the fancy display and the ping statistics, there is an additional advantage to using MTR. Unlike traceroute, MTR will not block when it hits a hop for which it cannot determine the router. That is, when traceroute sends out a packet with the TTL set to five, it will wait for the ICMP error response from the router five hops away before it goes on to send a packet with TTL six. If for some reason the router that is five hops away does not respond, traceroute will never learn about the routers later in the path. MTR, however, will try to access routers a few hops ahead, even if one of the earlier routers does not respond.

## 9.6   Netstat

The netstat program is a bit of a catch-all network reporting tool for Unix workstations. The default behavior is to print information about active network connections on a workstation, which it obtains from the operating system. This can be useful for examining problems on servers and client machines alike.

Netstat comes installed on every Unix operating system, though the options and behavior are very different from system to system. Running netstat with no arguments typically causes it to print a list of every open TCP connection on the machine and a list of active Unix domain sockets:[9]

```
Solaris% netstat

TCP: IPv4
   Local Address        Remote Address     Swind Send-Q Rwind Recv-Q  State
-------------------- -------------------- ----- ------ ----- ------ -------
workstation.63078    SERVER1.eklogin      24820      0 24820      0 ESTABLISHED
workstation.37318    SERVER2.telnet        2197      0 24820      0 ESTABLISHED
workstation.45954    ROUTER1.ssh           3953      0 25192      0 ESTABLISHED
workstation.telnet   CLIENT.61786          8460      0 25380      0 ESTABLISHED
workstation.47669    MAILSERVER.imap      64240      0 24820      0 TIME_WAIT

Active UNIX domain sockets
Address    Type         Vnode    Conn  Local Addr     Remote Addr
30002d95cb8 stream-ord 300027b6638 00000000 /tmp/.X11-unix/X0
```

---

[9]These are a network connection internal to a machine that programs use to communicate with each other.

In this example, you can see that this machine, workstation.example. com, has several established TCP connections.[10] One is an encrypted login (eklogin) session to server1.example.com, one is a telnet session to server2.example.com, and another is an ssh connection to a router. You can also see that the host client.example.com has a telnet session open to the workstation. Additionally, there is an Internet Message Access Protocol (IMAP) connection from the workstation that is in the TIME_WAIT state, which is a TCP state where the connection is all but terminated, pending a timeout to ensure that no extra data will be transmitted on the port.

The output on other operating systems may be organized in an entirely different fashion, but the general idea will be the same. This program is obviously a useful means to figuring out exactly what services a machine is trying to contact. On a server, it allows you to figure what clients are connecting and what state the connections are in.

Netstat is also a common way, and on some systems the only way, to view the routing table. Using the -r option:

```
Solaris% netstat -r

Routing Table: IPv4
  Destination            Gateway            Flags Ref   Use    Interface
-------------------- -------------------- ----- ----- ------- ---------
192.0.2.0                workstation        U      1    15116  eri0
BASE-ADDRESS.MCAST.NET workstation          U      1        0  eri0
default                  ROUTER1            UG     1   778357
localhost                localhost          UH     3 12485044  lo0
```

Other Netstat functionality varies so much from system to system that your best bet is to read the Netstat man page for details on which features are available. Most versions include an option that will allow you to view traffic statistics for each interface in real time. On Solaris, you can run Netstat as `netstat -i 1` and it will print second-by-second statistics for network traffic. This is an easy way to view the number of packets per second received and transmitted. A handy feature on Linux versions of Netstat is the -p flag, which causes it to print the program name and process ID associated with each network connection.

---

[10]The actual netstat output is not usually as well formatted as this; the spacing has been cleaned up a bit for the sake of clarity.

# Chapter 10

# CUSTOM TOOLS

Although many tools are available to aid in the tasks of network administration, there will often be some task for which you need a tool that does not yet exist. In this situation, you can either find a way to live without the tool, pay someone to make it for you, or create the tool yourself.

Most of the tools described in this book are relatively complicated and take a large effort to create. They require a mastery of the language the tool is written in, the ability to design and implement a large project, and experience with network programming. However, you can write a great number of simple tools using languages that were designed for just such a purpose. This chapter presents a brief introduction to two such scripting languages: the Bourne shell and Perl. Both of these languages are in very wide use. The Bourne shell in particular is present on every standard Unix system, and the Perl language is now installed on most modern systems.

In this chapter you will be expected to already have familiarity with programming in some language; most any of the commonly used languages will serve as a sufficient background for you to quickly pick up the basics of Perl and the Bourne shell.

## 10.1   Basics of Scripting

The world of programming languages can be divided in to two major categories: compiled languages and interpreted languages.[1] The source for a compiled program is stored in one or more files, and then a special program called the **compiler** translates those files into instructions for the processor. Those instructions are stored in a binary file. The text files can be thrown away if you wish; the binary file is all that is required to execute the program. The program has to be compiled only once, at what's called "compile time." After that the binary executable can be run repeatedly.

Most of the programs you run on a Unix system are compiled programs. You can check with the `file` command:

```
Solaris% file /usr/bin/date
/usr/bin/date:  ELF 32-bit MSB executable SPARC Version 1, ...
```

The text "ELF" and "SPARC" are tipoffs that the program is compiled.

An interpreted program, in contrast, is stored in one more files that are fed to a program called an **interpreter**, which decodes the program lines and executes the appropriate instructions on the fly. The program is interpreted every time it is run, and both the interpreter and script file must be present each time you wish to run the program. The term "script" or "shell script" always implies an interpreted language. The Perl and Bourne shell languages described here are both interpreted languages.

If you run the `file` program on a script, it will produce output like this:

```
Solaris% file test.pl
test.pl:        executable /usr/bin/perl script
```

What are the practical differences between compiled and interpreted languages? Compiled languages tend to run faster while interpreted languages are usually slower. Compiled languages produce a binary file

---

[1]Actually, the distinction between compiled and interpreted does not have to be inherent in the language itself, just to the way the program is run. Some languages can be either compiled or interpreted, and yet others, like Java, are somewhere in between. Typically, though, a given language tends to be considered a compiled language or an interpreted language based on the most common use.

that can be run on only machines of the same processor architecture and operating system, whereas an interpreted file can run on any machine. If the tool you need requires a good deal of performance (speed, memory, or anything else), a script is probably not the best way to create it. But if you need a low-performance program that can be created quickly and run anywhere, a script is just the right thing.

## 10.1.1   Running a Script

On Unix operating systems, there are two ways to cause a script to be interpreted. One is to invoke the interpreter program, passing it the filename of the script to be interpreted. For example, if you have a file called `testscript` with the following one line:

```
echo "Hello world"
```

it can be run as:

```
Solaris% sh testscript
Hello world
```

Note that `sh` is the interpreter program for the Bourne shell. In this example, the `sh` program reads the file `testscript` and takes action based on its contents. It would be nice if a script could be run like a normal program, though, without requiring you to specify the name of the interpreter first. This way, people using the script do not need to remember which language it was written in and they can type one less command. The operating system will let you do this if you place a special syntax at the beginning of the file. If `testscript` contains the two lines:

```
#!/bin/sh
echo "Hello world"
```

and you give it execute permissions:

```
Solaris% chmod u+x testscript
```

it can now be run directly:

```
Solaris% ./testscript
Hello world
```

When the kernel tries to execute `testscript`, it notices the `#!` as the first two characters, and upon finding them, it runs the interpreter named later on the line, feeding it all following lines of the file. It is also perfectly acceptable to give arguments to the interpreter on that special line:

```
#!/bin/sh -n
echo "Hello World"
```

The `-n` option is used simply for illustration; it instructs the Bourne shell to read the commands but not execute any of them. This is useful for checking the syntax of a script.

In many languages, including the Bourne shell and Perl, any line beginning with `#` is considered a comment and ignored by the interpreter. The first line is always treated as a special case by the operating system. Be aware that if you create an executable script file but do not include an initial `#!` line, the operating system will default to using the Bourne shell interpreter. You should not engage in this practice yourself, but you should at least recognize it when you come across it. For example, operators will sometimes give execute privileges to system startup scripts so that they can be invoked without the initial `sh` on the command line.

## 10.1.2   Naming Conventions

Often you will find that scripts are named with a suffix that reflects the language the script is written in. Bourne shell scripts commonly end in `.sh` and Perl scripts commonly end in `.pl`. This is not a requirement, and just as often, you may find scripts named without a suffix.

## 10.1.3   Local and Environment Variables

Every running program has an "environment" associated with it. The environment is a list of variables and their values. The command `env` will print the current environment:

```
Linux% env
PWD=/var/tmp/
XUSERFILESEARCHPATH=/usr/athena/lib/X11/app-defaults/%N
PAGER=less
VERBOSELOGIN=1
...
```

Scripting languages typically have a way to modify environment variables, but it is important to understand the distinction between modifying an environment variable and modifying a variable local to the program. If you modify an environment variable, the value will be passed on in the environment of other programs run from your script. If you modify a local variable, it has no impact on other programs.

## 10.2 The Bourne Shell

The Bourne shell serves a twofold purpose, as most shells do. It can be used as a command line interpreter, just like `bash` (Bourne-again shell) and `tcsh`, and it can be used to write simple programs. Of course, `bash` and `tcsh` can also be used for simple programming, but the Bourne shell is the preferred language. Though `csh` and `tcsh` were designed with a syntax similar to that in the C programming language, certain idiosyncrasies can lead to problems with even moderately interesting scripts. The Bourne shell and `bash` are closely related, and most programs written for one will work with the other. On many Linux systems, the Bourne shell program is really just a symlink to the `bash` binary anyway. Regardless, if you write a program with the Bourne shell in mind, it will work even on systems that do not have the `bash` program.

### 10.2.1 Basics of the Bourne Shell

Fundamentally, a Bourne shell script is a list of commands just as you would type on the command line. Unless the command is a reserved keyword, the shell uses the PATH environment variable to locate the command and then it is executed. For example the script:

```
#!/bin/sh
hostname
date
uptime
who
```

would run the commands `hostname`, `date`, `uptime`, and `who`, printing the output of each to the screen. If a command is not in your path, you can either specify an explicit path or modify the PATH environment variable. Thus:

```
#!/bin/sh
/usr/local/bin/myprogram
```

and

```
#!/bin/sh
PATH=${PATH}:/usr/local/bin; export PATH
myprogram
```

are both acceptable solutions.

Multiple commands can be listed on a single line if they are separated by semicolons. The preceding example could have been written as:

```
#!/bin/sh
hostname; date; uptime; who
```

## 10.2.2   Using Variables

Here is an example of setting and using a variable in the Bourne shell:

```
#!/bin/sh
a=foobar
echo $a
```

Notice that when a variable is set, no dollar sign is used, but when the variable is referenced, the dollar sign is used.

Because of the way quoting works in the Bourne shell, you will need to use quotation marks if you want to set a variable to a string with spaces in it:

```
#!/bin/sh
a="This is a test"
echo $a
```

But note that even though the variable a contains all four words and the spaces between them, when the variable is given to the echo command, each word is given as a separate argument. That is, the echo command is called here with four arguments. If instead you need to pass an argument containing spaces as a *single* argument to a command, you must use quotation marks when you reference the variable as well as when you set it. For example, if you want to use the grep command to search for the text "network administration," including the space, in the file book.tex it would look like:

```
#!/bin/sh
a="network administration"
grep "$a" book.tex
```

Here, only two arguments are passed to `grep`: first the search text and then the file name.

### 10.2.3   Local and Environment Variables

The Bourne shell has a slightly odd way of dealing with environment variables. The variable a, set and referenced above, is a local variable. Environment variables are accessed exactly the same way local variables are, except that they have the property of already being set for you. So:

```
#!/bin/sh
echo $EDITOR
```

prints the value of the EDITOR environment variable. Notice the convention that environment variable names are in uppercase while local variable names are in lowercase. This is not enforced but it is highly recommended so that you do not confuse others who read the program later. How did you know the EDITOR variable already had a value by virtue of its being in the environment? Only by convention. It is possible to figure out what variables have values set from the environment, but it is not usually necessary or worthwhile.

So does setting the value of an environment variable work just as above? The answer is no. The EDITOR variable as you accessed it is not really an environment variable at all. If you set its value with

```
EDITOR=vi
```

it will change the value of $EDITOR, but it is really only a local variable. This can be demonstrated with this script:

```
#!/bin/sh
echo $EDITOR
EDITOR=vi
/usr/bin/env | grep EDITOR
```

When run, it produces:

```
Solaris% ./testscript.sh
emacs
EDITOR=emacs
```

The value of the EDITOR environment variable is emacs even though
you changed the value of the local variable to "vi." The reason for
this is that when the Bourne shell starts up, *every* variable is a local
variable, and it places a copy of all environment variable *values* into a
local variable of the same name.

You can declare a variable to be an environment variable with the
**export** command. Once you do that, that variable is bound to the
environment, meaning that any value you set for it will automatically
be reflected in the environment and thus passed on to other programs.
If we modify the preceding example by adding an **export** command:

```
#!/bin/sh
echo $EDITOR
EDITOR=vi
export EDITOR
/usr/bin/env | grep EDITOR
```

the output now becomes:

```
Solaris% ./testscript.sh
emacs
EDITOR=vi
```

Often in scripts you will see the export command placed on the same
line as the variable is set, either with a semicolon:

```
EDITOR=vi; export EDITOR
```

or without:

```
EDITOR=vi export EDITOR
```

Both are valid Bourne shell syntax.

## 10.2.4   Exit Status

After a program is finished running, it returns an integer as its **exit
status**. Often a program returns an exit status of zero if it exits normally and an exit status of one if it does not. This is not always the

case, though; check the documentation for the program in question to find out its behavior.

In the Bourne shell, the return value of the last program run is stored in the variable $?. For example, this short script uses the $? variable to print the exit status from the touch program. The touch program tries to create a file if it does not exist; if it does already exist, it updates the modification time:

```
#!/bin/sh
touch /tmp/mytestfile
echo $?
touch /foobar
echo $?
```

When you run it, the result is:

```
Solaris% ./testscript.sh
0
touch: /foobar cannot create
1
```

The first use of the touch program exits normally with exit status zero. In the second instance, touch is not able to create the file /foobar, so a warning is printed and the exit status is set to one.

## 10.2.5   Conditionals

This script demonstrates the use of conditionals in the Bourne shell:

```
#!/bin/sh
a="green"
if [ "$a" = "red" ]; then
  echo "Found red"
elif [ "$a" = "green" ]; then
  echo "Found green"
else
  echo "Found a color other than red or green"
fi
```

Note that some of the spacing is very important. There must be a space after the open bracket, before the closed bracket, and both before and after the equal signs. Placing quotes around $a, while not strictly necessary in this example, is a good habit to develop. If the value of $a had been empty (""), the quotes would be required.

The if statement begins the set of conditionals. The elif command stands for "else if." The else statement catches any conditions not already met, and finally the fi ("if" backwards) command closes the set of conditionals.

There are a number of interesting details to be studied in how these statements are constructed and in shortcuts that can be taken. But the format above is clear and simple and will work wherever you need a conditional. However, it is worth mentioning that the brackets are not really Bourne shell syntax. The open bracket ([) is actually a separate program, usually a symlink to the test program:

```
Linux% ls -l /usr/bin/[
lrwxrwxrwx    1 root      root    4 Jul  1  2002 /usr/bin/[ -> test*
```

In the previous example, you compared strings to see if they were equal. Other tests are also possible, such as comparing numeric values:

```
#!/bin/sh
a=75
if [ $a -eq 0 ]; then
  echo "Zero"
elif [ $a -le 50 ]; then
  echo "Less than or equal to 50"
elif [ $a -lt 80 ]; then
  echo "Less than 80"
elif [ $a -ge 80 ]; then
  echo "Greater than or equal to 80"
fi
```

Also useful is the ability to test files. For example, you can use -r to test if a file is readable:

```
#!/bin/sh
a=/var/tmp/myfile
if [ ! -r "$a" ]; then
  echo "Warning: $a is not readable"
fi
```

The exclamation mark negates the test, which is to say that it will succeed when the opposite condition is true. Using -r alone will succeed when the file is readable; using ! -r will succeed when the file is *not* readable.

The **and** and **or** operators are −a and −o, respectively:

```
#!/bin/sh
a=1
b=1
if [ $a -eq 1 -a $b -eq 1 ]; then
  echo "Both"
elif [ $a -eq 1 -o $b -eq 1 ]; then
  echo "One"
else
  echo "Neither"
fi
```

The full list of tests is available on the **test** man page (type **man test** at the prompt). On some systems, this man page lists tests for a number of different shells, so make sure to look at the ones for **/bin/sh**, or if that is not present, the tests for the **bash** shell.

Do note that conditionals are particularly useful in conjunction with the status variable:

```
#!/bin/sh
touch /foobar
if [ $? -ne 0 ]; then
  echo "Warning: touch failed"
fi
```

## 10.2.6 Arguments

Often you will want use arguments from the command line as variables in your script. Say you have a script that tests a server for a security vulnerability. You would like to be able to invoke it as:

```
Solaris% ./scanhost myserver.example.com
```

In the Bourne shell, the arguments are stored in order as the variables $1, $2, $3, and so on. The variable $0 stores the name of the script itself, as invoked from the command line, and the variables $* and $@ store all of the command line arguments separated by spaces.[2] Our vulnerability testing program above might begin with:

```
#!/bin/sh
if [ "$1" = "" ]; then
```

---

[2]The difference between these two variables is in how they behave when quoted.

```
      echo "You must supply a hostname"
      exit 1
   fi
   host="$1"
   echo "Scanning $host"
```

Arguments can also be manipulated with the `shift` command. It will throw out the value of $1, store $2 in $1, store $3 in $2, and so on. A common example of argument processing using the `shift` command is presented in the next section, on Bourne shell loops.

## 10.2.7  Loops

The Bourne shell supports `for` loops as follows:

```
#!/bin/sh
servers="mail1.example.com mail2.example.com time.example.com"
for i in $servers; do
   echo $i
done
```

Support for `while` loops is also included. In this example, we use a while loop to perform argument processing:

```
#!/bin/sh
quiet=0
verbose=0
while [ "$1" != "" ]; do
  if [ "$1" = "-q" ]; then
     quiet=1
     shift
  elif [ "$1" = "-v" ]; then
     verbose=1
     shift
  else
     echo "Invalid argument"
     exit
  fi
done
```

## 10.2.8  Using Command Output

Many times you will want to use the output of a particular program in your script. Perhaps you wish to store the result of the `date` command in a variable so that it can be used several times later on in the script. You can do so by placing the command in single back quotes:

```
#!/bin/sh
date=`date`
echo The date is $date
```

Many scripts use this technique to perform simple changes to text using sed or awk:

```
gecos=`grep "$1" /etc/passwd | awk -F: '{print $5}'`
```

Note that $1 refers to the first argument on the command line, but the $5 is something else entirely. When single quotes are used in the Bourne shell, as they are in 'print $5', variables values are not substituted. Instead, the text string $5 is passed on to the awk program, which uses that syntax to represent the fifth field of text (in this case, the fifth field of the password file).

## 10.2.9  Working with Input and Output

Input and output redirection is straightforward in the Bourne shell. The standard output is redirected to a file with >*filename*:

```
#!/bin/sh
echo "Starting script at `date`" > /var/tmp/log
```

This will overwrite an existing file; if you wish to append to the file instead, use >>*filename*:

```
echo "Ending script at `date`" >> /var/tmp/log
```

You can redirect standard error by placing the number 2 in front of the greater-than sign.[3] The following will redirect both the standard out and standard error to the same file:

```
#!/bin/sh
make > /var/tmp/buildlog 2> /var/tmp/buildlog
```

The standard input can be redirected from a file with a less-than sign:

```
grep $user < /etc/passwd
```

---

[3]It is 2 because that is the file descriptor number of standard error.

It is also possible to read lines from the standard input and use them in your script. The following script, for example, can be used much like the cat program. Run it as `testscript.sh` *filename*:

```
#!/bin/sh
while read a; do
    echo $a
done < $1
```

The **read** command reads one line from the standard input and stores it in the named variable, here **a**. When the end of the file is reached, **read** returns a non-zero value. This allows the loop above to continue reading lines until no more are present.

## 10.2.10    Functions

Modern versions of the Bourne shell support user-created functions, though it is still possible to find some old versions that do not. Make sure to test out functions on your system before relying on them.

This program defines and uses a function called `logit`:

```
#!/bin/sh
logit () {
  echo "$*" >> /var/tmp/scriptlog
}
logit "Starting script at `date`"
# do some work here
logit "Finished script at `date`"
```

Notice that within a function, the variables $1, $*, etc., now refer to the arguments passed to the function instead of the arguments passed to the script command line. Functions can also return a value just as a program can. This allows you to check the success or failure of the function. As an example:

```
#!/bin/sh
myfunction () {
  return 1
}
myfunction
echo $?
```

This produces:

```
Solaris% ./testscript.sh
1
```

## 10.2.11   Other Miscellaneous Items

There are many other features available to you in the Bourne shell, all
of which are documented in the manual page. The following sections
describe a few odds and ends that you may find useful.

### Interpreting Another File

You can cause a Bourne shell script in another file to be interpreted by
placing the filename after a period and a space:

```
#!/bin/sh
echo This is my script
. /var/tmp/otherscript
echo Back to my script
```

All the commands in /var/tmp/otherscript will then be run just as
if they were present our script. Note that this means you do not want
/var/tmp/otherscript to start with a #!/bin/sh line.

### Exiting

You can exit a Bourne shell script with the exit command. If you give
it an integer argument, that will be the exit status of the program:

```
#!/bin/sh
if [ "$1" = "" ]; then
    echo "You must supply an argument"
    exit 1
fi
```

### Traps

Unlike many other simple scripting languages, the Bourne shell lets you
catch signals with the trap command:

```
#!/bin/sh
trap "echo Interrupted; exit 1" 2
sleep 30
```

This script, if run normally, will simply wait for 30 seconds and then
exit. Instead, run the script, but before it finishes, type <ctrl>-C to
send it an interrupt signal. The result is this:

```
Solaris% ./testscript.sh
^CInturrupted
```

The **trap** command takes two or more arguments. The first is the command to be run when the signal is caught. In this case, we wish to print "Interrupted" and then exit the script, so these two commands are placed in quotation marks so as to be one argument to the **trap** command. The second and following arguments to **trap** list the signals to be caught. Each signal is listed by number; the number assigned to the interrupt signal (SIGINT) is 2. The full list of signals available, in sequential order starting with signal 1, can be printed from the command line with:

```
Linux% kill -l
HUP INT QUIT ILL TRAP ABRT BUS FPE KILL USR1 SEGV USR2 PIPE ALA...
CHLD CONT STOP TSTP TTIN TTOU URG XCPU XFSZ VTALRM PROF WINCH P...
RTMIN RTMIN+1 RTMIN+2 RTMIN+3 RTMAX-3 RTMAX-2 RTMAX-1 RTMAX
```

This list may be different on different systems.

In a more practical setting, you might use the **trap** command to call a function that cleans up temporary files and the like, in case a script is interrupted unexpectedly.

### The Process ID

The process ID of the script itself is stored in the variable $$. This can be handy in creating temporary files so that they do not conflict with other instances of the script running at the same time.

```
#!/bin/sh
tmpfile=/tmp/scripttmp.$$
```

### Comments

Any line beginning with a pound sign (#) is a comment line and is ignored by the interpreter. The #!/bin/sh line at the beginning is an exception, as described earlier.

## 10.3   Perl

While the Bourne shell has many strengths, some things it is not particularly good at are manipulating text and dealing with lists and other complicated data structures. A programmer needing to manipulate text from a Bourne shell script usually calls other programs like `sed` and `awk`. But this can quickly become cumbersome. That's when many programmers turn to Perl. Perl is the ultimate language for text manipulation, and it has powerful tools for manipulation of lists and other data structures.

## 10.3.1  Basics of Perl

Using the Bourne shell, you can simply list Unix commands and they will be executed, unless the word you use happens to be one of the few reserved keywords like `if` or `while`. In Perl, this is not the case. Perl relies less on outside Unix commands, and as a result, it expects you to use Perl syntax by default. For example, instead of using the Unix echo command to print text to the screen, you will use Perl's print function:

```
#!/usr/bin/perl
print "Hello world\n";
```

Perl is often installed as `/usr/bin/perl`, but if it is installed elsewhere on your system, be sure to modify the `#!` line appropriately.

Notice that the line ends with a semicolon. Every line in a Perl program must end with a semicolon; it is not optional as it is in the Bourne shell.[4] Also notice that at the end of the print function, a newline is specified with `\n`. Unlike the Unix `echo` command, the Perl print function does not print a newline at the end by default.

## 10.3.2  Using Variables

One major difference between Perl and the Bourne shell is that in Perl, variable names are always preceded by a dollar sign, whether they are being set or read. For example:

```
#!/usr/bin/perl
$a=foobar;
print "$a\n";
```

---

[4]The term "line" here doesn't really mean a line of text. It would be more accurate to say that every command must end with a semicolon. A command can span multiple lines and the semicolon will be only at the end of the last line.

### 10.3.3   Local and Environment Variables

All variables in Perl are local to Perl. If you wish to access an environment variable, you can do it this way:

```
#!/usr/bin/perl
print "$ENV{HOME}\n";
```

This prints the value of the environment variable HOME. You can set it similarly:

```
$ENV{HOME}="/var/tmp/foobar";
```

The ENV variable here is really a special kind of data structure called a hash, which is described in more detail below.

### 10.3.4   Conditionals

Conditionals in Perl are similar to those C, except that the "else if" syntax is neither the **else if** used in C nor the **elif** used in the Bourne shell. Instead it is **elsif**:

```
#!/usr/bin/perl
$a=green;
if ($a eq "red") {
    print "Found red\n";
} elsif ($a eq "green") {
    print "Found green\n";
} else {
    print "Found a color other than red or green\n";
}
```

As you can see, strings in Perl are compared with the **eq** operator. Integer comparisons are as:

```
#!/usr/bin/perl
$a=75
if ($a == 0); then
    print "Zero\n";
} elsif ($a <= 50) {
    print "Less than or equal to 50\n";
} elsif ($a < 80) {
    print "Less than 80\n";
} elsif ($a >= 80) {
    print "Greater than or equal to 80\n";
}
```

Perl can also perform tests on files:

```
#!/usr/bin/perl
if (-r "/etc/passwd")  {
    print "Readable\n";
} else {
    print "Not readable\n";
}
```

The full list of tests is available in the Alphabetical Listing of Perl Functions section of the `perlfunc` man page.

The syntax for the **and** and **or** operators is **&&** and **||**, respectively:

```
#!/usr/bin/perl
if ( (12>5) && (3<2) ) {
    print "I bet this won't happen.\n";
}
if ( (12>5) || (3<2) ) {
    print "I bet this will.\n";
}
```

### 10.3.5  Text Manipulation

An in-depth discussion of the text manipulation capabilities of Perl is outside the scope of this book, but a sampling of the basic features gives you a good starting point. Perl uses regular expressions in a similar manner to `sed` and `awk`. The Perl operator for performing regular expression functions is =~ (an equal sign followed by a tilde). For example:

```
#!/usr/bin/perl
$a="foobar";
if ($a=~/oob/) {
    print "Contains oob\n";
} else {
    print "Does not contain oob\n";
}
```

The expression $a=~/oob/ evaluates true when the string "oob" is present within the text of $a. It is also possible to replace text using s/*text*/ *replacement*/ syntax:

```
#!/usr/bin/perl
$a="foobar";
$a=~s/oo/abcde/;
print $a."\n";
```

The result of running this program is:

```
Solaris% ./test.pl
fabcdebar
```

This program also demonstrates another useful tool of text manipulation: Placing a period between two strings concatenates them. The print statement on the last line prints $a followed by an appended newline (\n).

Details on the many regular expression options available in Perl can be found in the perlre man page. Additionally, the perlfunc man page lists many Perl functions that can manipulate text. For example, the chop function removes the last character from a string:

```
#!/usr/bin/perl
$a="foobar";
chop $a;
print $a."\n";
```

The result is:

```
Solaris% ./test.pl
fooba
```

This is a handy function when you are reading lines from a file or from the standard input. You can use chop to remove the newline present at the end of each line.

## 10.3.6    Lists

Most shell scripting languages have little to no support for manipulating lists, but Perl has excellent functionality for this. A list in Perl is a variable like any other, except that it is preceded by an at sign instead of a dollar sign. Here is an example of initializing and using a list:

```
#!/usr/bin/perl
@dances=("Waltz", "Foxtrot", "Tango", "Quickstep");
print "The first dance in the list is $dances[0]\n";
print "The entire list is:\n";
foreach $i (@dances) {
    print "  $i\n";
}
```

Note that when you refer to the variable `dances` in a place where a list is expected (**list context**), it is called `@dances`, but when it is referenced in a place where a normal variable is expected (**scalar context**), `$dances` is used.

Perl has several functions for manipulating lists. The `push` function appends a value to the end of a list, while the pop function removes a value from the end:

```
#!/usr/bin/perl
@dances=("Waltz", "Foxtrot", "Tango", "Quickstep");
push(@dances, "Viennese Waltz");
$a=pop(@dances);
print "The last dance is $a\n";
$a=pop(@dances);
print "The last dance is $a\n";
```

This script produces:

```
Solaris% /var/tmp/test.pl
The last dance is Viennese Waltz
The last dance is Quickstep
```

The `shift` function removes a value from the beginning of the list, and the `unshift` function prepends a value onto the beginning of the list:

```
#!/usr/bin/perl
@dances=("Waltz", "Foxtrot", "Tango", "Quickstep");
unshift(@dances, "Samba");
$a=shift(@dances);
print "The first dance is $a\n";
$a=shift(@dances);
print "The first dance is $a\n";
```

when you run this:

```
Solaris% ./test.pl
The first dance is Samba
The first dance is Waltz
```

The shift function is often used in parsing command line arguments, as demonstrated later.

One final trick that is useful to know: The variable `$#dances` will contain the index of the last element in the list `dances`. That is, it will be one less than the size of the list. The following code is another way to print the list of dances:

```
#!/usr/bin/perl
@dances=("Waltz", "Foxtrot", "Tango", "Quickstep");
for $i (0 .. $#dances) {
    print "$dances[$i]\n";
}
```

## 10.3.7  Hashes

Hashes are another useful data structure in Perl. A hash is a set of
key/value pairs. For example, the environment variables passed to a
Perl program are stored in a hash called ENV. The name of an environment variable in ENV is the key part of the key/value pair, and the
environment variable's value is the value part of the pair.

Much as you denote a variable representing an entire list by preceding it with an at sign instead of a dollar sign, you begin a variable
representing an entire hash with a percentage sign. The ENV hash is
then %ENV. But just as with lists, when you refer to an element of a
hash in a scalar context, use a dollar sign instead. The syntax for
accessing an element of a hash uses braces:

```
#!/usr/bin/perl
$vendor{"switch1"}="cisco";
$vendor{"switch2"}="enterasys";
print "The vendor for switch1 is " . $vendor{"switch1"} . "\n";
```

And the familiar example for accessing and changing environment variables is:

```
#!/usr/bin/perl
print "$ENV{HOME}\n";
$ENV{HOME}="/var/tmp/foobar";
```

## 10.3.8  Reading from a File

Reading lines from a file is easy in Perl:

```
#!/usr/bin/perl
open(FILE, "/etc/passwd");
while (<FILE>) {
    print $_;
}
close(FILE);
```

This will print every line from the password file. The variable $_ is special; it is set to successive lines of the file each time through the loop. Note that $_ will include the newline character at the end of each line. If you wish to remove the final newline character, you can use the chop function described in Section 10.3.5. In general, the $_ variable in Perl refers to whatever the "current thing" is. In this case, it is lines from the file.

Of course, it would be better programming practice to check if the file can actually be opened before you try to read from it, and you can do this in a variety of ways. The following will exit the script and print an error message if the file cannot be opened:

```
#!/bin/sh
open(FILE, "/tmp/myfile") || die "Could not open file";
while (<FILE>) {
    print $_;
}
close(FILE);
```

If you wish to read from the standard input, you can skip the open and close lines and use an empty file handle:

```
#!/usr/bin/perl
while (<>) {
    print $_;
}
```

## 10.3.9  Writing to a File

Writing to a file is also easy in Perl:

```
#!/usr/bin/perl
open(FILE, ">/var/tmp/foobar") || die "unable to write to file";
print FILE "This is the first line of text\n";
close(FILE);
```

The greater-than sign before the filename indicates that you wish to open the file for writing. You can also open a file such that writes will append to any text already present instead of overwriting the file. Using two greater-than signs instead of one:

```
#!/usr/bin/perl
open(FILE, ">>/var/tmp/log") || die "unable to append to file";
print FILE "This is the next log message\n";
close(FILE);
```

## 10.3.10   Arguments

Command line arguments are stored in a hash named **ARGV**. Unlike in other languages, **$ARGV[0]** does not contain the name of the script itself; it is the first argument on the command line. **$ARGV[1]** is the second argument and so on. You can use **$#ARGV** as the index of the last argument:

```
#!/usr/bin/perl
if ($#ARGV < 0) {
    print "You must supply an argument to this program\n";
    exit 1;
}
print "The first argument is $ARGV[0]\n";
```

## 10.3.11   Loops

Perl has the same kinds of loops as other languages, including **for** loops and **while** loops. A for loop is constructed as:

```
#!/usr/bin/perl
for $i (1 .. 4) {
    print "$i\n";
}
```

which produces:

```
Solaris% ./test.pl
1
2
3
4
```

Here's example syntax for a while loop used to parse command line arguments:

```
#!/usr/bin/perl
$verbose=0;
$quiet=0;
while (@ARGV) {
    $arg=shift(@ARGV);
    if ($arg eq "-v") {
        $verbose=1;
    } elsif ($arg eq "-q") {
        $quiet=1;
```

```
    } else {
       print "Invalid argument $arg\n";
    }
}
```

## 10.3.12   Using Command Output

Command output can be obtained in Perl with the use of single back quotes, just as in the Bourne shell:

```
#!/usr/bin/perl
$a=`date`;
print $a;
```

Perl has built-in functions for retrieving the date and time, but this example illustrates the use of back quotes to obtain command output.

## 10.3.13   Subroutines

Subroutines in Perl are defined through use of the sub keyword:

```
#!/usr/bin/perl
sub max {
   my $a=shift, $b=shift;
   if ($a > $b) {
      return $a;
   } else {
      return $b;
   }
}
print "The max of 5 and 12 is " . max(5,12) . "\n";
```

Arguments to the subroutine are passed in the variable @_, which is just like the variable $_ but now in the context of being a list, namely the list of arguments. Because this list of arguments is the "current thing," when the subroutine is entered you can simply call the shift function with no arguments to retrieve the first argument from the list. The word my is used to instruct Perl that the variables $a and $b are to be local to the procedure instead of visible to the entire script as Perl would have them be by default.

## 10.3.14   Exiting

There a number of ways to exit a Perl script. You can use the exit function:

```
#!/usr/bin/perl
exit 0;
```

Or you can use the `die` function, which prints an error message to standard error and exits with whatever the current error number is. The script:

```
#!/usr/bin/perl
die "This script failed"
```

produces the output:

```
Solaris% ./test.pl
This script failed at ./test.pl line 2.
```

### 10.3.15   Perl for Network Monitoring Scripts

Because Perl has such good text and list manipulation abilities, it is often the perfect tool for collecting output from several other programs. Perl can extract the relevant data from the formatted output that those programs produce and store it in data structures such as lists and hashes. This data can then be sorted or manipulated as required and finally printed in any format you desire.

## 10.4   Programming Monitors

Many administration tools will perform a task and then exit. For example, you may write a tool that queries SNMP variables on a device and then prints the results. This is a relatively straightforward program. However, you may also find that you occasionally want to write a program that runs all the time, monitoring a network service.

Ideally, you will not need to write a program like this yourself but can instead use the capabilities of other monitoring software. It is risky to have too many separate pieces of software performing monitoring functions. If one of them should die because of a bug or other problem, would you notice? If you have one central piece of monitoring software, you probably will, especially if you have software monitoring the monitor itself. But if you have 10 different scripts monitoring conditions of your network, all of which report only once in a while, how long will it take you to notice that one of them has stopped reporting? Regardless, the following sections provide a few tips that will help if you do find you need to write a monitoring script.

## 10.4.1   Loop Timing

Pay careful attention to the parts of your program that have loops in
them.  When writing a monitoring script, you will probably have at
least one loop: the large loop around the entire program that keeps
it going.  Be sure to add delays to the loop as needed!  You can do
this with the `sleep` command in both Perl and the Bourne shell, as
demonstrated below.  Remember that the computer will try to execute
your script as quickly as it can.  If your script is sending SNMP probes,
sending email, or doing anything that interacts with the rest of the
world, you will want to make sure you do not cause an operational
problem by overwhelming some resource.  Let's say you are going to
write a script that checks if a machine is responding to SNMP requests.
If the machine does not respond to SNMP, the script will send a piece
of email to the network administrators:

```
#!/bin/sh
host=www.example.com
to=admins@example.com
community=public
while [ 1 ]; do
  snmpget -v 1 $host $community system.sysDescr.0 > /dev/null 2> \
    /dev/null
  if [ $? -eq 1 ]; then
    echo "The host $host is not pinging" | /usr/lib/sendmail $to
    sleep 1800
  fi
  sleep 60
done
```

This script has a number of shortcomings:  It assumes **sendmail** is
available and it will repeatedly send email while the host being probed
is unresponsive. The latter point will be addressed in the next section.
It also does not include a subject line, which is a problem addressed in
Section 10.4.4.

The important thing to notice is that there are two `sleep` statements
in this example.  The first one is at the end of the while loop, and it
causes the program to sit and do nothing for a full minute.  This ensures
that the program does not do anything more often than once a minute.
If this `sleep` statement were not present, the script would send a flood
of SNMP requests to the host you wish to probe.  Also vital is the `sleep`

statement after email is sent, which causes it to wait 30 minutes (1800 seconds) after sending mail before doing anything else. If it were not present, and www.example.com stopped responding to SNMP requests for an extended period of time, the script would send a piece of email once every minute. Just imagine what would happen if neither `sleep` statement were included and www.example.com was down.

## 10.4.2   State Machines

Instead of receiving a piece of email every half hour in the above example, it would be preferable to receive a piece of email only when the machine either has been responding but stops or has not been responding but begins to respond. To make this happen, you must introduce the concept of **state** into your script. You will use a variable that indicates the current state of the SNMP status of the machine (we can call the states "alive" and "dead"), and when the state changes, the program triggers a message:

```
#!/bin/sh
host="www.example.com"
to="admins@example.com"
community="public"
state="alive"
while [ 1 ]; do
  snmpget -v 1 $host $community system.sysDescr.0 > /dev/null 2> \
    /dev/null
  response=$?
  if [ "$state" = "alive" ]; then
    if [ $response -eq 1 ]; then
      echo "The host $host has stopped pinging" | \
  /usr/lib/sendmail $to
      sleep 300
      state="dead"
    fi
  elif [ "$state" = "dead" ]; then
    if [ $response -eq 0 ]; then
      echo "The host $host has started pinging" | \
  /usr/lib/sendmail $to
      sleep 300
      state="alive"
    fi
  fi
```

```
    sleep 60
  done
```

If the SNMP state is "alive" but the machine is no longer responding, a notification is sent, and the state is changed to "dead." If the state is "dead" and the machine is responding, notification is sent and the state is changed to "alive." When the state stays the same (SNMP was dead and is still not responding or SNMP was alive and continues to respond), no message is sent.

A program that has different states like this is called a **finite state machine**. The possible states of the program, along with indications of how to transition between those states, can be represented in a simple **state transition diagram**, as in Figure 10.1. This program is simple and has only two states, making the state transition diagram useful only as an exercise. But add another state or two to your program, and it can easily become complicated enough that a state transition diagram will be a great help. It will ensure that you fully understand the structure of the state machine and that you do not forget to deal with any unexpected circumstances. It is surprisingly easy to forget about a state transition or two if you have even a modest number of states in your program.

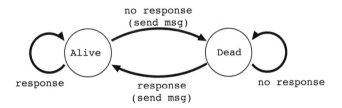

**Figure 10.1.** Simple State Transition Diagram.

### 10.4.3  Keeping It Running

When writing a monitoring tool, especially one that will remain silent when there are no problems to report, you must take care to write the program so that it is not likely to exit unexpectedly. For scripting languages like the Bourne shell and Perl, this mostly this means keeping the scripts simple and avoiding calls to `exit` and other functions that terminate the program. In languages such as C, you will need to take many additional measures to ensure the program does not exit because of memory corruption or other bugs that are unlikely to occur in a scripting language.

### 10.4.4   Sending Nicer Mail with Sendmail

The `sendmail` program does not have a convenient mechanism for specifying a subject line or other message headers on the command line. In order to send a message that includes these headers, you can create an appropriately formatted file and run `sendmail` with the `-t` argument. The following program fragment demonstrates one way to do this in the Bourne shell:

```
tmpmsg=/tmp/msg.$$
echo "To: admins@example.com" > $tmpmsg
echo "From: root@server.example.com" >> $tmpmsg
echo "Subject: Monitor for $host" >> $tmpmsg
echo "" >> $tmpmsg
echo "$host is not responding" >> $tmpmsg

cat $tmpmsg | /usr/lib/sendmail -t
rm -f $tmpmsg
```

Or, if you want to impress your friends, you can use this fancy shortcut:

```
tmpmsg=/tmp/msg.$$
cat > $tmpmsg <<EOF
To: admins@example.com
From: root@server.example.com
Subject: Monitor for $host

$host is not responding
EOF

cat $tmpmsg | /usr/lib/sendmail -t
rm $tmpmsg
```

Make sure the blank line is present between the subject line and the message body; this is how `sendmail` determines where the headers end and the message begins.

In Perl, the process is the same: Create a file with the message you wish to send and feed it to the standard input of `sendmail -t`:

```
open(SENDMAIL, "|/usr/lib/sendmail -t");
print SENDMAIL "To: admins\@example.com\n";
print SENDMAIL "From: root\@server.example.com\n";
print SENDMAIL "Subject: Monitor for $host\n";
print SENDMAIL "\n";
print SENDMAIL "$host is not responding.\n";
close(SENDMAIL);
```

Note that at signs (@) need to be escaped with a backslash and that a newline character is explicitly included at the end of each line.

## 10.5 Running Programs from Cron

You may wish to run scripts or other administration tools in an automated fashion on a regular basis. The Unix `cron` program will allow you to do this. If you run `crontab -e` from the command line, it will bring up an editor.[5] In this editor, you can add or edit the names of programs to be run. The account from which you run the `crontab` program is the account that will execute the programs later on. If the program should be run as root, make sure to run `crontab` as root when you add the entry.

Each line of the file specifies one program to run. The first five fields denote the time the program should be started. They are, in order:

- The minute (0–59)

- The hour (0–23)

- The day of the month (1–31)

- The month (1–12)

- The day of the week (0–6, 0 is Sunday)

An asterisk can be used in any of these fields to indicate that every value is acceptable. For example, `00 1 * * *` would mean that the program should be run every day at 1:00 a.m.

Following the timing information is the name of the program to run and its arguments. For example:

---

[5]If you are not happy with the default editor, which may be `ed`, you can override it by setting the EDITOR environment variable to the editor of your choice.

```
Solaris# crontab -l
37 * * * *       /usr/lib/sendmail -q > /dev/null 2> /dev/null
```

As you can see, running the `crontab` program with the `-l` option will
print the current configuration. Here the mail queue is run every hour
at 37 minutes past the hour. The standard output and standard error
are redirected to `/dev/null` because, otherwise, cron will send output
in email, and in this case, it was decided that it would be preferable
not to receive any error messages.

Here's another example:

```
Solaris# crontab -l
05 9 * * *       /usr/local/bin/report.pl -e > /dev/null
```

This runs a report program every day at 9:05 a.m. The program
sends email to administrators about problem conditions that have arisen
within the past day.

After you edit the `crontab` file, save and exit the editor, and the
changes will be complete. You should test the script to make sure it
works correctly from `cron`.

## 10.6    References and Further Study

The Bourne shell is well documented in the `sh` man page. There are
many extensive references on the Perl language, both in books and
on-line. The web site `http://www.perldoc.com/` is a good, canonical
source for on-line documentation and also contains links to other sites
with information on Perl. There is so much information in the online
Perl manuals that the man page has been split into many different
man pages. Typing `man perl` will list an index of the other perl man
pages. Particularly useful are `perlsyn` for Perl syntax, `perlfunc` for
information about Perl functions, `perlop` for information about Perl
operators and `perlre` for information about Perl regular expressions.
The books *Programming Perl, 3rd ed.*, (O'Reilly and Associates, 2000)
by Larry Wall, Tom Christiansen, and Jon Orwant and *Learning Perl,
3rd ed.*, (O'Reilly and Associates, 2001) by Randal L. Schwartz and
Tom Phoenix are commonly used references for Perl.

# INDEX

. character, Oak and, 119, 120
\+ modifier, Oak and, 120
\* modifier, Oak and, 120
[ ] operator, Oak and, 120–121
\- character, Oak and, 121
$ character, Oak and, 121
$_ Perl variable, 221
$? Bourne shell variable, 207
~ character, Oak and, 121
/ character, Oak and, 122
( ), substitution with in Oak, 122
# comment character, 202, 214
#! script startup character, 202

## A

access-list counters, 86
access privileges, SNMP, 12–13
action command, Oak, 124–125
action-limits statement, Oak, 125
anchors, Oak, 121
Apache Web server, 115
arguments, command line. *See* command line arguments
ARGV hash, 222
ARP cache, querying, 24–25, 66, 77–78

## B

bash program, 203
binary files, compiled languages and, 200–201
boards, 62–63, 69–71, 73–74. *See also* ports
Bourne shell scripts, 8, 58, 203–214, 230
    arguments as variables in, 209–210
    bash program and, 203
    comment lines (#) in, 202, 214
    conditionals in, 207–209
    disadvantages of, 214–215
    environment variables and, 205–206
    exiting of, 213
    exiting status and, 206–207
    initial line (#!) of, 202
    input/output redirection, 211–212
    interpreting those in another file, 213
    loops and, 210
    mail formatting with, 228
    multiple commands on one line, 204
    names of, 202
    output, using in, 210–211
    PATH environment variable and, 203–204
    process ID of, 213–214
    running, 201–202
    trapping of, 213–214
    user-created functions in, 212
    variables in, 204–205
bridge MIB (dot1dBridge), 25
bridging. *See* switching
bugs, notifying developers of, 8
burst variable, Neo, 65, 76–77

## C

cfgmaker command, MRTG, 44–46, 51–52
chop function, Perl, 218, 221
Cisco devices
    Cisco Catalyst 2948, ports on, 63
    configuring syslog on, 118–119
    monitoring with tcpdump, 170–172
    NetFlow and, 83, 86, 87, 89–90
Cisco Express Forwarding (CEF), 86
Cisco IOS ping, 182
command line arguments, scripting and, 75–76, 209–210, 222
comment character (#), 202, 214
commercial software, open source vs., 3–6
community name, SNMP, 12, 13
compiled languages, interpreted languages vs., 200–201
compilers, 200
conditionals, scripts and, 207–209, 216–217
contact lists, storing in variables, 150–151
continuous ping tests, 179–180

cron program, 229–230
crontab, MRTG and, 49–50
csh program, 58, 203
custom tools. *See* scripts

### D

denial of service attack, debugging, 78–80,
        84, 157–158
devices, 9
        costs of managing, 1–2
        managing with SNMP. *See* SNMP
        (Simple Network Management
        Protocol)
        Neo location syntax for, 60–62
        ping testing, 178–179, 182–183
        querying with Neo, 54, 57, 63, 68–72
        setting Sysmon, 141–147
domain name server (DNS) lookups,
        Neo, 57, 76
domain name server (DNS) options,
        Sysmon, 149
dot1dBridge SNMP variables, 25–26

### E

e-mail messages. *See* messages
elif command, Bourne shell and, 208
elsif command, Perl and, 216–217
environment variables, scripts and, 58, 203,
        205–206, 216
environmental conditions, Neo queries of,
        54, 57, 71
error messages, logging of, 111–112. *See also*
        syslog messages, Oak and
        Ethereal
exec command, Neo, 76
exec queue action, Oak and, 124, 125
exit status, script, 206–207, 227–228

### F

facilities, syslog message, 115
files, testing with scripts, 208, 217
finite state machine, 227
fire statement, Oak and, 125
flap detection, Nagios and, 153
flow-capture program, 90–91, 93–98
flow-cat program, 91, 105–106
flow collectors, 86–87
flow-dscan program, 91, 99, 103, 105
flow-expire program, 91, 107
flow-fanout program, 91, 97, 107–108
flow-filter program, 91, 108
flow-header program, 91, 107
flow-merge program, 91, 105–106

flow-print program, 91, 98, 99–100, 101
flow-receive program, 90–91, 92–93, 97
flow-report program, 91, 99, 100–102
flow-send program, 91, 108
flow-split program, 91, 106
flow-stat program, 91, 99, 102–103, 104
Flow-Tools, 7, 83, 90–108
        capturing flows with, 90–96
        compression of flow data, 97
        filtering data, 108
        header meta information, printing, 107
        installation and configuration, 88–89
        merging data files, 105–106
        multiple host/ports, sending data to,
                107–108
        programs included with, 90, 91
        references for, 108
        remote clients, enabling, 98
        removal of flow data, 107
        splitting data files, 106
        stopping flow capture, 97–98
        viewing flow data, 98–105
flow-xlate program, 91
flows, network traffic, 84–86, 90–96
for loops, 210, 222
forwarding tables, 54–55
Fullmer, Mark, 83
functions, user-created, 212

### G

GD library, MRTG and, 41, 42–43, 52
get-next-request SNMP PDU type, 13, 19,
        20, 33
get-request SNMP PDU type, 13, 20
get-response SNMP PDU type, 13
GNU General Public License, 39
GNU readline library, 58, 81
graphs, MRTG. *See* Multi Router Traffic
        Grapher (MRTG)
grep command, 119, 120

### H

hardware address translation
        with Neo, 53, 55–56, 66
        with SNMP, 24–25
hashes, 220
header command, Oak, 125
help command, Neo, 75
hostinfo command, Neo, 76
hosts, 9
        finding and disabling with Neo, 77–80
        locating with forwarding tables, 54–55
HTML index pages, generation of MRTG,
        47–49

## I

ICMP protocol, 175, 178–180
    ICMP packet flow and, 84–85, 86
    ping and, 178, 179, 180
if statement, Bourne shell
    conditionals and, 208
ifNumber variable, SNMP, 22
ifSpeed variable, SNMP, 23
ifTable variable, SNMP, 22, 23
ifType variable, SNMP, 24
input redirection, Bourne shell, 211–212
interface bandwidth, SNMP and, 23–24
interface index numbers, SNMP and, 25
interfaces SNMP variables group, 22–24
Internet Standard MIB, 14
interpreted languages, 200–201. *See also* scripts
interpreter, 200
IOS ping, 182
IP addresses
    changing ping source, 181
    translation of with ip.ipNetToMediaTable,
        24–25
    translation of with Neo, 53, 55–56, 66
    translation of with SNMP, 24–25
IP packets
    tracing path of with MTR, 195–197
    tracing path of with traceroute,
        189–191, 192–193
    viewing with tcpdump, 156–157
IP protocol, 175
IP time-to-live value, ping, 181
ip.ipNetToMediaTable, 24–25, 55–56

## J

Jacobson, Van, 155
Juniper routers, 83

## K

kern syslog facility, 115
key, flow-report, 102
keyfiles, Neo, 61–62, 80

## L

lexicographic order, listing SNMP
    variables in, 19
licenses, open source software, 2
linkDown trap, 19
Linux, 8, 41, 58, 158–159, 175, 191, 194, 203
list context, 219
lists, manipulating with Perl, 218–220
local variables, scripts and,
    203, 205–206, 216

locate command, Neo, 66–67
location print command, Neo, 60, 76
locking command, Oak, 125–126
logger program, 117
logging command, Cisco IOS, 118–119
logwatch program, 130
loops, 210, 222–223, 225–226

## M

macmode variable, Neo, 65, 68
mail, formatting sendmail with scripts,
    228–229
mail queue action, Oak, 124
mail syslog facility, 115
management agent, SNMP, 11
Management Information Base (MIB),
    14–15, 37–38
    bridge MIB, 25–26
    downloading and installing, 36
    net-snmp tools and, 36
    reverse lookups and, 25
    SNMP variable hierarchy and, 15–16
    tables and, 17–19
mark syslog facility, 115
Matt's traceroute. *See* MTR (Matt's
    traceroute)
message queues, Oak and. *See* queues,
    Oak and
messages
    message headers and subject lines,
        228–229
    syslog. *See* syslog messages, Oak and
    Sysmon and, 144, 145–146, 148,
        150–151
MIB. *See* Management Information Base (MIB)
MIB-II, 14, 15
monitoring scripts. *See* network monitoring
    scripts
MRTG. *See* Multi Router Traffic Grapher
    (MRTG)
MTR (Matt's traceroute), 8, 194–197
Multi Router Traffic Grapher (MRTG),
    5, 7, 39–54
    configuration, 43–46
    data gathering settings, 49–50
    faulty data in, 50–51
    HTML index page generation, 47–49
    initial data generation, 47
    installation, 41–43
    maintenance of, 51–52
    missing data from, 51
    references for, 52
    review of network patterns with, 39–41
    SNMP and, 39, 41, 45

## N

Nagios, 8, 135, 152–154
nc program. *See* Netcat
ND tool, 81
Neo, 7, 53–81
    board and port information from,
        54, 67–72
    bugs in, reporting, 58, 81
    built-in variables, 64
    command line arguments, 75–76
    command prompt, 59
    degraded network conditions and,
        76–77
    device info command, 71–72
    device summary command, 68–71
    domain name server (DNS) lookups,
        57, 76
    general device information and, 54, 57,
        71–72
    hosts, finding and disabling problem,
        77–80
    installation and configuration, 57–58
    IP address translation with,
        53, 55–56, 66
    keyfiles, 61–62, 80
    locate command, 66–67
    location syntax used by, 59–64
    maintenance of, 80
    online help system, 75
    ports, administrative status of, 67, 68
    ports, enabling/disabling,
        54, 56–57, 67–68
    power and environmental status reports,
        54, 57, 71–72, 80
    printer information from, 57
    references for, 81
    scripts and, 75–76, 80
    shell command execution with, 57, 76
    SNMP and, 53
    switch ports, determining host,
        53, 54–55, 66–67
    traffic statistics and, 53, 54, 56, 72–75
    variables, 64–65
    Web sites for, 57, 59, 80
net-snmp package
    installation and configuration, 27–29
    maintenance of, 37
    Management Information Base (MIB)
        and, 36
    scripting and, 36–37
    SNMP tools in, 29–36
Netcat, 8, 98, 185–189
NetFlow, 7, 83–109
    configuration of on router, 89–90
    data filtering and, 108
    export of data by routers, 86–87

    file rotation rate, 96
    flow capture by, 90–96
    flow collectors and, 87
    flow data compression, 97
    Flow-Tools package for, 83, 88–89
    flows, information in, 87–88
    merging data files, 105–106
    monitoring network traffic with, 83, 84
    multiple host/ports, sending data to,
        107–108
    printing of meta information, 107
    process ID files, 96
    references for, 109
    remote clients, enabling, 98
    removal of flow data, 107
    routers and switches offering, 83
    splitting data files, 106
    stopping flow capture, 97–98
    switching paths and, 86
    versions of, 88
    viewing flow data, 98–105
NetFlow Accounting. *See* NetFlow
NetFlow Switching. *See* NetFlow
netstat, 8, 197–198
network management, 1–2
network management tools. *See specific tools*
network monitoring scripts
    inactive, preventing exiting of, 227–228
    loop timing in, 225–226
    SNMP tools and, 36–37
    state changes and, 226–227
    *See also* Bourne shell scripts; Perl
network traffic, monitoring
    with MRTG, 39–41
    with Neo, 53, 54, 56, 72–75
    with NetFlow. *See* NetFlow
    with tcpdump, 157, 173
networked devices, growth in numbers of, 1
newline syntax, Perl and, 215
node, 9
numeric values, scripts comparing, 208, 216


## O

Oak, 7, 111–131
    condensing redundant messages,
        112, 113
    configuration, 122–130
    critical message notification, 112, 114
    global options, 123
    installation, 114
    invoking and running, 128–129
    maintenance of, 130
    queue definitions, 123–126
    regular expressions and,
        119–122, 126–128

report generation, 112–113
syslog configuration and, 115–119
unimportant messages, ignoring,
    112, 113
object identifiers (IDs), SNMP variable,
    15–16
objects, Sysmon, 141–147, 154
Oetiker, Tobias, 39
OID. *See* object identifiers (IDs)
open source software, 2–6. *See also specific
    tools*
Open System Interconnection (OSI) network
    models, 8–9
OpenView, HP's, 81
optimum switching, 86
output redirection, Bourne shell, 212


P

packet analyzers, 155–156, 175, 176
    snoop, 159
    Snort, 175
    tcpdump. *See* tcpdump
packet flood, tcpdump analysis of, 173
packet loss rate, 179–180
packet matching primitives, tcpdump,
    165, 166
parentheses ( ), substitution with
    in Oak, 122
passive tests, Nagios, 153
PATH environment variable, Bourne shell scripts
    and, 203–204
pause command, Sysmon, 139
pcap library, 155, 159–160
PDU type. *See* Protocol Data Unit (PDU)
    type
period (.), Oak and, 119, 120
Perl scripts, 8, 52, 214–224, 230
    collecting output from several
        programs, 224
    command line arguments in, 222
    command output, using, 223
    conditionals and, 216–217
    environment variables and, 216
    exiting of, 223–224
    hashes and, 220
    initial script line (#!), 202
    list manipulation with, 218–220
    loops and, 222
    mail, formatting of with, 228–229
    Multi Router Traffic Grapher (MRTG)
        and, 41
    names for, 202
    reading lines from a file, 220–221
    subroutines, 223
    syntax of, 215

text manipulation with, 217–218
variable names, 215
writing to files, 221
ping, 8, 177–183
    behavior of on different platforms,
        177, 178
    continuous tests, 179–180
    ICMP packet size and, 180–181
    options for, 180–181
    pinging from network devices, 182
    round-trip time (RTT) and, 180
PNG library, 52
PNG (Portable Network Graphics), MRTG
    and, 39, 41, 42, 52
polling software. *See* service monitors
port commands, Neo, 67–68
port mapping, bridge MIB (dot1dBridge) and,
    25–26
port numbers, interface index
        numbers and, 22
ports
    enabling/disabling with Neo,
        54, 56–57, 67–68
    information on from Neo, 54, 55,
        68–69, 70–71
    Neo syntax for, 62–64
    Neo traffic statistics for, 72–75
    SNMP tables of, 17–19
    *See also* boards
power status, Neo queries of,
        54, 57, 71–72, 80
prescan command, Oak and, 125, 126
primitives, tcpdump, 165, 166
print command, Neo, 64–65
privacy, packet analyzers and, 155–156
process ID file, changing, 96
process ID, storing script, 213–214
programming languages, compiled vs.
        interpreted, 200–201
promiscuous mode, tcpdump and, 161
proprietary programs. *See* commercial
        software
Protocol Data Unit (PDU) types, SNMP and,
    13, 19–20, 33–34


Q

quality, open source software, 5–6
queue time, Sysmon, 148–149
queues, Oak and, 122, 123–124
QuickPage, 154


R

-r Bourne shell conditional, 208
Rand, Dave, 39

readcom variable, Neo, 65
Red Hat Linux, 2–3
regular expressions, Oak and,
        119–122, 126–128, 131
relative sequence number, TCP, 168
reload command, Sysmon, 139
remote clients
     sending flow data to, 98
     Sysmon and, 140
remote hosts, sending messages to,
        117, 118–119, 131
repeaters, 54
resume command, Sysmon, 139
reverse lookups, SNMP and, 25
root node, Sysmon configuration and, 141
root privileges, 161, 195
round-trip time (RTT), 180
routers, 41
     flow expiration and, 86
     management by SNMP, 11
     message logs of activity on, 111
     monitoring with MRTG, 41, 49–50
     NetFlow and, 83, 86–87, 89–90
     tracing path of packets through,
        189–191, 192–193, 195–197
routing tables, viewing with netstat, 198

### S

scalar context, Perl and, 219
Scotty/Tkined, 81
scripts, 199–230
     Bourne shell, 203–214
     comment lines (#), 202, 214
     cron program and, 229–230
     environment variables and, 202–203
     inactive, preventing exiting of, 227–228
     initial line of (#!), 202
     interpreted languages and, 200–201
     local variables and, 203
     loop timing and, 225–226
     mail, formatting of with, 228–229
     naming of, 202
     Neo and, 75–76, 80
     Perl, 214–224
     SNMP tools and, 36–37
     state changes and, 226–227
     Unix and, 201–202
security, 6, 12, 13, 76
semicolon (;), Perl syntax and, 215
sendmail program, 228–229
service monitors, 8, 133–155
     benefits of running, 135–136
     Nagios, 135, 152–154
     Sysmon, 135, 136–152
severity levels, syslog, 116

set command, Neo, 65
set-request, SNMP PDU type, 13, 20
set writecom command, Neo, 67–68
severity level, syslog message, 115, 116–119
shell commands, executing with Neo, 57, 76
Simple Network Management Protocol (SNMP).
        *See* SNMP (Simple Network
        Management Protocol)
simple variables, request for SNMP, 17
sleep script command, 225–226
SMI standard. *See* Structure of Manage-
        ment Information (SMI) standard
snaplen tcpdump option, 162
snmp-options variable, MRTG and, 45
SNMP (Simple Network Management
        Protocol), 7, 11–38
     access privileges, 12–13
     community name and, 12, 13
     device information available for retrieval,
        20–26
     get-next-request and, 13, 19–20, 33
     management agents, 11
     Management Information Base (MIB)
        and, 14–15
     packet header information, 12–13
     Protocol Data Unit (PDU) types, 13,
        19–20, 33–34
     references for, 37–38
     tools for. *See* SNMP tools
     trap PDU type and, 13, 19–20, 33–34
     User Datagram Protocol (UDP)
        and, 12
     variables. *See* SNMP variables
     versions of, 11–12
SNMP tables, 17–19, 22, 24–25
SNMP tools (net-smnp)
     maintenance of, 37
     Management Information Base (MIB)
        and, 36
     net-snmp installation and configuration,
        26–29
     scripting with, 36–37
     snmpbulkget, 34
     snmpbulkwalk, 30, 31, 34
     snmpcmd, 30
     snmpd, 35
     snmpdelta, 35
     snmpdf, 35
     snmpget, 29–31, 37
     snmpgetnext, 34
     snmpnetstat, 35
     snmpset, 30, 31, 32
     snmpstatus, 35
     snmpstatust, 35
     snmptable, 35, 36
     snmptest, 35

snmptranslate, 35
snmptrap, 35
snmptrapd, 33–34,
snmptrapm, 35
snmpwalk, 19, 30, 31, 33
Web sites for, 27
SNMP variables, 14–15
    bridge MIB (dot1dBridge), 25–26
    getting value of writable (snmpset), 32
    hierarchy of, 15–16
    interfaces group, 22–24
    ip.ipNetToMediaTable, 24–25
    lexicographic ordering of, 19
    Management Information Base (MIB)
        and, 14–15
    naming of, 15
    object identifiers for, 15–16
    requests for simple, 17
    retrieving contiguous segment of
        (snmpwalk), 33
    retrieving value of (snmpget), 29–31
    system group, 20–22
snoop packet capturing program, 159
Snort, 175, 176
Solaris, 8, 41, 58, 115, 159, 191, 194–195
spawn command, Sysmon, 145–146
state machines, 226–227
state transition diagram, 227
station learning, 54
stats command, Neo, 72–75
statsdelay, Neo, 65, 75
status file, Sysmon, 147
Structure of Management Information (SMI)
    standard, 14
subroutines, Perl, 223
support services, open source software
    and, 6
Swatch, 130
switch ports, determining host, 53
switches, 54, 55, 66–67
switching, 25–26, 86
sysContact SNMP variable, 20, 21
sysLocation SNMP variable, 20, 21
syslog messages, Oak and, 111, 112
    condensing redundant information,
        112, 113
    ignoring unimportant messages, 112, 113
    message facility types, 115, 117
    message severity levels, 116–118
    notification of critical messages,
        112, 114
    report generation, 112–113
    sending messages to remote hosts,
        117, 118–119, 131
    sorting of messages by priority, 116
syslog protocol, configuration of, 115–119

syslogd program, 131
Sysmon, 8, 135, 136–152
    command line options, 140–141
    configuration file organization, 151
    global options in, 147–152
    installation, 136–137
    maintenance of, 152
    objects and dependencies in, 141–147
    online documentation for, 154
    pausing, 139
    placement of on server, 136
    reloading the configuration file, 139
    remote clients, enabling, 140
    root node configuration and, 141
    starting/stopping the Sysmon daemon,
        137–138, 139
Sysmon variables, 150–151
sysName SNMP variable, 20, 21
sysObjectID SNMP variable, 20, 21
sysServices SNMP variable, 20, 21, 22
system facility, syslog message, 115
system group SNMP variables, 20–22
system information, querying with Neo, 71
system logs, monitoring with Oak. *See* Oak
sysUpTime variable, SNMP, 14, 15, 20

### T

tcpdump, 8, 155–176
    binary format, storing data in, 164–165
    Cisco CatOS devices and, 170–172
    Cisco IOS devices and, 172
    command line options, 161–165
    data capture, setting amount of, 162
    data that can be viewed with, 156–157
    debugging with, 157–158, 172–174
    displaying packets on detection, 164
    DNS queries, 162, 163
    Ethernet header information, 164
    example command lines, 166–167
    example output, 156–157
    filtering and, 165
    hexadecimal output, 163, 168
    installation, 160
    interfaces, specifying, 164
    limitations, 158
    maintenance of, 175
    packet matching primitives, 165, 166
    pcap library and, 155, 159–160
    pre-installed on Linux, 158–159
    printing bytes as characters, 168–169
    printing detailed packet information, 163
    printing less packet information, 163
    promiscuous mode, enabling, 161
    switched network configuration,
        169–170

tcpdump, *Continued*
    TCP output format, 167–168
    types of problems solved with, 157
    UDP output format, 167
    versions of, 155, 159, 175
TCPslice, 176
tcsh program, 58, 203
telnet, 8, 183–185
test plug-ins, Nagios, 153
time stamp, syslog message, 115
timeout variable, Neo, 65
traceroute, 8, 189–193
    installation, 191–192
    MTR (Matt's traceroute), 194–197
    root privileges and, 191–192
    special characters used by, 192
    testing with, 192–193
traffic flood, analyzing with tcpdump, 173
Transmission Control Protocol (TCP)
    flows and, 84, 85–86
    tcpdump and, 167–168
trap command, Bourne shell, 213–214
trap, SNMP PDU type, 13, 19–20, 33–34
TTL field, IP packet, 190

**U**

Unix, 8, 115–118, 177, 183, 191, 197, 199,
    200, 201–202
User Datagram Protocol (UDP), 12, 86, 167,
    175, 188

**V**

variables. *See specific types*

**W**

Web pages
    generating MRTG HTML, 47–49
    retrieval of and telnet, 183–184
while loops, 210, 222–223
workstation, 9
writecom variable, Neo, 65

**Z**

zephyr queue action, Oak and, 124
zlib library, MRTG and, 41